D1563151

BLACK THEOLOGY II

BLACK THEOLOGY II

Essays on the Formation and Outreach of Contemporary Black Theology

EDITED BY
Calvin E. Bruce and William R. Jones
YALE UNIVERSITY

Lewisburg
Bucknell University Press
London: Associated University Presses

© 1978 by Associated University Presses, Inc.

Associated University Presses, Inc.
Cranbury, New Jersey 08512

Associated University Presses
Magdalen House
136–148 Tooley Street
London SE1 2TT, England

Library of Congress Cataloging in Publication Data
Black theology II.
Includes bibliographical references.
1.   Black theology—Addresses, essays, lectures.
I.   Bruce, Calvin E.   II.   Jones, William Ronald.
BT82.7.B57   230   75–39113
ISBN 0–8387–1893–0

The editors wish to thank Doubleday for permission to quote from
BLACK RELIGION AND BLACK RADICALISM, copyright © 1972
by Gayraud S. Wilmore. Reprinted by permission of Doubleday &
Company, Inc.

PRINTED IN THE UNITED STATES OF AMERICA

to
our families, for their encouragement,
and to
DR. C. SHELBY ROOKS,
for sustaining a vision of what black religious scholarship can
mean to the black community, and for sharing that vision
with many talented, young scholars.

CONTENTS

PREFACE

The title of this book is a metaphor. We have chosen it to suggest a series of moves that contemporary black theology must make to strengthen its objectives and broaden its horizons. *Black Theology II* represents an attitude of respect and scholarly eagerness, shared by a number of thinkers, intended to advance the concerns of black theological discourse. We are fortunate to have a few of this growing number of thinkers contribute to this forum. Yet we regret that, because of space limitations, the insights of a number of other scholars will be missing from these pages.

Our trust is that both the serious advocate of black theology and the casual reader will profit from fresh perspectives on what makes black theology what it is and what its future development should look like. Each writer speaks for himself/herself. But the views shared are meant to further the dialogue into which all appreciative minds can be drawn.

Last, it would be too long a list to recognize by name the many persons whose encouragement, suggestions, and intellectual stimulation made this volume possible. To all who had a hand in this enterprise, we offer our heartfelt thanks.

C. E. B.

W. R. J.

9

ACKNOWLEDGMENTS

We wish to thank the following publishers for permission to quote from copyrighted material:

Abingdon Press, for permission to quote from Major J. Jones, *Black Awareness: A Theology of Hope.*

Alkebu-Lan Books, for permission to quote from Yosef ben-Jochannan, *African Origins of the Major "Western Religions."* Permission granted by The Publishers, Alkebu-Lan Books Assoc. (209 West 125th Street, Suite 218, New York, N.Y. 10027).

Cambridge University Press, for permission to quote from Alfred N. Whitehead, *Religion in the Making.*

Harper & Row, Publishers, Inc., for permission to quote from Allen B. Ballard, *The Education of Black Folk: The Afro-American Struggle for Knowledge in White America.*

Johnson Publishing Company, Inc., for permission to quote from *The Negro Mood,* by Lerone Bennett, Jr., © 1964, Johnson Publishing Co., Inc., Chicago; and from *Before the Mayflower,* by Lerone Bennett, Jr., © 1961, Johnson Publishing Co., Inc., Chicago.

J. B. Lippincott Company, for permission to quote from *A Black Theology of Liberation* by James H. Cone. Copyright © 1971 by James H. Cone. Reprinted by permission of J. B. Lippincott Company.

Macmillan Publishing Company, Inc., for permission to quote from *Religion in the Making* by Alfred North

11

INTRODUCTION

Theology is concerned with making sense of a faith that is worth sustaining at all costs.

Theology is a particularly paradoxical enterprise. In a sense, it is timeless. But there is something that makes all theology bound by time and conditioned by culture.

Theology is strengthened by tradition, but it is not boxed in by any generation's interpretation of tradition as it has received it. In fact, as the Reformers taught us, theology is as much fortified by reaction against tradition as by unchallenged allegiance to it.

Theology is articulated in the medium of culture, and the impact of culture permeates its warp and woof. Just as there is no acultural theology, there is no articulation of theology apart from the cultural self-expression of those who contend for the faith.

Its quality of "mutability" makes theology active in the lives of the faithful as a growing body of thought, not as a stultified mass of intellectual dead weight. Theology changes by virtue of reason's urging us to see old truths in new ways.

A living theology is an abrasive one. Its cutting edge gnaws at all the stubborn obstacles that obscure both fresh illumination from divinity and novel observations of man in relation to his fellow man.

A theology that perpetuates itself rubs against the grain of unquestioned acceptance of the human condition. It dares to ask Why? and is restive until it finds some suitable answers.

Theology joins philosophy in the quest for understanding life's dearest truths and profoundest enigmas. Yet theology resigns itself to a level of trust that may not pass the test of philosophic credibility. For theology does not deny our experiences with the supramundane.

Experience does not validate theology's pronouncements on every score, but theological perspicuity makes sense of our most common everyday experiences.

The faithful have a testimony, and theology frames that testimony on the canvas of ecclesiastical history and against the background of sacral availability to God's presence. Theology convinces us that the Highest is both knowable and approachable.

Theology is not an end in itself. It embraces qualities for living in the here-and-now and fosters hope that endures even after death. Thus, theology looks beyond itself to insure in us a strong measure of confidence in that to which we are ultimately committed.

II

Black theology endeavors to understand and transmit a faith that has nurtured black people's souls that have been tested and tried by oppressive circumstances.

Black theology is paradoxically self-assertive. It is old and new, oral and written, eloquent and simple. It defines itself over against all theological enterprises that fail to account for the realities of the black struggle. But it is somewhat hard put to proclaim, in every case, what it stands for on its own.

Black theology is strengthened by the respectful challenge of the tradition that has made its inception so indispensable. Black theology recognizes that the history of black people's belief is both glorious and inglorious. While not denying the inglorious, black theology presses forward to make the present circumstances of blacks' existence less bitter and more joyful.

Cultural reawakening is the backbone of black theology. Its spokesmen understand that the soulfulness of blacks' existence, distinctive in many respects, demands some reformulation of traditional theological insight. Black culture sees in theological demonstration of God's love a source of pride in the re-creation of black humanity.

Black theology is nourished by active and imaginative hearts and minds. Dogmatization of black theological insight would deplete its vital life force. Flexibility of method makes the constancy of doctrine an impetus for intellectual rethinking of the truths we cherish because they set us free.

Black theology is both incisive and abrasive. Its prophetic thrust cuts to the core of social ills and exposes the sins that fester beneath the deceptive veneer of social progress. The black theologian waits for a word from the Lord and the moving of the Spirit to tell him what is *really* happening. The word he receives is bound to rub someone the wrong way.

For the black theologian employs his theology as a tool for asking the questions that show disrespect for ecclesiastical propriety. Less concerned with what was, black theology gives a contemporaneous witness that questions what is and what will be the course of the black church.

Metaphysics as much as politics supports the philosophic relevance of black theology. All the profound questions of life are part of black theology's struggle to comprehend the good and the evil that inescapably color our lives. Black theology is not ashamed to admit that the faith that has motivated black believers to endure has heretofore had metaphysical valuation attributed to it without question. Now it recognizes that faith invites a critique of the answers it gives concerning suffering and evil.

Many experiences constitute "the black experience." Metaphorically, the totality of black experience is the testing board for the "ontologic validity" of black theology. If black theology speaks to and through our individual experience, we can be sure that what it attempts to say is worth hearing. Black theology respects the testimony of the black church, and it acknowledges that within the composite story of the church's will to survive are included personal testimonies of liberative character. The spiritual, even ecstatic, quality of black religion backing black theology assures us that if ultimacy is discernible, we can know it for ourselves.

Never is black theology an end in itself—it is faith seeking understanding, and understanding requestioning faith. Theology aids us in living life to the fullest, while assuring us that death does not end the soul's quest for greater peace. Black theology bolsters our courage to realign ourselves with the loyalty to which we are ultimately committed. In most cases, this is God himself.

Not satisfied with past expressions of its liberative truths, contemporary black theology searches for new ways to tell the old, old story of grace and freedom.

III

There has always been theological reflection upon the life and faith of the black church. In this regard there has always been a black theology flowing, like love, from "breast to breast" among those devoted to the cause of Christ. However, there has not always been sustained academic examination of how black belief interlaces the varied cultural expressions of newly enlightened black communities.

Black theology did not commence with the theopolitical writings of black churchmen in the 1960s. The oral/aural tradition of black theologizing is lasting and convincing evidence that black Christians have always sought to expound, interpret, and apply the content of Christian faith to the specific contexts of its advocates. This tradition is currently with us, as evidenced by the appreciative "ear to hear" that most black congregations have sensitively developed. The written tradition of black theologizing, slightly more obscure and hence more different to trace, is equally persuasive of the sincerity with which black believers have examined matters that concern the professional theologian.

We need not point to the impressive attempts made by black churchmen in bygone centuries to construct a systematic theology pertinent to black Christians to make the point of the endurance of black theology. Afro-American cultural history has been sustained by informal theological insistence that the will to live need not be obliterated by oppressive opposition.

The early writings of those doing theology-in-black uttered the primal cries of those questing for full spiritual and political liberation. Later literary endeavors spawned the mounting urgency in the collective psyche for clearer articulation of the interplay of black existence and black belief in the fulfillment of that quest. Black theology has endured because the plaintive cries have reechoed and because methodolgical dissatisfaction has prompted, among black churchmen, more ambitious expressions of truths that speak to the spirit of black humanity.

The influence of secular history is telling. It was not until the resounding salvos of Black Power captured the minds of complacent Christendom that black theology began to proliferate outside the black church as well as to endure within it. Certainly many persons had already understood the power of black pride and the theological ramifications of Black Power before the late 1960s, when black theology so dramatically announced itself to the church universal.

The words of black theological awareness had been uttered ages ago by many informed churchmen recognizing the mission we have both as blacks and as black Christians. With the explosion of the new black consciousness, however, what had formerly been whispered from the pulpit was shouted from the podium. And the intellectuals picked up the message—seeking to respeak it to those in the academy. Therein lay a new challenge for black theology.

A different metaphor speaks to the point. Though the threads of black theology appear boldly in the fabric of

black church history, the concerted attempt to interlace
those threads with the weaving of unrelenting intellectual
rigor is a new undertaking.

Black religionists addressing both the black church and
the white academy faced this novel undertaking with passion and conviction. Imaginatively and sensitively, the
liberation-minded black theologians informed us that the
black agenda for freedom must correlate with the theological
teachings of Christian identity and purpose. Their messages
of liberation, reconciliation, hope, and nationalism were
geared toward promulgating the intellectual integrity of the
black community's struggle, and toward underscoring the
political expediency of its achieving corroborative victory in
its mission.

The writings of James H. Cone, J. Deotis Roberts, Sr.,
Major J. Jones, and Albert B. Cleage highlight the strength
of that new undertaking. We allude to their publications as
"Black Theology I." They represent some of the first recent
literary endeavors to make the gospel of black liberation
touch base with rediscovered black awareness, the new black
politics, and the reassessment of the mission of the black
church to the world.

Black Theology I has made an indelible impression on
the rethinking of Christian faith and action. Not only has
black-leberation theology paved the way for feminist and
third-world theologies to make their bid for ecclesiastical
attention, it has impelled "white" or standard theology to
reevaluate its formulations and strategies for representing
Christ amid the suffering, poverty, and death that surround
us.

Black Theology I has become standard curricular fare
in many universities and most seminaries. The rather limited
number of writings under that rubric serve as principal
source material for courses on black theology (understandably) and for courses on black religion that accord a respectful nod to the liberation ambitions of the black church.
Somewhat expectedly, the initial writings in the discipline
of black theology tend to lend themselves to sacrosanct

acceptance as "authoritative." In the minds of some people, the early material on black theology is both the first and last word in the matter.

This book challenges that assessment. It demonstrates that Black Theology I opens the discourse but does not end it. In fact, it would be in violation of the historic growing edge of black theology if further articulation were discounted.

We have suggested what theology is in general, and also something of the enduring character of black Christian theology. We are convinced that the texture of black theology is undergoing modification, inasmuch as new insights and observations flow into the articulation its spokesmen are now giving it. What is emerging is a broadening and deepening of theological sensitivity attached to the movement of black spiritual-political liberation..

We refer to that emergent step as "Black Theology II."

IV

Black Theology II is as much an attitude as a cautious statement of how black theology can be redirected in the coming decades.

It is an attitude shared by both black and white theologians (male and female) that black theology should forge ahead toward the *eventual* accomplishment of systematic construction. It is an awareness that the good of Black Theology I should be preserved, but its dross discarded. It is a mentality that is open to the points of strength offered by analysis of the phenomenon of black theological liberation from a variety of intellectual vantages.

Black Theology II is a transitional movement from the initial self-declaration of black theology's integrity (sometimes still questioned) to the making more fully explicit the outreach potentials derived from that integrity. More precisely, Black Theology II reflects a series of movements that aid the bolstering of black theological discourse as both a self-sustaining academic enterprise and an engaging program of political strategy for the black church.

The writers consenting to address the question of where black theology is headed share a belief that a decisive advancement is needed. Differing in background and ideology, these individuals are convinced that a number of crucial issues attend the task of black theology's making the next important step in its growth: that of "critical expansion." Each is willing to suggest a specific point for focusing the redirective step that will take black theology beyond its apologetic "rage stage."

In some cases, this is a step backward as well as forward. It is a step into black history that traces the sense of vocation that black theology has sustained as part of its historical proclamation of the availability of liberation. Similarly, Black Theology II is a step into the history of higher education, wherein black theological affirmation found mutual support with black cultural identification. The impact of black theology on the collegiate scene gives testimony to the fact that it has an educational ministry that supports it even when it challenges it.

Black Theology II also takes a Janus-like glance at the primal beginnings of black faith. In order to progress toward the adoption of the kind of theological model that best suits the struggles for liberation of black humanity, it is necessary to reconsider the theological formulations of historical black theology. There is an African religious component in this body of early theological self-understanding of Afro-Americans. Yet there are decisively non-African components that inhere in black Christian belief.

Both foci are part of a broader horizon of theological assertion that correlates with a particular method for advancing contemporary black theology.

The second section of the book considers the outreach potentials of black theological scholarship.

Urgent among the concerns of this facet of Black Theology II is the need to broaden the dialogical strength of black theological discourse. On the one hand, this demands that black theologians be in spirited dialogue among themselves and with all segments of the black church. On the other hand, this need for communicative redirection urges that black theologians profit from the dialogue into which many white theologians are willing to enter. A philosophic reexamination of black theology's essential tenets is another part of its next step. Although the theistic emphasis of black theology is acknowledged in the history of the black church, a humanistic rethinking of black suffering cannot be ignored. The issue of black theodicy, already becoming more important, calls for a critical response from a black theologian who insists that black theism can be ransomed from philosophic peril and is, indeed, liberative.

A third perspective on black theology's philosophical frame of reference is included. When black suffering is analyzed in the light of process thought, some dramatic implications hold true for the expression of faith that is qualified by, but not circumscribed by, the totality of the suffering event.

Also, it is felicitous for black theology to reach out to embrace other vanguards of the human liberation movement. Whether or not black and feminist theologies eventuate a concerted effort to attack both racism and sexism may depend upon black theologians' realizing the importance of sexist issues for the black community, especially its females. At least the dialogue among blacks and feminists should be opened, and the obstacles barring it recognized from the outset.

BLACK THEOLOGY II

PART I

Black Theology in Formation

1
Vocation and Black Theology

WILLIAM H. BECKER

Vocation—the sense of being called to perform some special task, carry some burden, play some significant role—is a concept and a symbol deeply rooted in the experience of the black American. The black sense of vocation has at least four historical roots; two are shared with white Americans, two are distinctly black, and all four are very much intertwined in this multicolored American soil.

THE ROOTS OF BLACK VOCATIONAL CONSCIOUSNESS

First is the biblical concept of Israel as a people chosen by God, whose vocation it is to "choose life, that you and your descendants may live, loving the Lord your God, obeying his voice, and cleaving to him" (Deut. 30:19–20). Just as the New England Puritans understood themselves to be a New Israel, bound in covenant with God, so, too, did the black slaves. The parallel is drawn in early spirituals:

> Go down, Moses
> 'Way down in Egypt land,
> Tell ole Pharaoh,
> To let my people go

It is found in post-Emancipation sermons, such as Alexander Crummell's "The Destined Superiority of the Negro" (1877):

> When God does not destroy a people, but, on the contrary, trains and disciplines it, it is an indication that He intends to make something of them, and do something for them. It signifies that He is graciously interested in such a people. In a sense, not equal, indeed, to the case of the Jews, but parallel, in a lower degree, such a people are a "chosen people" of the Lord.[1]

The second root of the black American's sense of vocation goes back not to Hebrew revelation but to French Enlightenment philosophy: the philosophy of the natural rights of man, as expressed by Thomas Jefferson and embodied in what is often called the "American Creed." This creed, as described by Gunnar Myrdal, affirms the "ideals of the essential dignity of the individual, of the basic equality of all men and of certain inalienable rights to freedom, justice, and fair opportunity," ideas that "represent to the American people the meaning of the nation's early struggle for independence."

> The American Negroes know they are an oppressed group experiencing, more than anybody else in the nation, the consequences of the fact that the Creed is not lived up to in America. Yet their faith in the Creed is not simply a means of pleading for their rights. They, like the whites, believe, with one part of themselves, that the Creed is ruling America.[2]

In 1829 David Walker addressed this vocational question to white America: "Do you understand your own language? Hear your language proclaimed to the world, July 4, 1776— 'We hold these truths to be self evident—that All men are created EQUAL!!' "[3] In 1903 W. E. B. DuBois wrote: "There are today no truer exponents of the pure human spirit of the Declaration of Independence than the American Negroes."[4]

Suffering is a third source of the black sense of vocation: the suffering of slavery, the suffering of the "dream deferred" after Emancipation. Oppression, if it does not destroy a people, sometimes functions as a crucible from which that people emerges with a new sense of identity and mission. Why is this so—that sometimes suffering leads to the acceptance of a calling? In a moving article entitled "I Hear Them . . . Calling," Vincent Harding gives us a hint: to hear the voices out of one's past, from one's suffering people, is to be called:

> I hear my people. I hear them calling. . . . I hear them, mourning, weeping, wailing, prostrate around the thousands of trees where brothers and sisters were hung and burned and mutilated beyond recognition by a savage people. I hear them vowing never to give in, never to turn back. . . . I hear Nat Turner and David Walker, . . . I hear Garvey and Du Bois, . . . I hear my mother, sighing. . . . I hear . . . my children. . . . I hear their voices, and I know what it means. It means I am called.[5]

The minority group has been defined as "any group of people who because of their physical or cultural characteristics, are singled out from the others in the society in which they live for differential and unequal treatment, and who therefore regard themselves as objects of collective discrimination." [6] This means that there are dynamics built into the situation of the minority group that may encourage the development of a special sense of vocation. Discrimination creates a special sense of group identity—even where it did not exist before—and out of that identity there may naturally arise certain questions that have a vocational thrust: What are the special characteristics that lead us to be set apart? What should be our attitude toward these characteristics: affirmation or denial? What should be our response to those who reject us: opposition or assimilation? In short, what is our proper calling with respect to our particular identity?

African soil produced the fourth of these vocational roots: the call to understand, nurture, and be faithful to the African heritage of the American black. One need not be troubled by the fact that most American blacks have never stood on African soil, nor that the issue of whether there are significant "African survivals" among North American blacks is so moot.[7] The vocational meaning and power of the African heritage for the American black derives, not from conscious memory or cultural-linguistic survivals, but from its symbolic meaning. For many American blacks in many periods—particulary periods of black nationalism—Africa has functioned as a symbol of black origin, black identity, black freedom, and black authenticity. The name *African* was used in the titles of innumerable black American voluntary associations, both religious and secular, and the "back to Africa" theme played a central role in many black movements well before Marcus Garvey made it a famous slogan.[8]

> So even if he had no conscious memory of Africa, the image of Africa played an enormous part in the religion of the black man. The image of Africa . . . constitutes the religious revalorization of the land, a place, where the natural and ordinary gestures of the black man were and could be authenticated. In this connection, one can trace almost every nationalistic movement among the blacks and find Africa to be the dominating and guiding image.[9]

What Charles Long says here of black religion and nationalism can without distinction be applied to the black sense of vocation: Africa has been a "dominating and guiding image" in defining and empowering that vocation, and it is still.

These four roots of the black American's sense of vocation are, as I said above, intertwined in our American soil. Some black prophets have given vivid expression to this intertwining, describing black identity and vocation in terms that insist that all the roots be retained, none cut off. W. E. B. Du Bois, writing of the black man's "twoness,—an American, a Negro; two souls, two thoughts, two unreconciled strivings," affirmed the black man's longing "to merge his double self into a better and truer self."

In this merging he wishes neither of the older selves to be
lost. He would not Africanize America, for America has too
much to teach the world and Africa. He would not bleach
his Negro soul in a flood of white Americanism, for he knows
that Negro blood has a message for the world. He simply
wishes to make it possible for a man to be both a Negro and
an American, without being cursed and spit upon by his
fellows, without having the doors of Opportunity closed
roughly in his face.[10]

Other black prophets and leaders have concluded, in various
periods, that one or more of these vocational roots is dead
or moribund, diseased or dysfunctional—and hence should
be cut away. Henry M. Turner and Marcus Garvey argued
for the need to cut off the diseased American root, and with
it the root of oppression and suffering, and nourish the
African and biblical roots. Malcolm X insisted, on the other
hand, that biblical Christianity, too, having been corrupted
by white racism, must be rejected as a root of the black
vocation. Yet, in spite of the efforts of these and other black
prophets, all four of these vocational roots still seem alive
and firmly established, capable, in various possible combinations, of continuing to nourish the tree of black vocational consciousness. In the next section I will consider the
question, what continuation of roots is being selected to
nourish the vocation of this small but robust sapling called
Black Theology?

The Vocation of Black Theology

Black theology is a "theology of peoplehood," that is, a
theology that finds God revealed in the experience of a
particular community, and is devoted to the interpretation
of that experience. There are many forms of such theology
now in process of development in the United States: the
new particularism in Judaism, the "theology of women," the
"theology of youth," and the "new ethnicity." The 1972
edition of the annual collection of articles entitled *New
Theology* is devoted to "The New Particularisms—nation,
tribe, race, clan, ethnic group, gender and generation." [11]

Particularist or inclusive? The first and most basic question to be asked about the vocation of black theology is the one that must be asked of all the "new particularisms" I have mentioned: how inclusive or exclusive is your calling? How does your vocation relate you to those who are not part of your particular community?

> Theology related to the experience of a people will tend to be dynamic, concrete, unitive, totalist—and it may be dangerous. When a transcendent reference is related to tribe, clan, race, people, or nation—whether the appeal is made to Yahweh or Allah, the God of Our Fathers or the God of Battles—the dangers of messianism, destructive missionism, and pride are all present.[12]

In South Africa, for example, the policy of apartheid derives at least in part from the Afrikaner conviction that God created His people with the special mission of civilizing that land.

There will inevitably be strong resistance from proponents of the new particularisms to questions about the dangers of exclusivism and pride, particularly if they are raised by those outside the particular community. Resistance is inevitable because, in the first place, such questions will be viewed—and indeed may sometimes be intended—as attacks. Insofar as one sees his identity and integrity as rooted in the life of a particular community, efforts to question, deemphasize, or overcome the particularities of his people will appear threatening, even deadly. If these efforts originate with outsiders, they are easily dismissed as at best the foolishness of those who know not whereof they speak, and at worst the activity of Satan. White criticism of Black Theology, writes James Cone, "will not reveal the weakness in Black Theology but only the racist character of the critic." [13]

Resistance occurs, secondly, as a political-rhetorical tactic. Often it is simply easier to make one's case, to further one's cause, by refusing to consider questions that, though neither unfair nor irrelevant, can be pursued only at the cost of blunting one's weapons. James Cone provides a nice example in point: "I *do not intend* to qualify this statement [i.e., that the humanity of the oppressed is "inseparable from man's liberation from whiteness"] *because too much is at stake*—the survival of the black community."[14]

A third reason that the particularist may resist questions about the inclusiveness of his position is this: he may not yet know the answer. At the early stages in the development of a theology of peoplehood it may not be fully clear to anyone, insider or outsider, just how parochial or inclusive this people and their God will turn out to be. We do not yet know whether statements such as "Black Theology will accept only a love of God which participates in the destruction of the white enemy"[15] or "His [God's] Word is our word; his existence, our existence"[16] are to be understood as a form of militant, particularist rhetoric, or taken as careful theological statements.

But whatever may be the resistance to evaluating the particularism of black theology, and whatever may be the difficulties involved, it is a job that has to be done, and indeed the work has already begun. From the moment the terms *black* and *theology* were coupled, certain basic questions were implicitly raised: Precisely what does *black* mean; does it refer to (1) black skin, or to (2) a certain life-experience, or to (3) a certain attitude or perspective on life, on suffering? Do meanings 1, 2, and 3 go together, or can they be separated? Is this theology called *black* because it is produced only *by* blacks (defined as 1, 2, or 3), or only *for* blacks, or rather because—whoever may produce it or read it—it has reference to the black community, black experience, or black perspective? Obviously these are basic questions, literally fundamental to the enterprise. Answering these questions is part of the vocation of black theology, and the answer(s) accepted will in turn determine the nature and scope of that vocation.

At this preliminary stage, one can identify a broad spectrum of different answers to these questions, ranging from those of Albert Cleage and James Cone on the left, to traditionalist "in Christ there is no black nor white" positions on the right, with spokesmen like Vincent Harding, Major Jones, J. Deotis Roberts, Joseph Washington, and others at various points between. Cone and Cleage generally employ these equations: black theology = concern for the oppressed = true Christianity = black power = where Christ is present in America today. On the other hand, white theology = viewpoint of oppressor = false Christianity = white racism = Antichrist. Using these formulas, one obviously must conclude that only black people can hear and understand God's Word and obey His will. Moreover, there is no danger that black people will misunderstand or disobey His will, since in the last analysis their will and God's will are incapable of conflict.

> White religionists are not capable of perceiving the blackness of God because their satanic *whiteness* is a denial of the very essence of divinity. . . . Because black people have come to know themselves as *black*, and because that blackness is the cause of their own love of themselves and hatred of whiteness, God himself must be known only as he reveals himself in his blackness. The blackness of God, and everything implied by it in a racist society, is the heart of Black Theology's doctrine of God. There is no place in Black Theology for a colorless God in a society when people suffer precisely because of their color. The black theologian must reject any conception of God which stifles black self-determination by picturing God as a God of all peoples. . . . Black Theology cannot accept a view of God which does not represent him as being for blacks and thus against whites.[17]

Other spokesmen for a Black Theology argue, to the contrary, that no matter how much God may be "for blacks" he must be for other men as well. "Black Theology," writes Major Jones,

> must be concerned with securing for the black man's aspirations the blessings of God, but these blessings cannot be only for God's chosen people; they must be for the whole human family.[18]

J. Deotis Roberts insists that black theology must "be aware of the perils as well as the promises of the idea of a chosen people." Only if "they correctly understand the role of a suffering servant" and "are not led to consider themselves as superior or favored people before God" can "black people overcome the danger of assuming the posture of a chosen people and at the same time fulfil the promise" of chosenness.[19]

The debate among black theologians concerning the meaning of black *chosenness* and the scope of the black vocation has just begun, but already one point is abundantly clear. That is, that the crucial question to be faced is, what exactly does *black* mean, and to what extent does the vocation of black people derive from their blackness? How crucial this question is can be seen by a careful examination of the two-fold definition of blackness provided by James Cone:

> First, blackness is a *physiological* trait. It refers to a particular black-skinned people in America who have been victims of white racist brutality. . . . Black Theology believes that they are the *only* key that can open the door to divine revelation. Therefore, no American theology can even tend in the direction of Christian theology without coming to terms with the black-skinned people of America. Secondly, Blackness is an *ontological* symbol for all people who participate in the liberation of man from oppression. This is the universal note in Black Theology. It believes that all men were created for freedom, and that God always sides with the oppressed against the oppressors.[20]

At first sight this definition may seem clearly reasoned, in that it recognizes that blackness may have more than one meaning, makes an important distinction between its literal and symbolic meaning, and so on. Also it may appear to face squarely the tension inherent in the claim that a particular people has a mission of universal significance, in that it identifies a "universal note" in black theology, and relates the meaning of blackness to "all men." Actually, however, the reasoning of the definition is thoroughly polemical

36 BLACK THEOLOGY II

and does not stand up under careful scrutiny. Its motif of universality serves to disguise the most radical sort of racial or tribal exclusivism. I find two basic logical-theological problems in the definition.

First, Cone finds the "only key" to divine revelation in blackness as skin color. Since Cone is well aware of the distinction between literal and symbolic meaning, one can fairly assume that he means what he says here : that black skin color, *as a literal physiological trait,* is the only key to an understanding of God's will. This literalism in his definition provides a basis for the radically literalistic statements concerning the relation between blacks and God that permeate his theology. One example : "His [God's] Word is our word; his existence our existence." This literalism, no matter how noble may be the cause it claims to serve, deserves to be called by its true name : black racism and blasphemy.

The second problem is more complex and concerns the relation between a symbol and the meaning to which it refers. Following Paul Tillich's analysis of symbols (as Cone claims to do), a symbol (in this case, blackness) points to a reality beyond itself (in this case, "all people who participate in the liberation of man from oppression") and serves to disclose that reality; but there are no *a priori* grounds for claiming that a particular symbol is the only one through which that reality can be approached or disclosed. The flag is a major symbol of America, the Cross a major symbol of the Gospel, but in neither case are these the *only* adequate symbols. Yet Cone argues not only that blackness symbolically points to liberation from oppression, but that the latter must somehow also point *back to the former.* "To decide the blackness of a particular perspective, we need only ask, 'For whom was it written, the oppressed or the oppressors?' If the former, it is black; if the latter, it is white." [21] In this formulation, being oppressed is defined as *identical* with blackness : whatever is oppressed is black, whatever is black is oppressed. There is a very great difference between this (once again) literalistic formulation and one that genuinely understands blackness to be symbolic. If blackness and oppressed, whiteness and oppressor, are literally identical, then it is not possible to speak of the oppressed who are white or oppressors who are black. If, on the other hand, these terms are understood to function symbolically, one can assert that blackness can serve as a powerful disclosure of human oppression and liberation, while by no means insisiting that it is the only meaningful disclosure of this reality in our time.

Theological or sociopolitical? Is the vocation of black theology genuinely theological, or is it more accurately described as sociopolitical? Let me stress that though I employ the term *or* in this question, I am by no means assuming or arguing for the separation, a la Martin Luther, of the spiritual and temporal realms. However, given the inextricable relation between these two realms, it remains true that one is likely to have different objectives, choose different terms, employ different standards of judgment, depending upon whether his basic purpose is to reflect upon the faitn of a community (the task of the theologian), or to direct, support, and encourage a community with effective ideological propaganda (the task of the sociopolitical leader and polemicist).

The concrete difference between the two is well illustrated by Cone's definition of blackness, which I have just analyzed. Theologically considered, it is careless and irresponsible. But viewed as the basis for an effective sociopolitical polemic, it is a triumph. What better way to affirm black pride and negate white racism than to define genuine humanity as black and whiteness as sin! There is not much subtlety here, little of humor or the light touch—but it is nevertheless a very effective polemic.

"James Cone," writes one critic, "is on the fence between the Christian faith and the religion of Black Power. It will be necessary for Cone to decide presently where he will take his firm stand." [22] Cone, and black theology in general, will need to decide what the term *theology* is to mean in this context. Does theology have its own integrity, norms, and authority, derived from the biblical revelation to which it refers, or does it instead derive from the black community to which and for which it interprets this revelation?

Since Cone is "on the fence" with respect to this basic question, one can find statements in his writings that would seem to support different answers. Here he stands on the side of biblical revelation: "Whatever is said about the nature of God and his being-in-the-world must be based on the biblical account of God's revelatory activity. We are not free to say anything we please about him." [23] Here he seems to have jumped to the other side: "Black Theology refuses to accept a God who is not identified totally with the goals of the black community. If God is not for us and against white people, then he is a murderer, and we had better kill him. The task of black theology is to kill Gods who do not belong to the black community. . . ." [24] Here he straddles the fence: "Black Theology seeks to create a theological norm which is in harmony with the black condition and the biblical revelation." [25]

There are tremendous rhetorical-polemical advantages to be gained from the freedom to slip back and forth over such a fence, and sometimes to sit and rest on top—but there is also a great spiritual risk. It is the risk of self-deception and the double standard, to which American white racism has so thoroughly succumbed. One is free to express at top volume the rage and hatred that black people feel, and even sanctify it is God's word, while insisting that the view of white men should not be expressed at all, for they are by definition racist and satanic. One is free to argue, and perhaps even believe, that what one's own people does is wholly righteous and without sin; what one's enemy does is wholly evil. One is free to present one's position as a Christian theology, while accepting no responsibility for affirming and living the ethics of Christ.

Other spokesmen for Black Theology have recognized the self-deception in a gospel of blackness = grace/whiteness = sin. They have recognized the need for black theology to take up that extremely difficult, delicate, and unpopular position of articulating liberation for the oppressed, and reconciliation between the oppressed and the oppressor, at the same time.

> A Christian theologian is not an interpreter of the religion of Black Power. . . . He runs the risk of being misunderstood by black militants and moderates as well as by white radicals and liberals. . . . His theological task is a type of ministry to blacks and whites. It is a priestly ministry to blacks. As he speaks of deliverance, he can bring comfort and assurance to those who have been victimized by inhuman treatment much too long. But to many blacks reconciliation will come as harsh judgment. The black theologian's role is that of a prophet as well. His message will often be unwelcomed by blacks as well as by whites. But insofar as he speaks the Christian message in the area of race, he will need to speak of reconciliation beyond confrontation and liberation whatever the risk and whatever the personal cost.[26]

These are profound words, honest enough to face the most difficult truth of the Christian faith: even the one who has already suffered much, even he especially, cannot escape the Cross. The vocation of black theology, if it is to be a genuine theology, includes the acceptance of this truth, this anguish.

America, Third World, or Mankind? One finds a certain ambiguity among black theologians concerning the vocational focus and purpose of black theology. Is it an expression of the black situation in America, or does it adequately express the religious needs of oppressed peoples everywhere? James Cone, here again, seems to be on the fence:

> "Black Theology" is a phrase that is particularly appropriate for contemporary America. . . . However, I am convinced that the patterns of meaning centered in the idea of Black Theology are by no means restricted to the American scene, since blackness symbolizes oppression and liberation in any society.[27]

Given Cone's insistence that liberation theology "is always theology identified with a particular community," that "it is not possible to transcend the community" because our community "decides our being," [28] one wonders whether he has not too casually assumed a "community of being" between blacks in America and the dark-skinned or oppressed elsewhere. Many of Cone's central theological statements presuppose the white-black conflict in American society, and would not seem applicable in, say, India, Nigeria, or Brazil.[29]

Joseph Washington escalates Cone's ambiguity, in that his definitions of the black vocation alternate between the United States and all (rather than simply the third-world) nations. Sometimes he describes this vocation as distinctively American: "The great mission of the Negroes has yet to be accomplished: to witness to the one humanity of the one God here in the United States where groups reside in devisiveness." Washington recognizes that certain tactics effective in America, such as nonviolence, may be "irrelevant to South Africa." Moreover, he limits the messianic role of the American black: "It is presumptuous to believe that God has called the Negro to redeem mankind from war, nationalism, pride, and other human weaknesses." [30] Yet on these same pages Washington asserts that "the Negro is called to be the servant whereby all nations, not just America, will be redeemed. . . . The mission of the Negro must be to unify mankind through acceptance of group differences as blessings rather than punishment." [31]

No doubt there is something built into the dynamics of a minority group that leads to the escalation of its vocational aims during periods of rising self-consciousness: women's liberation promises to liberate men, too; youth culture promises to restructure all of society through its new consciousness; black theology promises to liberate all the oppressed, and/or all mankind. Yet there is something special in the dynamics of black theology, I believe, that drives it to move outside America in a way that a "black theology" developing in Nigeria or even South Africa would not need to do. Black theology in America, as the expression of a minority whose very humanity has been denied by a hostile white majority, has been and still is forced to look *beyond*

America for those fundamental myths and symbols that provide the foundation for a people's sense of identity and vocation. St. Clair Drake speaks of the "great *myths,* the source of every people's deepest strengths," that were necessary to help preserve the dignity and self-esteem of American blacks during slavery and after. In self-defense against the white man's definition of the black as without a soul, without a culture, and without a home, the slaves developed a "counter-image of themselves . . . that they were Africans." This mythological self-image, which Drake terms *Ethiopianism,*

> emerged as a counter-myth to that of Southern white Christians (and many Northern ones). It functioned on a fantasy level giving feelings of worth and self-esteem to the individual, but also as a sanction for varied types of group action. It generated concern for the "redemption" of black men in the Motherland as well as the Diaspora so that the ancient state of power and prestige could be restored. It was the duty of black men who were "saved" to try to "convert" and "save" others—to preach the gospel to their brothers wherever they may be, to enlighten them, to "civilize" them, to lift them from "their fallen state," to "redeem" them.[32]

The Ethiopianism that caused nineteenth-century black churchmen to speak of a "Special Mission of the A.M.E. Church [and other black denominations] to the Darker Races" is still alive in the black theology of the 1970s. Indeed, it has broadened its scope in that now, in some of its expressions, it dreams of redeeming not only "black men in the Motherland as well as the Diaspora," but all of the oppressed and indeed all mankind.

There is great power in this myth of vocation,[33] but also great potential danger. The danger is that the myth of a trans-American vocation may carry the energies and dreams of the homeless American black ("Sometimes I feel like a motherless child—A long way from home") away from this land, which, though inhospitable, is now his only possible homeland, to a myth-land that, though once home, can no longer be so. On the other hand, what American can deny

the grave dangers also inherent in a strictly American vocation for American blacks: that this land will be forever
inhospitable, the American Dream always a lie. "At . . .
times America seems to be the forever unfaithful lover of
the Blues, the lover who is always lamented but never left—
until the last, inevitably bloody scene." [34]

CHRISTOLOGICAL MODELS FOR BLACK VOCATION

Until some of the questions raised in the preceding
sections have been resolved, it will not be possible to define
the vocation of a Christian as understood by black theology.
There will be many possible interpretations of the Christian's
calling, as there are many alternative directions in which
black theology itself may move.

Nevertheless, it is possible to identify some "models" of
Christian manhood that have been so central to the black
experience in America, so dominant in the black tradition,
that one can safely expect that they will continue to inform
and direct black vocational self-understanding, whatever
specific new directions that understanding may take. Since
each of these models is Christological, one could speak of
only one model: Jesus the Christ. I have chosen to speak
of three different Chistological models, in order to emphasize
the distinctive aspects of black vocational identity that are
informed by these models. The models are: Christ Crucified,
Christ Resurrected, and Christ Incarnate. [35]

Doubtless the American black, denied access to the
models of his African religious-cultural heritage, has undergone a more intense and searing quest for appropriate
models of manhood than have most men. He has had to
look with critical distance upon the models presented to
him by a white and racist society and has, often with regret,
perceived the "clay feet" of American models that on the
face of it seem especially tailored to his needs. Thus in 1876,
on the occasion of the unveiling of the Freedman's Monument in memory of Abraham Lincoln, Frederick Douglass
spoke these words:

It must be admitted—truth compels me to admit—even here in the presence of the monument we have erected to his memory, that Abraham Lincoln was not in the fullest sense of the word, either our man or our model. In his interests, in his associations, in his habits of thought and in his prejudices, he was a white man. He was preeminently the white man's President. . . .[36]

But there was one man presented to the slaves as a model, yet capable of sitting in judgment on the slave society presenting him, to which many blacks responded with complete identification. "The glorious manhood of Jesus Christ," said Daniel Payne in an 1888 sermon, "is the only true type of real manhood. I pray thee, then, I beg you, to study it, study it, study it as your only model; study it, study it, until it penetrates your hearts and souls, and guides every movement of your hearts, wills and intellects. Be like Jesus. . . ."[37]

Christ Crucified. "Through some miracle no man can explain," writes Lerone Bennett, "some of the slaves believed." The Cross of Christ, though it may not explain this miracle, was the *sine qua non* of its occurrence.

Going straight to the heart of the matter, the Negro slave gave central importance to that which Christians have been fleeing for almost two thousand years: the cross.

Were you there when they crucified my Lord?
Were you there when they nailed him to the tree?
Oh, sometimes, it causes me to tremble, tremble,
tremble.

the implication here is that the slave was *there,* that he knew something about Jesus that no man who did not stand with him, or near him, could possibly know.[38]

Likewise, Jesus knew something about the slave nobody else could know:

Nobody knows the trouble I seen,
Nobody knows but Jesus.

Knowing the Cross and bearing the Cross is one model central to any theology of the black vocation. But the Cross, always a stumbling block, is a very difficult model for the black theologian to deal with today! The crucified one, the lamb led without complaint to slaughter, fades imperceptibly in our fevered vision into a cosmic Uncle Tom. As I have argued elsewhere, American blacks today resemble Jews in insisting "Never again!", though both communities have long claimed a special insight into the potentially redemptive character of suffering.[39]

The arms of the cross stretch so wide, however, as to embrace us even when we are most determined to flee them. No better illustration of their reach could be found than in the ambivalence of James Cone's position on suffering. Cone vehemently rejects any God who would be an accomplice to black suffering, insisting that the God of black men "has chosen them not for redemptive suffering but for freedom." Seventy pages later, however, the reader learns that "freedom is inevitably associated with suffering."

> The existence of Jesus Christ . . . discloses that freedom is bound up with suffering. It is not possible to be for him and not realize that one has chosen an existence in suffering.[40]

Though it involves a mixing of metaphors to say it, there is a circular character to the logic of the cross: to have been *there* once is to be brought back again and again, even against one's will. To know oneself as oppressed is to know that all oppression—even that of one's own oppressor—is fundamentally wrong. One must therefore suffer a limitation on one's own anger that was not suffered by one's oppressor. Camus recognized this in *The Rebel*. Vincent Harding acknowledged it when he asked, concerning Black Power's preoccupation with self-defense, "Does manhood indeed depend on the capacity to defend one's life? . . . Is there perhaps a certain kind of bondage involved when men are so anxious about keeping themselves alive that they are ready to take the lives of others to prevent that occurence?"[41] And likewise Martin Luther King, Jr., wrote that "the central quality in the Negro's life is pain—pain so old and so deep that it shows in almost every moment of his existence," and went on in the same book to insist that, in spite of this, further suffering is necessary and might well have creative effect. "By recognizing the necessity of suffering in a righteous cause, we may achieve our humanity's full stature." [42]

Christ resurrected. "Whether a man has been helped by a miracle," Kierkegaard wrote, "depends essentially upon the degree of intellectual passion he has employed to understand that help was impossible, and next upon how honest he is toward the Power which helped him nevertheless." Even resurrection—the possibility of new life out of the very jaws of defeat and death—is no miracle unless the resurrected have the passionate understanding and honesty to see it as such, to say with the father in Jesus' Parable of the Prodigal Son, "My son was dead, and is alive again; he was lost, and is found."

In their centuries-long American experience, American blacks have known, within and beyond the agony of crucifixion, the power of resurrection in life. Resurrection has been experienced, first of all, in the very endurance by which American blacks, though oppressed, have remained alive and creative as a people.

> *The Negro endured:* let us begin with that . . . inestimable contribution to his posterity and to his native land. . . . In other places and in other climes, brown and red men drank the white man's whiskey, read his Bible, became demoralized and wasted away into nothingness. The Negro drank the white man's whiskey, read his Bible, did his work—and his tribe increased. He descended into the hell of slavery, was denied books, pencil and paper, was denied the sanctity of marriage —was crucified, in fact, and rose again some three hundred years later in Chicago and Harlem and Atlanta and Washington. *The Negro endured.*[43]

Endurance here means more than simply physical survival. The Mountain People of Colin Turnbull's book of that name have survived, but they are no longer a people; they have no contribution to make to themselves or anyone else—

except as a frightening example. But the endurance of the American black has by some special grace been permeated in every period by a spirit of affirmation that Lerone Bennett has called "the sun of a fierce and irresistible will to life." Howard Thurman found this spirit strongly present in the sorrow songs of the slaves, along with all the anguish, and even yearning for death, that these songs express. "This is the miracle of their achievement . . . they made a worthless life, the life of chattel property, a mere thing, a body, *worth living*." [44]

Resurrection has become a part of the black vocation in a second way, a way that concerns the endurance, not of black people themselves, but of the great visions and fundamental ideals of the Bible and the American creed. The practitioners of slavery stole, sold, chained, beat, and raped their slaves, and murdered these visions and ideals; how then can they still be alive for the American black? Part of the answer must be, of course, the candid recognition that for many blacks they are not alive. The vision of a brotherly love in which even the enemy is to be included, for example, becomes obscene when it is preached by a master to his slave. "Many black militants," writes James Cone, "have no time for God and all that religious crap with its deadly prattle about loving your enemies and turning the other cheek." [45] Addison Gayle accuses Christ: "You are the greatest slave master of them all. You taught us to be good to our enemies, to love them, to forgive them. Holding out promises of heaven, you tied our hands and made us weak." [46]

But—and this is the resurrection—there is much more in blacks' hearts than bitterness, disappointment, and the rejection of great visions because they have been corrupted by hypocrites, know-nothings, and savage men. There is, and there has been from the time of the early sorrow songs, a black awareness of the difference between the biblical vision itself (or the vision of the American creed) and those who, in affirming it, consciously or unconsciously corrupt and deny it.

Heaven, Heaven,
Everybody talkin' bout heaven ain't goin' there.

In his *Narrative* of 1845, Frederick Douglass put the distinction with great force:

> Between the Chistianity of this land, and the Christianity of Christ, I recognize the widest possible difference. . . . I love the pure, peaceable, and impartial Christianity of Christ; I therefore hate the corrupt, slaveholding, women-whipping, cradle-plundering, partial and hypocritical Christianity of this land.[47]

It is a part of the crucifixion-experience of black Americans that this distinction had to be so constantly drawn; it is part of their resurrection-experience that they had the grace to draw it, to appropriate for themselves the substance of great visions, while rejecting as hypocrites many of the whites who first told them of these visions. And it is only because resurrection is part of the black experience and a model for the black vocation that these words, imprinted in our memories, could have been spoken:

> Even though we must face the difficulties of today and tomorrow, I still have a dream. It is a dream deeply rooted in the American dream. . . . I have a dream that one day on the red hills of Georgia, sons of former slaves and sons of former slave-owners will be able to sit down together at the table of brotherhood.[48]

Our dream was dead, and is alive again; it was lost, and is found.

Christ Incarnate. If the Word of God became flesh in the Christ, then there can be no essential discontinuity or conflict between spirit and matter, the sacred and the secular, holiness and daily life. This is the logic of the incarnation, a logic that is central to the Protestant insistence that every worthy vocation is a proper expression of service to God, and that every Christian, whatever his work, has the religious vocation to serve as a priest to his neighbor. In spite of this basic logic, Protestant Christianity—particularly in

America—has become infected by a legalism that tends to classify human activities into "the good" and "the sinful," and to distinguish categorically "righteous" from "immoral" men. Langdon Gilkey, with dismay, recognized this tendency among many of his more religious fellow Protestants during a period of imprisonment in a Japanese internment camp. He said:

> It was ironic that these Protestants here described seemed to incarnate even more than their monastic brothers the very view of Christianity they repeatedly deplored, namely, a Christianity which removed itself from men to seek salvation away from the actual life of real people. In their frantic effort to escape the fleshly vices and so to be "holy," many fell unwittingly into the far more crippling sins of the spirit, such as pride, rejection, and lovelessness. This, I continue to feel, has been the greatest tragedy of Protestant life.[49]

"If *that* is morality, then I want none of it," was the response of many internees to these self-righteous Christians.

Black Americans, it would seem, have to a large extent avoided the world-denying legalism and moralism so characteristic of much white American Protestantism. Some suggest that this is due to their African heritage, in that the traditional religions of Africa make "no formal distinction between the sacred and the secular, between the religious and the non-religious, between the spiritual and the material areas of life." [50] Whatever its source, there is an insistence in the black tradition on holding together in their tension and complementarity "the poles of pain and joy, agony and ecstasy, good and bad, Sunday and Saturday." As Lerone Bennett points out, this black attitude is "un-Anglo Saxon in its balance and complexity" and has affinities with Zen Buddhism in understanding that "good and evil, creative and destructive, wise and foolish, up and down, [are] inseparable polarities of existence." [51]

> Sometimes I'm up
> Sometimes I'm down
> Oh, yes, Lord.

Incarnation, an insistence upon holding together in their creative tension the worldly and the spiritual, Saturday and Sunday—this, too, is a major Christological model for the black vocation. The biblical picture of Jesus the Christ as incarnate, crucified, and resurrected promises to provide today's black theology with rich and compelling models of the black Christian vocation. And even if this be a black messiah, one may hope that some nonblack Americans too will have ears to hear his calling.

NOTES TO CHAPTER 1

1. Alexander Crummell, "The Destined Superiority of the Negro: A Thanksgiving Discourse, 1877," in *The Greatness of Christ and Other Sermons* (New York, 1882), p. 351.

2. Arnold Rose, ed., *The Negro in America: The Condensed Version of Gunnar Myrdal's An American Dilemma* (New York: Harper and Row, 1964), p. 2.

3. David Walker as quoted in W. E. B. Du Bois, *The Gift of Black Folk* (New York: Washington Square Press, 1970), p. 85.

4. W. E. B. Du Bois, *The Souls of Black Folk* (New York: Fawcett, 1961), p. 22.

5. Vincent Harding, "I Hear Them . . . Calling (And I Know What It Means)," *Katallagete* 4, nos. 2–3 (Fall–Winter): 24–25.

6. Helen M. Hacker, "Women as a Minority Group," in Betty and Theodore Roszak, eds., *Masculine/Feminine* (New York: Harper and Row, 1969), pp. 131–32.

7. E. Franklin Frazier took the position, in *The Negro Church in America* and other books, that the experience of the middle passage and slavery effectively destroyed the African heritage of North American blacks. Melville Herskovits in *The Myth of the Negro Past* finds significant African survivals, particularly in the religious life of North American blacks. Whatever the extent of African cultural survivals, it is important to recognize that Africa as "homeland" has functioned as a powerful relgious-secular symbol for American blacks. This argument is stressed in the sources cited in notes 9 and 32.

8. Cf. Edwin S. Redkey, *Black Exodus: Black Nationalist and Back-to-Africa Movements, 1890–1910* (New Haven, Conn.: Yale University Press, 1969).

9. Charles H. Long, "Perspectives for a Study of Afro-American Religion in the United States," in *History of Religions* 11, no. 1 (August 1971): 58.

10. W. E. B. Du Bois, *Souls of Black Folk*, p. 17.
11. Martin Marty and Dean Peerman, eds., *New Theology No. 9* (New York: Macmillan, 1972).
12. Ibid., p. 13.
13. James H. Cone, *A Black Theology of Liberation* (Philadelphia: J. B. Lippincott, 1970), p. 33.
14. Ibid., p. 28 (italics mine).
15. Ibid., p. 136.
16. Ibid., p. 62.
17. Ibid., pp. 122, 120, 131.
18. Major J. Jones, *Black Awareness: A Theology of Hope* (Nashville, Tenn.: Abingdon Press, 1971), p. 119.
19. J. Deotis Roberts, *Liberation and Reconciliation: A Black Theology* (Philadelphia: Westminster Press, 1971), pp. 49, 59.
20. Cone, *A Black Theology of Liberation*, p. 32.
21. Ibid., p. 28.
22. Roberts, *Liberation and Reconciliation*, p. 21.
23. Cone, *A Black Theology of Liberation*, p. 116.
24. Ibid., pp. 59–60.
25. Ibid., p. 76.
26. Roberts, *Liberation and Reconciliation*, pp. 21–22.
27. Cone, *A Black Theology of Liberation*, pp. 11–12.
28. Ibid., pp. 25, 175.
29. For a discussion of the differences between Black and African Theology see David G. Gelzer, "Random Notes on Black Theology and African Theology," *The Christian Century* 87, no. 37 (Sept. 16, 1970): 1091–92
30. Joseph Washington, Jr., *The Politics of God* (Boston: Beacon Press, 1969), pp. 158, 161.
31. Ibid., p. 160.
32. St. Clair Drake, *The Redemption of Africa and Black Religion* (Chicago: Third World Press, 1970), pp. 50, 18, 11.
33. For a discussion of the "symbol of the black man as missionary to other men of color" and its power, see my article, "The Black Church: Manhood and Mission," *Journal of the American Academy of Religion* 40, no. 3 (Sept. 1972): 316–33.
34. Vincent Harding, "The Religion of Black Power," *The Religious Situation: 1968*, ed. Donald Cutler (Boston: Beacon Press, 1968), p. 20.
35. Two comments about this trinity of models. First, the three titles, believe it or not, were not chosen first, and the content then found to fill in these orthodox forms. Rather, the titles came to mind as appropriate ways to sum up the material studied. Second, I am aware that chronology, at least the chronology of Jesus' life, requires the order: incarnation, crucifixion, resurrection. But the logic of my discussion, and perhaps also the chonology of the black experience in America, is better served by the order I have used.

36. Frederick Douglass, *Life and Times of Frederick Douglass* (1892), reprint ed. (New York: Bonanza Books, 1962), p. 484.

37. Daniel A. Payne, *Sermons and Addresses, 1853–1891*, ed. Charles Killian (New York: Arno Press, 1072), p 58.

38. Lerone Bennett, Jr., *The Negro Mood and Other Essays* (Chicago: Johnson Publishing Co., 1964), p. 68.

39. Cf. William H. Becker, "Black and Jew: Ambivalence and Affinities," *Soundings* 43, no. 4 (Winter 1970): 413–37.

40. Cone, *A Black Theology of Liberation*, p. 181.

41. Harding, "Religion of Black Power," pp. 21–22.

42. Martin Luther King, Jr., *Where Do We Go From Here: Chaos or Community?* (New York: Bantam Books, 1967), pp. 122, 54.

43. Bennett, *The Negro Mood*, p. 63.

44. Howard Thurman, *The Negro Spiritual Speaks of Life and Death* (New York: Harper and Bros., 1947), p. 56.

45. Cone, *A Black Theology of Liberation*, p. 110.

46. Addison Gayle, *The Black Situation* (New York: Horizon Press, 1970), p. 132.

47. Frederick Douglass, *Narrative of the Life of Frederick Douglass, An American Slave, Written by Himself* (New York: Signet Books, 1968), p. 120.

48. Martin Luther King, Jr., "I have a dream" (Speech delivered in Washington, D.C., August 28, 1963, The March on Washington for Civil Rights).

49. Langdon Gilkey, *Shantung Compound* (New York: Harper and Row, 1966), p. 188.

50. John S. Mbiti, *African Religions and Philosophy* (New York: Praeger Publishers, 1969), p. 2.

51. Bennett, *The Negro Mood*, p. 51.

2
Black Theology and Blacks on Campus

EDWARD LeROY LONG, JR.

One focus for this discussion is the development of black theology, the object of specific attention for most essays within this volume. Black theology has transformed black religion by moving from the acceptance of suffering in this world—compensated for by the hope of glory in the next life—to an assertive and challenging declartion that blackness has central significance for present existence and is a unique condition from which to proclaim the Gospel. Liberation has always been a theme in black religion, but the difference between treating it as a postponed hope and affirming it as something to be grasped through the present celebration of a unique ethnicity constitutes a major transformation in perspective. This transformation has been accompanied by important changes in the posture of the black toward society, and may itself have contributed to such changes.[1]

The other focus for this discussion is the experience of blacks on campus. The changes that have taken place in this regard are manifold and have broken in upon the American institution of higher learning with poignant forcefulness and moral urgency. The expansion of educational opportunities

for minority groups—particularly for those once called
Negroes—started with efforts to recruit a cadre of black
students for institutions that had become ethnically colorless
and representative of economic privilege. Institutions discovered that a merely "open" policy of nondiscrimination
was not enough to bring about ethnic balance, and that only
a deliberate counterbalancing would effect justice. Even
institutions that had for years admitted people of color without hesitation came to realize that their whole educational
and pedagogical milieu was not attracting the constituency
that their ideals called for. A passive policy of nondiscrim-
ation merely drew from a pool of applicants that was already
skewed along cultural and economic lines endemic to a
racially unjust society. The special efforts instituted to coun-
teract this situation had unforeseen and striking impacts
upon campus life and pedagogical assumptions—impacts
that still elicit lingering uncertainties for many members of
the academic community.

The late nineteen sixties saw the crossing of a decisive
cultural divide in both theology and education. With regard
to the theological changes, this proclamation is typical:

> Black Theology is a theology of black liberation. It seeks to
> plumb the black condition in the light of God's revelation in
> Jesus Christ, so that the black community can see the gospel
> is commensurate with the achievement of black humanity.
> Black Theology is a theology of "blackness." It is the affirma-
> tion of black humanity that emancipates black people from
> white racism thus providing authentic freedom for both white
> and black people. It affirms the humanity of white people in
> that it says "No" to the encroachment of white oppression.²

With both similarity and contrast there is the following
assessment of the campus agitations during the same period,
agitations that were aspects of the black thrust for identity,
recognition, and authenticity in the campus scheme of
things:

> The demands the students brought to the attention of the
> status-quo administrators and faculties of those predominantly

white institutions spoke in wholesale form to the need for the universities to become more responsive to human needs, and to incorporate perspectives and values outside the one-dimensional premise of the "superiority" of Anglo-Saxon Western culture. The students' particular demands addressed the need to have black values reflected at every level of the academic experience—in curriculum changes, in faculty and administrative changes, and in the involvement of greater proportions of students who come from backgrounds traditionally excluded from the university experience.[3]

Both of these statements, which refer from different perspectives to a similar transformation of consciousness, herald the crossing of a great theological and educational gap. The divide itself, where the excitement is concentrated, may not be the only important object for attention. The sign marking the exact watershed has monumental implications, but it may not stand at the most important part of the journey. Every part of the landscape approaching it, including some of the temporary "downs," is part of a movement upwards; every descent from the dividing line, including some of the temporary "ups," is part of a movement into a new valley of promise. In the transformation of consciousness that concerns us, the prelude had advances and retreats, and the postlude will have excitements and failures. But the great line has been crossed, and the flows of circumstance and history will not be subsequently reversed—except at pain of cultural disaster and wholesale folly.

I propose five modalities for discussing the approaches to, crossing of, and journey after this transformation of consciousness. These modalities are admittedly abstract— as are all reflective and interpretive schemes—and they involve certain sequential implications. The sequential implications call for a special caveat. Not all blacks have moved through the modalities at the same pace. Indeed, some of the most severe tensions within the black community, as well as between blacks and other groups, are the results of interaction between people standing in different modalities at the same time. Moreover, because each modality has in its own way served certain needs and values important to its time, it is often difficult for people to shift their assumptions quickly from one to another of these perspectives.

Assimilative accommodation: The first modality in religion and education. For decades before and since their legal emancipation, black Americans were subject to severe deprivations in both religious practice and educational opportunity. The deprivation was so great that it affected Negro experience for almost a century, truncating or frustrating even the best efforts to overcome it. In the practice of religion the slave traders and owners sought to expunge all identifiable native African practices from the life of indentured slaves. ". . . the African's native drum was not allowed the slave because it was as readily adaptable to a call for escape or insurrection as to a call to dance."⁴ Similarly, many whites of the time, even following legal emancipation, reasoned that since "blackness of skin placed an individual in the animal species, then whites were justified in treating such creatures, after taming them, in the same fashion they would treat a dog, horse, or cow. And dogs, horses, and cows do not go to school."⁵

Religion maneuvered under the harsh blanket of oppression more successfully than did education. The American Negro did evolve a religion of depth and power based upon a transformation of biblical idioms by African practice. Dance, drama, music, and story telling—the emotive modes of preaching and worship in the black church— were mostly African in heritage and flavor, but were used to embody a Christian content. The Christian element made the religion more plausible to white overlords, who loved the Bible more than they understood its implications. "Go down, Moses" could be sung in ways that conveyed the full realization of promise to the indentured and disinherited, but to those who heard it superficially it was "good biblical stuff,"

Some religion accessible to slaves was made available paternalistically by owners. Usually the owner's white minister was permitted to hold services for slaves. He often preached on the duty of obedience and drew upon the conservative passages in Paul to support admonitions to subservience. But there were also religious services and events conducted by slave preachers. Sometimes monitored by representatives of the owners (at least whenever suspicions arose) these services were still able to convey a sense of meaning and identity to many who participated in them under the conditions of those times. Howard Thurman has recounted how his grandmother, who was a slave, reacted negatively to the services conducted by the owner's white minister, but positively to those conducted by the slave preacher. Speaking of the latter, his grandmother gave this report:

> It didn't matter what the text was, the minister always ended up at the same place. . . . He would stand up, start very quietly and then look around to all of us in the room and then he would say, "You are not slaves, you are not niggers—you are God's children.[6]

Thurman points to the pride that that experience instilled in his grandmother's heart and the seriousness with which he and his sister heard her recount it as they sat at her knees in their childhood.

There was no equivalent cultural vitality of an educational nature in Negro experience at the time of emancipation, nor was there any concern for some time following the Civil War to emancipate the minds of black people through an adequate and systematic education even remotely equivalent in significance to their group religious consciousness. In time provisions were made, mainly in isolated pilot projects, for higher education for Negroes. Hampton Institute and Tuskegee College were founded, under white missionary auspices, to meet the needs as perceived at the time. From the standpoint of contemporary perspectives, the way in which these needs were perceived is open to question and may even have helped to perpetuate

Negro accommodation to white culture. However, as initial steps these undertakings did much to prepare the way for a longer and different odyssey to come, an odyssey that might never have taken place without such first steps. Booker T. Washington, most influential during the years from 1895 to 1905, became the spokesman for educational programs designed to provide vocational and industrial training in close connection with intellectual learning. Washington's agenda was bound into the context of the time, and may have been successful in part because it was less abrasive to white prejudice and less threatening to white prerogatives than agendas envisioned by men like W. E. B. Du Bois. Washington's prescription for the advancement of his race involved manual training, which Washington described movingly as an important means of personal satisfaction. While acknowledging the importance of Negro religion, Wasington put more stress upon the economic attainments available through practical ability in trades open to the Negro and the Negro's own willingness to take advantage of options open to him.

> Much will depend upon the sense of justice which can be kept alive in the breast of the American people. Almost as much will depend upon the good sense of the Negro himself. That question, I confess, does not give me the most concern just now. The important and pressing question is, Will the Negro with his own help and that of his friends take advantage of the opportunities that now surround him? When he has done this, I believe that, speaking of his future in general terms, he will be treated with justice, will be given the protection of the law, and will be given the recognition in a large measure which his usefulness and ability warrant.[7]

Washington's expectation that the cultivation of individual competence would rout systemic injustices has not proved well founded, but it did make a contribution. Graduates from schools he either nurtured or inspired moved into black communities in the South (finding themselves barred from employment in white culture) and raised the literacy rates among their own people. Describing the impact of this process, Allen B. Ballard notes: "The Black college graduates had heeded Washington's advice 'to cast down their buckets' but had brought up books instead of agricultural tools. Black colleges provided a higher educational base, no matter how limited, for the development of a Black bourgeoisie, and the formation of a nascent middle class was crucial in creating the present Black assertiveness." [8] Moreover, the black institutions that were created in response to Washington's (and related) efforts kept alive a scholarship among blacks that would serve as precursor to the later creation of Afro-Americanism as a field of study.

Both the Negro vocational institute and the Negro college were oriented toward the preparation of leaders. The trained and educated Negro would emerge from these institutions prepared to raise the conditions of his race. He would do this by the successful pursuit of many values generally associated with success in America regardless of ethnic identity. The curriculum of the Negro college up to the middle sixties was patterned heavily on the curriculum of white institutions, and even collegiate styles were "well-ivied." Patterns of control and governance were traditional and even, at times, paternalistic and autocratic. Students attending such institutions were expected to manifest gratitude for the opportunity through diligent scholarship and appropriate behavior. Problems of financing were present and grew increasingly difficult in later years; the academic quality of the Negro institutions was warmly debated; but the overwhelming problem was a growing ambivalence between orientation to a white educational world and service to a segregated Negro community.

Integrative "equalism": The second modality in religion and education. Segregation in the United States—in public services, public schools, economic opportunity, higher education, and religion—has continued, even in face of massive moral condemnation on idealistic grounds and court decisions making overt discrimination illegal. In 1970 the

estimated enrollment of blacks in twenty-six hundred
American institutions of learning above the high school
level was 5.8 percent of a total of 8,050,000 students.[10] A
hundred traditionally black institutions accounted for a
third of this number, so that the percentage of blacks in
white institutions was under 4 percent. This was a fourfold
increase over the situation in 1954, when only 4,080 out of
480,000 (less than 1 percent) of the entering classes at
white colleges were black.[11] That, in turn, was an increase
over the nineteenth century. Up to 1890 less than a hundred
blacks had earned degrees from white institutions—and
over half of these had been granted by one institution noted
for its special concern about these matters.[12]

Considered in isolation these statistics might imply
gradual change for the better, but considered in relationship
to standards of justice applicable to society at large, they
reveal but a miserably token achievement. While many institutions of higher learning had accepted in theory the
importance of equal treatment for all regardless of color,
the practice did not fulfill the ideal. In the late nineteen
sixties many institutions had gone one step beyond the
passive openness of nondiscrimination to special programs
for the recruitment and support of minority students—
though in other places policies of deliberate exclusion were
still operative as late as 1960. These efforts were heartening,
but at the time they were based on an ideal of integrative
"equalism" made functional by the realization that special
efforts would be required to overcome the de facto differences in opportunity between blacks and whites. In Novem-
ber of 1971 the Ford Foundation gave a hundred million
dollars to Negro higher education, half of which went to
Negro colleges with the hope that they also would move
toward integration by including whites in their student
bodies, even as blacks should be included in the student
bodies of other institutions. The Report of the Foundation,
upon which this grant was premised, stated the integrative
ideal as follows: "[Negro colleges] . . . clearly have an
opportunity to play unusual and important roles in preparing

black and other youth for a complex, multiracial, multiethnic society. . . ." [14] Both the special opportunity programs and the gift of the Ford Foundation moved toward fairness, toward an ideal of equality, and indicated a concern to open doors to those excluded by or left beyond the orbit of the system. They were well-intentioned and essential steps in an ongoing development.

Meanwhile, in the theological realm much emphasis was placed upon the ideal of integrative equality. The emphasis in the theology during the nineteen fifties and early nineteen sixties was on overcoming segregation, on achieving racial justice, and on "The Kingdom Beyond Caste." Liston Pope, a representative Christian ethicist writing at this time, summarized the moral case for integration in this way:

> Integration calls for a society in which the individual is free and has equal opportunity to make the most of his life and to participate in the direction of the affairs of the society. He will naturally have certain limitations put on his freedom; absolute freedom for each person would lead to anarchy. But the limitations will not be arbitrary in that they apply to him or to his group alone. He may not end with power or privilege exactly equal to that of every other member of the society; exact quantitative quality has not been the democratic social goal. But he will continue to have equality of access to the general privileges of the society—the franchise, jobs, educational opportunities, cultural and religious activities. [15]

Pope then went on to point out that integration meant not only the elimination of barriers but a joining together of all groups in a search for common commitment to central goals. Nor was this perspective shared only by liberal theologians. Even a popular evangelist like Billy Graham came to acknowledge that an integrated society was both inevitable and morally demanded.

Religious leaders and educators invested much effort in attempts to overcome the systems of segregation and exclusion that prevented the black minority of the nation from sharing fully and equally in the privileges of churchmanship, scholarship, and citizenship. Churchmen became active in the civil rights movement, thus placing both moral influence and even visible presence behind the effort of blacks to break the color barrier. Not all encounters were easy, and the system continued to reveal its deep-seated injustices—as, for instance, in the relative ease with which whites arrested on trespass charges in the South could post bonds in contrast with the difficulties the blacks had in doing so.

The basic premise of the integration movement was the belief that blacks should have opportunities equal to those of whites in obtaining and enjoying the rewards of the economic order and the fruits of culture. Differences between blacks and whites were minimized in the effort to eliminate the very distinction at the root of the differentiations upon which segregation depended. But this effort neglected the importance of ethnic identity and peer encounter within the black community. Now that blacks are telling about integration as they experienced it, they are coming to appreciate the intense personal isolation and agony that many felt who were the first (and often isolated) ones to be "integrated" into a white-dominated system. The sense of isolation was particularly acute in small, white institutions in rural locations that offered little or no access to black communities. Moreover, as Allen Ballard says, speaking of his own experience as the first of his race to enter a midwestern white college: ". . . it is clear that— with some exceptions—our existence on that campus was defined not by us but by the constant necessity to be everything that negated the white man's concept of niggers." [16] Excluded automatically from fraternity life, forced to adopt manners, speech, and dress styles foreign to his upbringing, and even often placed in leadership position as an "exhibit" of white tolerance, the Negro in these circumstances underwent an "eight-semester social ordeal." Integration proved morally vulnerable because its zeal to open doors on the basis of fairness was not matched by a realization that true bringing together of white and black required more than black access to a white-dominated situation. While the ideal of integration was premised on equality of opportunity, the

realities involved forced blacks to assimilate to whites rather
than for the two to combine in forming a new societal
gestalt. As Frank Hercules suggests:

> Within the racial caste structure of the American society,
> . . . the integration of blacks has long since occurred. What
> the present-day proponents of "integration," therefore are
> actually clamoring for is something quite different. They are
> really demanding a fundamental change in the racial caste
> structure, whereby blacks will no longer occupy the position
> of "untouchables." By integration they mean, not the assimi-
> lation of blacks into the life and values of the society, for this
> has already taken place, but a change in their caste level
> from inferiors to equals; which is to ask, in terms, for the
> radical reshaping of the American society as a whole. The
> use of the term "integration" is, accordingly, as misleading
> as it is offensive to the dignity, and destructive of the self-
> respect, of blacks.[17]

*Black self-awareness and the imagery of black power:
The third modality.* One fruit of the special-opportunity
programs developed under the impetus of the integrative
ideal, however limited it was in understanding the situation
of the black when plunged into a white ethos, was the
bringing to campuses blacks in sufficient numbers to permit
ethnic peer support to develop among them. With such
support blacks were enabled to respond to the campus
scene quite differently from the way they did as isolated
Negroes in situations of token integration. They were able
to say, sometimes with actions rather than with words,
that education as carried out in the main-line American
institution of higher education was "Whitey's thing." They
grew restive under conditions in which accommodational
or assimilative realities were functional, even though the
ideology was integrationist.

Black awareness crystallized as the standing ground from
which assumptions about color-blinded fairness and neutrality as professed by the university were smoked out
from behind the cultural façade of white dominance. These
assumptions are the normal ideological stock and trade of

the academy, which believes that it transcends the prejudices of a crasser culture. Had not the campus evidenced its good faith and idealism by deliberately opening its doors to the ethnically dispossessed? Are not the facts and skills of the learned life equally real for all?

Black awareness broke upon the campus in a confrontational manner. From Harvard to the University of California at Berkeley, and at most quality institutions in between, blacks came together to protest against the failure of the white university to include black interests, styles, and concerns on an equal basis with the traditional (and largely "whitened") curricular and extracurricular instrumentalities of university life. This process took place mainly between 1967 and 1970, at a time of much ferment and discontent within many segments of society, and particularly those segments with backgrounds in, or connections with, the campus. It was a time marked by great frustration with the continuation (mostly by executive authority) of an unpopular war. Universities were being criticized for their involvement with various activities that directly or indirectly supported the war, making their professions of neutrality hollow.

The confrontational style was nourished further by the fact that radical white movements, like the Students for a Democratic Society, were demonstrating that overt pressures bring responses from authorities that rational discussion does not seem to attain. There was little in the experience or life of the nation during the period to bolster confidence in progressive change instituted by cooperative discussion and carried into practice by voluntary good will. Much that mainstream America did or did not do, whether directly or indirectly, functionally or dysfunctionally, encouraged the belief that protest and confrontation are the only way to get things done. When Martin Luther King was assassinated in 1968, the credibility of the nonviolence he advocated suffered cruel erosion and the plausibility of his vision— totally integrationist—was undermined. A white America given to violence seemed hypocritical in urging blacks to keep it cool. Rap Brown emphosized this pointedly when he remarked, "Violence is as American as cherry pie."

Black demands upon the university were of two types. Some focused, as in the gymnasium strike at Columbia or in the protests at Yale related to the trial of the Black Panthers, on university responsibilities to oppressed blacks in surrounding neighborhoods. Most demands, however, were related to internal policies. Blacks demanded the development of, and control over, programs of black studies. They asked for places on campus where blacks could be together as blacks, including dormitory space and activity centers. They wanted to exercise control over such places. They asked that the universities (or colleges) become even more open to blacks, until the percentage of blacks on the campus more nearly reflected that of the larger society and was large enough to result in a cadre supportive of black identity. They asked for special aid, both financial and pedagogical, in order that the disadvantages affecting most blacks upon entering college could be compensated for in decisive ways. Demands of this sort arose, not only from blacks in white institutions, but from black students in black institutions, where attitudes and curricular patterns were basically copies of those in white schools.

These demands can be understood as efforts to establish identity, to develop a standing ground from which to participate in the university on an equal footing with other groups. When first enunciated, many of these demands were forefully expressed in terminology uncongenial to academic elegance. They were often declared "nonnegotiable." The making of such demands may well have created an *esprit de corps* among blacks that had interwoven with it the expectations of unquestioning support and loyalty that frequently occur in early phases of mass movements.[18]

Theological developments taking place in this same period also embodied a growing awareness of black identity. In 1969 Albert B. Cleague, Jr., published a volume of sermons entitled *The Black Messiah*. These sermons articulated a new posture, in which affirmations of black uniqueness replaced those of fearsome subservience. In the introduction to this book Cleague declared:

> we are building a totally new self-image. Our rediscovery of the Black Messiah is part of our rediscovery of ourselves. We could not worship a Black Jesus until we had thrown off the shackles of self-hate. We could not follow a Black Messiah in the tasks of building a Black Nation until we had found the courage to look back beyond the slave block and the slave ship without shame.[19]

Cleague's theology discovered essential parallels between black theology and black revolution. "As black preachers we must tell our people that we are God's chosen people," he declared, "and that God is fighting with us as we fight. When we march, when we take to the streets in open conflict, we must understand that in the stamping of feet and the thunder of violence we can hear the voice of God." [20]

In the same year that Cleague published his sermons, James Cone published *Black Theology and Black Power*. Cone wrote as one convinced that Black Power is Christ's central message to twentieth-century America, that "if the Church is to remain faithful to its Lord, it must make a decisive break with the structure of this society by launching a vehement attack on the evils of racism in all forms." [21] He admitted his angry mood, which he declared to be a legitimate and prophetic stance in the face of flagrant evil. According to Cone,

> Black Power, in short, is an *attitude*, an inward affirmation of the essential worth of blackness. It means that the black man will not be poisoned by the stereotypes that others have of him, but will affirm from the depth of his soul: "Get used to me. I am not getting used to anyone." And, "if the white man challenges my humanity, I will impose my whole weight as a man on his life and show him I am not the 'sho good eatin' that he persists in imagining." This is Black Power, the power of the black man to say Yes to his own "black being," and to make the other accept him or be prepared for a struggle.[22]

Consolidation, liberation, and hope: The fourth modality.
The vigor and declaratory assertiveness of black awareness,
both in black campus activism and in black theology, carried
blacks across a great psychological watershed. The crossing
of this watershed remains the basic achievement of the last
few years. The struggle to attain awareness of independence
and to make it felt in a recalcitrant society has been enormous. The struggle is not over by any means, yet something
different is taking place among blacks as they seek to consolidate their new position. The shift to the fourth modality
has not been marked by sharp delineations or self-heralded
changes of outlook, but it is no less real or less important
because of this fact.

Without in any way compromising their insistence upon
the authentic beauty of blackness and its significance for
understanding the Gospel, black theologians have begun to
write and speak with reference to a wider range of theological concerns than was the case when they first developed
their position. James Cone, for example, a year after publishing *Black Theology and Black Power* brought forth a
second volume, entitled *A Black Theology of Liberation.*
In the preface to the second book, which Cone addressed
primarily to the black community, he interprets blackness
as representative of a condition of oppression regardless of
who suffers it. He indicates that any man is able to become
black in spirit to the extent that he casts his lot with the
oppressed and opposes the oppressor. ". . . Blackness is an
ontological symbol and visible reality which best describes
what oppression means in America." [23] Cone looks at liberation in relationship to biblical thought, moves through
questions of authority and revelation to the doctrine of God,
of Christ, and of the church, the world, and eschatology.
He finds that Karl Barth and Dietrich Bonhoeffer, and even
Reinhold Niebuhr, qualify as at least quasi-black theologians
because they looked at the Gospel with reference to oppressed peoples.

While he would insist that both books have essentially

the same message and posture, and while he can point to the fact that his first book ended with a discussion of reconciliation (a reconciliation to follow becoming black, i.e., having a soul, mind, and body where the dispossessed are),[24] there is a sense in which Cone's second work differs significantly from his first. In the second book there is a broadeing (not softening) of the conceptual framework, a reaching away from the primary concern with power to other themes that also illumine black experience. There is an effort to meet criticism through explanatory apologetic. This is what is entailed in consolidation. It appears, perhaps even more explicitly, in the inaugural address Cone delivered at Union Theological Seminary when he was installed as Professor of Theology there. "I admit readily that the social context of my existence plays an important role in my understanding of the gospel message. However, it would be ridiculous to claim that there is some secret language by which Africans could be persuaded by what I say while non-Africans could never understand it. Clearly there is a basis for speaking across cultural lines, namely the Bible." [25]

As black theology develops, expansions in its use of categories and even transformations in its tone are bound to occur. Major J. Jones has focused upon the category of hope in his effort to interpret black religious identity. Jones contends that "merely to assert a black self-identity to counter a white self-identity, which has traditionally refused to reciprocate, is not enough in the black man's quest for a usable black self-identity." [26] Jones criticizes the demand for separatism that was present, perhaps for strategic reasons, in the initial or militant mode of early black theology. He also aligns himself—all the critics and detractor who have argued otherwise having been heard—with Martin Luther King's belief that nonviolence when embraced as a total way of life does provide a ground on which blacks can come to a fullness of selfhood. He says that ". . . to feel the need to respond to violence by becoming violent seems to make one a slave to the person or persons who called forth the act of violence as a means of self-defense. The self-defense adherents cannot escape the cogent question as to just who is the master." [27]

The "consolidation" of black theology does not mean the development of a single uniform position; indeed, it should mean almost the opposite—namely, the development of diversity and of interaction between different black theologians who differ among themselves, in order to ferret out truth and adequacy through dialogue. J. Deotis Roberts, in his *Liberation and Reconciliation: A Black Theology*,[28] takes explicit issue with his fellow black theologians regarding priorities and emphases. He raises questions about the conditions under which black separatism can be productive and fruitful and about the conditions under which it may do a disservice to its own professed aims. This book is important, not because it represents a break in a phalanx, but because it shows that breadth, independence, and candid disagreement will become possible in black theology as its main themes are consolidated.

Blacks will not consolidate their position if they feel, or are forced to feel, any obligation to whites in seeking conciliation. They can pursue universality and fairness only if they stand as fully and authentically on their own as do any other groups. Preston Williams accepts the metaphor of reconciliation that appears in the thinking of black theologians like J. Deotis Roberts but pleads that it be kept free of the taint of subservience. "Reconciliation demands a new metaphor, one symbolizing the white's acceptance of the black's worth and dignity as well as solidarity with him. What the new metaphor will be is not yet known, but it is my belief that it cannot employ such tarnished concepts as human relations and integration. Rather it will spring from the universalizing of some black particular." [29] Williams also suggests, speaking more as a black ethicist than as a black theologian (if these can be separated in any satisfactory fashion), the importance of concepts like promise-keeping, reparations, and accountability in a future society in which social justice becomes operative.

If in black theology consolidation has meant the movement toward a broader use of conceptual categories and the exploration of the possible black base for a new universalism, on campus the emergence of black awareness has moved from the stage in which demands are uppermost and concern about power central to an exploration of the structural ways in which the standing of blacks can be made equivalent to that experienced by whites. Except on a few campuses the demand for black studies programs met resistance [30]—a resistance that has had several causes, including devotion to the ideal of integration that separatist postures connected with black studies seem to contradict and, at times, a deep-seated white ethnocentrism in traditional academic fare. Some particularly vexing issues stemmed from special-opportunity programs designed to redress the disadvantages suffered by most blacks in their preparation for college work. Colleges were asked to engage in compensatory educational endeavors that called for new and different expectations for classroom attainment.[31]

Securing a right to have black studies programs requires one posture; conceiving and executing an adequate curriculum requires another. Considered as a historical phenomenon, the growth of black studies as a new, or newly recognized, discipline has been remarkably rapid. To be sure, some material from which to build such programs was latently present on the sidelines, so that the accomplishment has not given birth to a complete nova. Yet black studies are not the mere polishing up of matured concerns. They are an outgrowth, in response to a felt need and a newly won opportunity, of enormous effort expended under the urgency of time. The wonder is not that the results have, at times, been short of established expectations for other fields, but that so much has come forth in the way of materials and insights within such a short span of time. Critics of black studies, including a black like Martin Kilson of Harvard, have raised questions concerning the intellectual adequacy and orientation toward achievement fostered in separate programs for blacks.[32] Black study programs have been suspected of having too great an ideological content, of lacking adequate resources and the instructional personnel for their distinguished implementation, and of fostering a separatism inimical to the universality professed by the academic institution.[33]

Black studies programs have sometimes left things to be desired in the way of adequacy and attainment. This failing plagues almost every educational venture, especially innovative ones. Moreover, black studies have struggled to develop in a cultural context in which the traditional methodologies of scholarship have been under attack from another source, the largely white (and middle-class) counterculture. The sensitivities of the scholarly world have been tenderized by some challenges from the counterculture and its disdain for pedagogical rigor, and the backlash engendered by this source has sometimes found black studies as its target. It has required a perceptive awareness beyond that commonly evident in academic policy-making to see a difference between two movements, both of which have been raising questions about the adequacy of the educational status quo, yet doing so from different premises.

In the area of institutional governance, the fiery rhetoric of sit-in days, in which the concept of black power carried with it coercive overtones, has largely given way to a steady, yet rationally argued, demand for distinctive representation of minorities on policy-making bodies. Black communities on the campus have watched the development of more broadly based schemes for decision-making. They have keenly felt the need to consolidate their place within such schemes, even to the point of asking for quota-based or specially structured representation. In an ideal community such representation might come naturally and proportionately, but in the situation of our time it can be relied upon only if provided for on a deliberate, and admittedly unique, basis.

The modality of consolidation is reflected in the following statement of goals or purposes from the Third World Organization of Hampshire College.

The goals of the Third World body at Hampshire College are: first to unite and form a cultural bond among ourselves; second, to make certain that full resources are available at Hampshire for the enrichment of Third World people; third, to attempt to create in the non-Third World students and faculty an awareness, an understanding, and a knowledge of the global situation of Third World people and the situation faced by Third World students at Hampshire College; and finally, to convert this philosophy into some concrete, tangible action and involvement which may take form in community work or some kind of *active concern* that will constantly remind us of who we are and from whence we came.[34]

Internal self-scrutiny and creative interaction: Toward the fifth modality. There is every reason to believe that the development of black awareness will continue to consolidate and grow. As it does so it will undoubtedly move through those same transitions that are common to most historical movements—including both success and failure with its own agenda. The experience of liberation is most exhilarating at that special juncture when it first seems real as a historical promise, within actual reach. Prior to that stage submissiveness anesthetizes hope; following liberation self-satisfaction can arise that blinds a group to continued need for change. While prophetic criticism is out of place with a people still trying to cross the sea from the land of repression, it is easy for a promised land to become the location for corruption once it seems to feel secure. Questions of enormous import loom the minute a movement consolidates itself sufficiently to exercise authority and power rather than be merely victimized by it. Black theology has been largely concerned with identifying the spiritual slavery of its people, in condemning the Egypts of white dominance, and setting forth the need and hope of release. Nothing about this task is diminished in importance by noting that to the extent it produces a successful agenda it also will be called to respond in a different way to the same God who has been its liberator. The special problem for a movement so large and widespread and important as black awareness will be to realize that the crossing of the sea from repression to liberation will come in stages. Unlike a little Hebrew band that knew when the waters covered the Egyptians decisively, blacks will experience liberation incrementally. It will not be easy to identify the points at which internal prophetic criticism and judgment is appropriate (if indeed it has ever been easy to do that), and there will always be more than sufficient lingering evidence of repressive conditions to render plausible any efforts to fasten blame for inadequacies elsewhere.

No taskmaster or "associate-of-a-taskmaster" from "Egypt" can serve as a prophet to a liberated band, even if he could perceive things that might call for judgment according to the assumptions and covenants of the liberated group. But someone in an Egypt of colorlessness can tell whether or not prophetic ingredients are developing as a phenomenon within black awareness. He can tell whether or not, in the course of time, an agenda moves from consolidation to internal scrutiny, from calling/destiny to repentance/redemption. He can tell whether or not the imagery remains modeled entirely on the exodus and chosen people or whether it moves to servanthood in a new sense and a messianism that involves transcendence. He can observe whether a perspective enlarges from in-group loyalties to a universality that uses particularity as an instrument to redeem others as well.

Similarly, black studies, once the preoccupation with winning the right to academic recognition is no longer needed, will be enriched only as criteria develop for judging adequacy and competence. The inappropriateness of traditional grounds for making judgments about many aspects of black studies does not abrogate the fact that such judgments will have to be made. Already canons for measuring rigor and adequacy are coming to black studies, in accordance with which successful programs can be distinguished from unsuccessful ones. The further development of such criteria will bear along with them all of the dangers that inhere within establishment status, and also the values that are served by having structure, discipline, and standards for adjudication and evaluation.

Allen Ballard has commented upon the necessity for spread and breadth within black studies. His observations reflect consolidation and even point to a subsequent posture:

> The real end of Black studies is not therapy but education to give young Black people a solidly grounded knowledge in things Black as well as a conceptual framework within whose contours they can begin to develop their own strategies for solving the problems of the Black urban masses. In this context it is absolutely necessary that courses be rigorously constructed and that they provide the broadest possible exposure to all schools of Black thought. . . . Basic and necessary to good teaching . . . is the obligation of a professor to expose a student first to all the facts pertinent to the subject under scrutiny and second to the various schools of criticism as they interpret those facts. Having done this, the professor should be free to examine critically and freely both the facts and the scholarly interpretations of those facts. And the students, likewise, should be encouraged to argue and question the assumptions and ideology of professors and books as they deal with the topic under discussion. These techniques must be followed in the case of Black Studies. Within the context of Black togetherness, the broadest possible discussion and intellectual stimulation must take place lest the student be stifled. They must be given the opportunity to find new ways of interpreting the Black experience which may lead to different solutions from those presently proposed by the Black intelligentsia.[35]

What more could any practitioner of an academic discipline want, except to share in dialogue with such a process?

The relationship between black theology and black experience on campus has been only implicitly considered in this analysis. Both have been viewed as products of some larger set of cultural conditions rather than as factors directly affecting each other. Indeed, it is impossible to draw many conclusions about the impact of black theology on the black experience on campus, or the other way around.

The center of black experience during the time when the assimilative and integrationist modalities were most operative (or whether they may still be operative in traditional terms) may have been located more in the religious community than in the academic scene. It may turn out that the many efforts to bring blacks to campus in significant numbers and under new conditions will do much to shift the center of black experience to the campus. There is a real danger that blacks anxious to make it academically will, despite their profession to eschew white attitudes, adopt the suspicion of religion and of theology often found in the academic situation as a whole. If they do this, remaining ignorant of the rise of black theology as a new stance within the Christian community, they may very well miss one of the important religious phenomena taking place around them and become as limited in their perception of what is going on religiously as are many academic whites.

Moreover, while the campus experience, both curricular and extracurricular, may express the modality of black awareness very well, and even the modality of consolidation, there are many aspects of the fifth modality—with its ingredient of prophetic self-criticism—that can become richly developed only in a theological matrix. If blacks on campus do not come to appreciate and operate in relationship to such a matrix, then those most able to make a contribution to the maturing of religious stances will have absented themselves from the process. Conversely, a secularized blackness will develop less richly than would a blackness in which theological sensitivities are significantly operative.

NOTES TO CHAPTER 2

1. The issue whether black theology as such is a causal factor or merely a barometer of the cultural atmosphere cannot be settled here, if indeed it can be decisively settled by any reading of the circumstances around its growth. This issue is just as baffling with respect to black theology as it is to all theological reflection, but this uncertainty on the analytical level does not make black theology any less important to the thinking of blacks about religious identity or any less momentous for all of us.

2. From a statement of the National Committee of Black Churchmen produced by the Committee on Theological Perspectives. Issued at the Interdenominational Theological Center in Atlanta, Georgia, June 13, 1969.

3. George Napper, *Blacker Than Thou: The Struggle for Campus Unity* (Grand Rapids, Mich.: Eerdmans, 1973), pp. 15f.

4. Joseph R. Washington, Jr., "How Black is Black Religion?" in James J. Gardiner, S.A. and J. Deotis Roberts, Sr. ed., *Quest for a Black Theology* (Philadelphia: Pilgrim Press, 1971), p. 25.

5. Allen B. Ballard, *The Education of Black Folk: The Afro-American Struggle for Knowledge in White America* (New York: Harper and Row, 1973), p. 10.

6. Mary E. Goodwin, "Racial Roots and Religion: An Interview with Howard Thurman," *The Christian Century*, May 9, 1973, pp. 533f.

7. Booker T. Washington, *The Future of the American Negro* (Boston: Small, Manard and Company, 1902), pp. 231f.

8. Ballard, *Education of Black Folk*, p. 23.

9. Particularly controversial has been the evaluation offered by Professors David Reisman and Christopher Jencks in *The Academic Revolution* (New York: Doubleday, 1968).

10. Data from Fred E. Crossland, *Minority Access to College: A Ford Foundation Report* (New York: Schocken, 1971), p. 13.

11. Data from W. E. B. DuBois and Augustus Evanville Dill, "College-Bred Negro American," *Atlanta University Publications* (New York: Arno Press, and *New York Times*, 1968), p. 46.

12. Ballard, *Education of Black Folk*, p. 52.

13. For example, the famous Lawson case in the Divinity School of Vanderbilt University.

14. Crossland, *Minority Access to College*, p. 42 (Quoted in *The New York Times*, October 11, 1971, p. 26).

15. Liston Pope, *The Kingdom Beyond Caste* (New York: Friendship Press, 1957), pp. 81f.

16. Ballard, *Education of Black Folk*, p. 4.

17. Frank Hercules, *American Society and Black Revolution* (New York: Harcourt Brace Jovanovich, 1972), p. 416.

Black Theology and Blacks on Campus 77

18. The allusion here is to the "true believer" phenomenon identified by Eric Hoffer in a book by that title. For supporting evidence from a black scholar see Napper, *Blacker Than Thou.*

19. Albert B. Cleague, Jr., *The Black Messiah* (New York: Sheed and Ward, 1909), p. 7.

20. Ibid., p. 6.

21. James H. Cone, *Black Theology and Black Power* (New York: Seabury, 1969), p. 2.

22. Ibid., p. 8.

23. James H. Cone, *A Black Theology of Liberation* (Philadelphia: J. B. Lippincott, 1970), p. 27.

24. Cone, *Black Theology and Black Power*, p. 151.

25. James H. Cone, "The Dialectic of Theology and Life, or Speaking the Truth," *Union Seminary Quarterly Review* 29, no. 2 (Winter 1974): 89.

26. Major J. Jones, *Black Awareness: A Theology of Hope* (Nashville, Tenn.: Abingdon, 1971), p. 68.

27. Ibid., p. 82.

28. J. Deotis Roberts, *Liberation and Reconciliation: A Black Theology* (Philadelphia: Westminster Press, 1971).

29. Preston N. Williams, "The Price of Social Justice," *The Christian Century*, May 9, 1973, p. 529.

30. See Prince E. Wilson, "Some Aspects of the Education of Black Americans, 1968," in Patricia W. Romero, ed., *In Black America: 1968: The Year of Awakening* (Philadelphia: United Publishing Corp., 1969), pp. 89–131.

31. I have found Leonard Kriegel's autobiographical account of his experience (and satisfactions) teaching in the S.E.E.K. Program of the City College of New York a helpful insight into compensatory education as viewed from the teaching side of the desk. See especially chapter 6 of *Working Through: A Teacher's Journey in the Urban University* (New York: Saturday Review Press, 1972).

32. Martin Kilson, "The Black Experience at Harvard," in *New York Times Magazine*, September 2, 1973, pp. 13ff.

33. These charges against black studies are based on the list provided by Ballard, *Education of Black Folk*, chap. 6.

34. Article Two, printed in Hampshire College pamphlet *Third World Perspective.*

35. Ballard, *Education of Black Folk*, pp. 113f.

3
African Religion:
A New Focus for Black Theology

GEORGE B. THOMAS

I AFRICAN RELIGION AS A NEW WORLD FORCE

Just as John S. Mbiti makes the observations (1) that African religions "should be regarded as preparation for the Christian Gospel," (2) that "Christianity may be seen as fulfillment of traditional African religions," and (3) that "African traditional religiosity can become an enrichment for Christian presence in Africa," [1] I would also propose that African Christianity in America makes a parallel claim upon the relevance of African religion as preparation for and enrichment of the black religious experience in America. The assumption in both instances is that traditional African religions are wellsprings of spiritual resources in the African and African-American Christian experience.

In the same way that traditional African religions are spiritual resources for African Christianity (the Christianity from which the African Christian church evolves), traditional African religions have also been resources for that Christianity in America identified as "Black religion," [2] the religion from which the black church has evolved. Just as African

79

theology is emerging from the life, culture, traditions, and faith of the African church, black theology is emerging from the life, culture, traditions, and faith of African peoples in the black church in America. I am, therefore, setting forth the position that African Christianity is both an evolutionary process in the African and black religious experiences and church movements and the main source and resource of African and black theology. Also, Pan-African theology evolves from Pan-African Christianity, now being manifested in black and African theology.

At this point, it is not possible to directly estimate a relevant relationship between African religion and Euro-American Christianity. Euro-American Christianity has lost much credibility on some essential and existential issues. It is evident that wherever the Euro-American economic systems have demeaned the African heritage and black experience, Christianity has ofttimes conducted economic exploitations under the banner of evangelistic enterprises. (No doubt the time will come when Euro-American Christianity will be prepared to respond creatively to the role and relevance of African religion to Christianity.) Nevertheless, the African and the African-American are probing more seriously the self-evident and self-fulfilling value of rooting Christianity in the soil of the African religious heritage—in spite of the lures of a dominating ideology from the West or the East. African Christianity is its own ideology, and it struggles to link and liberate African peoples and to exercise a mission of liberation and salvation for humanity.

The West, viewed as the Euro-American systems that have spawned capitalism,[3] has historically used Christianity to help colonize African peoples. African religion was regarded as having little or no intrinsic value. Christianity in America, looking back through European eyes, would recognize the built-in difficulties of disengaging those structures[4] and stigmas that have abused the religious experiences of African peoples. Now Euro-American Christianity is in a "twilight zone"[5] of credibility. This is true in part because traditional African religions in Africa, as well as black religion in America, are still viewed as having little or no relevance, or at best peripheral relevance, to the mainstream of Christianity in America or in the West.

The East, dominated by the Euro-Asiatic systems that have spawned Communism,[6] would likewise ignore the essential validity of the African religious heritage. Communism has attacked Christianity and has sought to parallel it, if not establish itself as an ideological substitute[7] for it, in a function of salvation-history. The religion of Communism, however, lacks a spiritual, critical principle in its basis. Notwithstanding these views, African Christianity has its own ideology as it struggles to link and liberate African peoples and to exercise a mission of liberation and salvation for humanity.

Neither the West nor the East seems to be able to provide man with a relevant spiritual consciousness or energy that transforms, renews, and sustains the most meaningful and total life-style. African peoples have embraced Christianity as a folk religion, as an integral part of the heritage in the nature of the human life-style, indeed as the soul of experience. African Christianity, it seems to me, is moving to reforge some of the broken links and to restore the broken relationships—beginning with African peoples and continuing with all peoples. It may be that African peoples engaging in Christianity will restore soul and spiritual consciousness as the axis around which the affairs of existence and the universal human purpose must turn. Consequently, African Christianity might yet become one of the most dynamic forms of religious energy on the world scene.

At this point in history, it seems evident that neither the West nor the East, in terms of ideology, can provide or support a genuine universal folk religion, a folk religion indigenized and expressed from the soul-center of the human experience. There are, however, some spiritual resources in traditional African religion that can "enrich" Christianity, providing an authentic base of spiritual power by permeating personality and community. I am proposing, therefore, that, given some elements of the African heritage of traditional African religion, Christianity can reemerge in history as a new and essentially humanizing world religious force. African religion in Christianity undergirds the spiritual nature of the Christian experience and is dynamically active as liberating and life-supporting.

In the context of this paper, *African Christianity* will be taken to mean that Christianity integrated by Africans into their traditional religious experiences. These questions may now be raised: How is traditional Christianity related to traditional African religions? How is Christianity to be understood as an African religion? And how is traditional African religion relevant to Christianity in America?

II CHRISTIANITY AS AN AFRICAN RELIGION—IMPORTED, IMPOSED OR INDIGENIZED?

First, Christianity must be disengaged from being defined as an exclusively white Western or Western-oriented religion. There is a dominating form of European Christianity that is prevalent in America at this stage of history. However, Christianity has its own history, only a part of which is tied in with European Christianity. This may also be true of the branch of Christianity emerging out of the black religious experience in America. Therefore, it is important to exponents and adherents of black religion in America that Christianity in Africa be inherently appreciated as an African religion, shaped in part by traditional African religions. To more fully understand Christianity as African religion, let us examine some of Christianity's African origins.

a *African origins in the Judeo-Christian tradition*

There are some definite African sources implicit in the evolution of historical Christianity. There were African sources of influence in the background and beginnings of the Bible (the Old and New Testaments)—and in Judaism and Islam as well as in Christianity. As outlined in Robertson Smith's work:

No positive religion that has moved man has been able to start with a *tabula rasa*. . . . The new system must be in contact all along the line with the older ideas and practices.[8]

In addition, Yosef ben-Jochannan writes:

no major religion of today is exclusive of moral and philosophical concepts of any of the peoples with whom it had contact in its earliest development.[9]

If, for example, Moses is the founder of Judaism and the major reference in the Pentateuch, the Bible would be its own witness to these certain truths: Moses was born in Egypt and educated in Egypt. Egyptians were and are Africans and from time immemorial have been under the influence of the peoples of central Africa. Religious and commercial influences have long been exchanged along the river on which the baby Moses was found "floating down the Nile." The Nile begins in Uganda and Ethiopia; to understand Egyptian religion, one might well study the traditional African religions, during the prebiblical period, of the peoples along the Nile and down the Rift Valley into the civilizations of south-central and east Africa. Jochannan states:

The Ten Commandments spoken of in each of the so-called Western Religions' moral code of ethics are based upon extensions of philosophical developments of indigenous Africans —the so-called Negroes and Bantus of the Nile Valley civilizations from pre-recorded history. The laws that say . . . Thou shalt not kill and Thou shalt not steal . . . etc., were used in Egypt (Sais) and Ethiopia (Cush) thousands of years before the birth of Moses and the Hebrew (Jewish) Torah.[10]

The inestimable influences of African religions are, therefore, significant presuppositions in the permeations in and emergence of the development of the Judeo-Christian heritage and history.

Another exponent who speaks to this issue of historical analysis from the black religious perspective is Albert B. Cleage, Jr. Cleage's basic position is that the nation of Israel is itself a synthesis of the African and Asiatic influences intermingling with the black people of central Africa:

> The intermingling of the races in Africa and the Mediterranean area is an established fact. The Nation Israel was a mixture of Chaldeans, Egyptians, Midianites, Ethiopians, Kushites, Babylonians and other dark peoples, all of whom were already mixed with the black people of Central Africa.[11]

Several black American scholars are reconstructing the interrelationships between the biblical and the traditional African religious resources as a context of analysis of historical Christianity. Christianity is already clearly emerging as African in the black religious experiences in the New World.

There are definite philosophical and theological concepts in African religion that also appear in traditional Western Christianity. Janheinz Jahn's work, which draws from that of Alexis Kagame, may draw our attention to some basic conceptual processes in traditional African religions:

> *Ntu* is the universal force as such, which, however, never occurs apart from its manifestations Mantu, Kintu, Hantu and Kuntu. *Ntu* is Being itself, the cosmic universal force. . . . *Ntu* is that force in which Being and beings coalesce.[12]

As Greek thought shaped some Christian theology, for example, the Gospel of John, some authors have raised the connection between African philosophy and Greek philosophy:

> Greeks are treated as if they were in no way whatsoever influenced or taught by Egyptians, Ethiopians and other indigenous Africans along the Nile Valley—when the philosophical concepts, now called Greek Philosophy, were originated—thousands of years before the creation of the Greek nation.[13]

There is, of course, real need for more serious and inclusive study of the kinds of intercourse that must have taken place in all of these matters in the deepest reaches of Africa.

The earliest portion of church history, after the emergence of Christianity as an infant movement in Africa, was the pre-Roman Catholic or Greek Orthodox period, which covered the first two, possibly three, centuries. Some of the most outstanding Christians were Africans, some of whom became martyrs and forerunners of the church fathers. Namphano, Perpetua, and Felicita are described in the works of C. P. Groves as follows:

> A certain Namphano, claimed as the first martyr, also came from Numidia. . . . Added with Namphano were . . . Perpetua and Felicita, both of whom were also indigenous Africans.[14]

St. Cyprian, Tertullian, and St. Augustine were renowned church fathers and representatives of early African Christianity. St. Cyprian, the Bishop of Carthage (A.D. 249–258) was martyred by the Romans, who sought to stamp out the Christian movement. Jochannan reminds us:

> It must be remembered that the Christians of Carthage were indigenous Africans brought in from the neighboring state called "Numidia" as slaves for Rome.[15]

Tertullian was an outstanding African Christian scholar:

> one of the most outstanding scholars in rhetoric Latin and Greek . . . and it was his depth in and love for Latin which caused him to make it the official language of the Roman Catholic Church [in part an outgrowth of the North African Church].[16]

Augustine was one of the greatest contributors to the philosophical and theological formulations in the Western Christian church. Jane Soames states:

> We learn a great deal about the civilization from the Confessions, the product of a mentality strikingly sympathetic to the European mind, though bearing the imprint of its African origin.[17]

George Sabine writes of Augustine:

his mind encompassed almost all the learning of ancient times and through him, to a very large extent, it was transmitted to the Middle Ages. His writings were a mine of ideas in which later writers, Catholic and Protestant, have dug. . . . He also fathomed the inner secrets of neo-Platonism and Manichaeism which he moderated by linking them with his understanding of indigenous African mythology and Ancestral Spirit worship. The latter two are fundamentally indigenous African theology and [sic] moral principles.[18]

Sabine's conclusion is radically different from other conclusions on Augustine's writings

[which] . . . show much of the insight he revealed to his fellow Christians which made them adopt his teachings as the basic concepts of Christianity as developed in North African Church under indigenous Africans from the fourth through the present twentieth century.[19]

African-Americans are becoming more perceptive and appreciative of the new revelations that illustrate the contributions made by African peoples and African religion to the basic style and substance of the Christian religion. Hopefully, man will further understand and accept Christianity as an indigenous folk religion rather than rejecting and incorrectly stereotyping it as the white man's religion for African peoples, including black people in colonial America (Christian faith came into the black experience via white Euro-American Christianity).

Interpreting Christianity in the black or African relgious experience, one must approach the case from another perspective in attemping to get at the whole matter of the relevance of African religion to Christianity in America.

b *Christianity—imported, imposed or indigenized?*

The African-American analysis of the relevance of African religion to Christianity, including Christianity in America, views the relationship between the African religious experience and the Christian religion from three points of view :

1. Christianity was imported by Africans and represents
    Africans Christianized.
2. Christianity was imposed upon Africans and represents
    Christianized Africans.
3. Christianity was indigenized by Africans and represents
    African Christianity.

First with regard to imported Christianity, Africans are
spoken of as being "Christianized." The original and direct
thrust of the Christian movement in the first century penetrated Africa directly. In this way the Africans Christianized
were in a continuous experiential relationship with the
Judeo-Christian movement as an African experience. This
occurred across North Africa, in Egypt, and down into
central Africa to Ethiopia. These linkages were already
evident in several biblical accounts of communication and
contact in the Old and New Testaments—Jesus in Egypt[20]
and Phillip and the Eunuch of Ethiopia.[21] There are two
implications here:

1. The original institutionalization of the African Church
    was independent of and prior to the development of
    European Christianity.
2. There was continuous incorporation of traditional Afri-
    can religion and influences seen in the schisms in north
    and east Africa where Christianity was imported.

Africans, like any people, may accept or reject the im-
portation and/or creative development of a religion. However, Africans importing Christianity infused and precipi-
tated various ideas and movements. Schisms resulted, as
David Barrett states:

> Ecclesiastical schisms were frequent during the first six
> centuries of Christianity in North Africa, particularly in
> Egypt. By the fifth century the Church was divided into
> Dyophysites, Monophysites, Arians and Nestorians, and by
> the year 500 several inner-monophysitic divisions had merged.
> In 634 A.D. Muslim rulers conquered Egypt, and within a few
> centuries all traces of Christianity had disappeared from North
> Africa with the sole exception of the Coptic Orthodox Church
> along the Nile Valley.[22]

Second, as to Christianity's being imposed, one speaks of Christianized Africans: that is, those who came under the influence of the movements of the European church, colonial or missionizing activities in Africa, beginning in the fifteenth century. The various European Christian powers—the Holy Roman Catholic Church in Portugal, Spain, and Belgium, a combination of Catholic and Protestant conquerors from France, and England (and later America)—were responsible for Christianizing Africans. Quite often this was a process of superimposing political, economic, and racial structures and relationships, including religious beliefs and practices, upon African peoples. As such, Christianized Africans came to believe in the de-Africanization of African people and the Europeanization of Africans as prerequisites to legitimizing the quality of the religious experience. In fact, to be Christian was to be less and less African in religious beliefs and practices and more and more European. At the same time, some negative aspects of traditional African religion were displaced and some creative aspects of European Christianity were positively embraced. Nevertheless, the making of European Christians out of Africans was to produce Christianized Africans.

Such Africans, like any people in the same position, represented, in their adoption of Christianity as a religious veneer, a convenient accommodation to the Euro- Christian society. As Christians, these Africans would lack self-definition and self-awareness, self-development and self-determination, resulting in an artificial, or at best superficial, Christianity.

Third, as to Christianity's being indigenous, one speaks of African Christianity, in which the essential Christian movement is "Africanized," assimilated, internalized, and nurtured in the very character of the African personality and community, whether the Christian movement was a part of the original extension of the faith, described above as Africans Christianized, or whether there was a breakaway, takeover, or transfer of leadership to the Christianized Africans as now evidenced by the upsurge of independent African Christian movements. Christianity is here *Africanized*, which is to say, authentically indigenized. Christianity Africanized is the process whereby African peoples are fully open to God's progressive revelation and will in the African community, church, and theology. The development of African Christianity is spoken of in these terms in any place or any time.

Ultimately, such streams of the Christian movement from Africa and Africans everywhere will flow toward the river of Christian world religion that gathers up the streams of Asia, Latin America, Europe, and America. African-Americans will more and more identify with and relate to the streams of Africans Christianized, and the whole movement of African Christianity will form that great river of Pan-African Christianity. Christian African-Americans are already analyzing the relevance of African religion to Christianity in the light of that Pan-African process and perspective, and are pressing on with the emerging knowledge of African Christianity at this historical stage of world Christianity.

III RELIGIOUS RESOURCES OF THE BLACK EXPERIENCE IN AMERICA

From the beginning of slavery in America, black religious thought and temperament, belief and practice drew upon traditional African religious folklore[23] and merged with elements of traditional Christian teachings.[24] Black religion creatively blended—in the message, melody, and mood of soul music, in the folksongs, worksongs, blues, and spirituals —subtle theological perceptions. Only as one sets before him the conceptions of traditional African religious folklore and the traditional folklore of Christianity, is he prepared to appreciate the continuities and similarities of African religion and black religion. Religious African conceptions that were harmonious with the Christian Scriptures were the sources of spirituals. Whereas Booker T. Washington described spirituals as originating "in the camp meetings, the

revivals, and in other religious exercises," according to Miles
Mark Fisher, W. E. B. DuBois described the spirituals as
"siftings of the centuries . . . first African songs, next Afro-
American then (as) mixtures with white songs. . . ." [25]

"De Lawd" is a spiritual conception of the High God
that was synthesized in black religion. The biblical expression of the Lord God Almighty manifested in the form of
Christ inspired the religion of Jesus in the black experience.
Knowledge of De Lawd did not come from book-learning
experiences, but from experience in the university of life.
Soulful prayer was the way to spiritual communion and
knowledge of De Lawd. Knowledge of the High God or De
Lawd came from deep down within, where religious instincts
blended with intuition in affirming a spiritual encounter:

> I know the Lord [De Lawd], I know the Lord has laid His
> hands on me.

The deep stirrings of De Lawd within create strange
feelings:

> Something within me I cannot explain . . . banishes pain . . .
> holdeth the reigns; that never doth tire, burning fire. . . . Then
> let the world know, there is something within.

Theologizing in the spirituals may also be seen in the
blending of the Africanism of the High God into the black
experience of De Lawd, as interpreted in the Scripture
(the High God is the big wheel, the power of Almighty
Grace, and the little wheel is the revelation of the Word
made flesh, "way up in the middle of the air"):

> The little wheel turns by faith and the big wheel turns by the
> grace of God; the wheel in the wheel, way up in the middle
> of the air.

The black-folk religious style was one that required a
testimony about an encounter of the presence of De Lawd.
One had to hear De Lawd speak or see De Lawd moving
or at least feel De Lawd in the power of the visitation of

the Holy Spirit. The feeling of the Spirit was so intense
that words of Jeremiah were appropriately sung—"feels like
de fire shut up in my bones." Dancing was therefore a
natural religious expression: [26]

> Sit down, servant; I can't sit down . . .
> Sit down, servant; I can't sit down . . .
> My soul's so happy that I can't sit down.

Whenever African Negroes assembled, they accompanied their
songs and dances with percussion, wind, and stringed instruments. They used their voices and their bodies as well as
instruments in making music.[27]

Black religion was grounded in spiritual perceptions and
feelings—where the inner revelation, the transsubjective
knowledge, penetrated through the depths of consciousness
into the blessed realms of assurance and trust. By this faith,
grace, intuition, and revelation, black religion was nurtured
and shaped by the religious sensitivities of African peoples
affirming the religion of Jesus.

1. *Parallels of God-interpretation in traditional African re-*
   ligion, Biblical Christian teachings, and black soul music
   a. God is omnipresent.
      Traditional African religion: God as the all-seeing and
      all-hearing; to convey the concept of God's omnis-
      cience, African peoples use metaphors of seeing and
      hearing, which are obviously easy to understand.
      Bamum say: "He who sees and hears everything . . .
      Bena believe God is everywhere at once." [28]
      The Bible: "Whither shall I go from Thy spirit or
      whither shall I flee from Thy presence? If I ascend.
      . . . If I take the wings of the morning. . . . Even
      there. . . . The darkness and light are both alike to
      Thee . . . Thine eyes did see my substance." [29]
      Spiritual: "De Lawd's got His eyes on you . . . sees
      all you do, hears all you say. . . . God's got His eyes
      on you."

b. God is transcendent.

Traditional African religion: The Shilluk prayer: "There is no one above Thee, Thou God." [30]

The Bible: "As high as the heavens . . . so high are My thoughts above your thoughts and My ways above your ways. . . ." [31]

Spiritual: "He's so high you can't get over Him . . . so wide, . . . so deep. . . ."

c. God is mysterious.

Traditional African religion: The Ila: "He has no-where or nowhen that he comes to an end." [32] The Pygmy: "In the beginning was God, today God, tomorrow will be God. The Word it is no more, IT IS PAST, AND STILL IT LIVES." [33]

The Bible: "Canst Thou by searching find out God? Canst Thou find out the Almighty unto perfection? It is as high as heaven; what canst Thou do? deeper than hell; what canst Thou know? The measure thereof is longer than the earth and broader than the sea. . . ." [34]

Spiritual: "Over my head I hear music in the air, over my head I hear music in the air, there must be a God somewhere. . . ."

d. God is omnipotent.

Traditional African religion: ". . . Power is viewed hierarchically so that God is at the top as the omni-potent. . . ." [35] "Nothing perishes without God's will."

The Bible: ". . . with God all things are possible." [36]

Spiritual: "He's got the whole world in His hands. . . ."

2. *Socio-religious parallels between traditional African religion, biblical Christian teachings, and black soul music*

There are definite theological and religious patterns in black religious music that have evolved from both the language and literature of African religions and folklore and the traditional Scriptures.

a. God's care.

In black religious music, especially the spirituals, the theme of God's care became very important in the sufferings of oppressed peoples. The African Shilluk pray, "Protect us, we are in your hand, and protect and save us. . . ." The Scripture carries a prophecy: "And God spake on this wise, that his seed should sojourn in a strange land; and that they should bring them into bondage, and entreat them evil four hundred years. . . ." [37] From the ethos of the black experience, as "children of God," black people have affirmed confidence in God's care in spite of suffering and oppression:

> We are all our heavenly Father's children
> And we all know that he loves us one and all . . .
> And he knows just how much we can bear . . .
> Though the load gets heavy.
> We're never left alone to bear it all . . .
> There is a God who rules . . . and He knows.

Christianity, as it emerged from the black religious experience in America, had a sad note because, whether slavery was felt as the punishment of God or the capriciousness of the white man, "African children" had been taken a long way from home. The exile paralleled, only more tragically, that of the children of Israel in Babylon:

> As by the waters of Babylon, we cried.[38]

As a consequence, the same theme appears in the black experience:

> I just hung my head and I cried, cried, cried,
> I just hung my head and I cried.

African children were taken away from mother Africa and made motherless, homeless, hungry, and utterly dependent, "a long way from home":

> Sometimes I feel like a motherless child . . . Sometimes I feel like a motherless child. A long way from home.

But the High God came near in America. The revelation came through King Jesus as De Lawd. From a transcendental absentee landlord, he became a present help and provider. He became everything one could depend upon for life:

He's everything to me.
. . . water in dry places . . . food on barren land,
He's my rock and shelter and holds me in his hands.
and when my way gets weary,
close by my side He stands
He is, yes my Lawd, is everything to me.

God's care could be sung in a deeper joy in the midst of
affliction. The Scriptures were a testimony, and spirituals
linked the individual with the word of God:

Why should I feel discouraged.
Why should the shadows fall . . . when my heart be lonely.
. . . Jesus is my portion, my constant friend is He.
His eye is on the sparrow and I know he watches me.

There is a balm in Gilead. . . . Sometimes I feel discouraged.
But when the Holy Spirit revives my soul again.

The High God knows, "King Jesus is a-listening," and
the Holy Spirit and angels come when necessary. In the
midst "of tribulation," he "stands by me." Remembering the
prisons of Paul and Daniel, blacks maintained the simple
but profound faith that a miracle would occur in the lion's
dens as well as in the prisons of black servitude and oppression:

Daniel in the lion's den [black people in white slavery]
He began to pray [Black religion], An angel of the Lawd
shut lion's mouth . . . That sho was a mighty day . . .
[liberation].

b. Personal and corporate strivings in the souls of black
   folk.
The inner and enriching dimension of the religious life of
the black experiences kept black people in a growing relationship with the Lord (De Lawd). The personal and corporate strivings were manifested in soul music:

Get right with God and do it now . . .

It's me, it's me, it's me, O Lawd, Standing Standing in the need of prayer . . .

I will trust in De Lawd, I will trust in De Lawd . . .

Everytime I feels the Spirit moving in my heart, I will pray . . .

I couldn't hear nobody pray . . . in the valley, on my knees with my Jesus, O Lawd . . .

We are climbing Jacob's ladder . . . Every round goes higher . . .

Lord I want to be a Christian in my heart.

Traditional African religion expressed worship through ideas and feelings couched in singing:

> God is often worshipped through songs, and African peoples are very fond of singing. Many of the religious gatherings and caremony are accompanied by singing which not only helps to pass on religious knowledge from one person or group to another, but helps create and strengthen corporate feeling and solidarity.[39]

In ceremonies of long traditions, the African worship life had behind it the force of spiritual reality. The meaning of the symbols and the process of the ritual were concretely functional in the pouring of the libations to the spirits, in the celebrations at times of seasons, and in the proper acculturation process in the rites of passage:

> Sacrifices and offerings constitute one of the commonest acts of worship among African peoples.[40]

Coming to America, Africans continued to express their religious symbolism in the deepest musical sense:

> The very first slaves brought to America and passed on to their descendants their own tonality, harmony and a rich treasure of musical means of expression.[41]

In black songs beyond the Christian influence, such as the spiritual, the memories were restored or rediscovered, and there was a perpetuation of the corporate experience:

> Let us break bread together, on our knees . . .
> Let us drink wine together, on our knees.

Perhaps the hand clapping replaced the drums, but the sticks or gourds filled with dried corn kernels set the rhythm in motion, and the vibrations of the spirits once again beat with the power of the "blood running warm in my veins." Tired bodies were regenerated, troubled spirits were refreshed, and struggling minds and visions were restored. In the black song content there were messages coming through; in the accompanying movement there was physical and social therapy coming through. Joints once stiffened by disease or hard labor would be "loosed" by the Spirit. Fisher discusses the Africanisms in the spirituals:

> First came the African. Traces of the ancient institution of the secret meetings survived in Negro spirituals. In spirituals, African beliefs and customs were preserved. The way in which Africans passed on the traditions of their ancestors from generation to generation through music, instrumental and vocal, and through rhythm or dancing and emotionalism was clearly evident. Professional people, prophets, and "doctors" were the human transmitters of the tradition.[42]

c. Black eschatology.

There are several eschatological concepts in the attitudes and expressions of black religion. The most widespread ones are: "one day," "by and by," "in the morning," and "over Jordan":

> Trials dark on every hand and we cannot understand
> All the ways of God . . . to that blessed promised land.
> But we'll understand it better by and by . . .
> When the morning comes. . . .
>
> I don't mind though dark and dreary my way may be,
> I don't mind . . . but when I cross the River of Jordan,
> When calling the roll, O Lawd, remember me.

In spite of the afflictions and troubles of this world, there will be a great joy in the land of milk and honey, where "every day will be Sunday and Sabbath will have no end":

When I get to heaven, I'm going to shout all over . . . heaven.

O when I come to the end of my journey . . . He'll say "well done."

Swing low, sweet chariot. . . . If you get there before I do, Tell all my friends I'm coming too . . . coming to carry me home.

Jesus has become a central character in the Christianity of black folk. The testimony is, "it's my determination to make heaven my home":

I'm going through, yes, I'll pay the price what ever I must do, I've started with Jesus and I'm going through.

Although the idea of heaven came through Western Christianity into the black religious experience in America, the double meaning began to emerge soon thereafter. Eschatology was not always meant as otherworldly, but sometimes as the escape to personal freedom, the return to the motherland, or signals for violent struggle. In the permanent knowledge of separation from kindred land, and freedom, the sea became the symbol of that separation and had to be crossed. The water had to be entered. This seemed to be the only way of returning to the promised land, which was heaven after death or heaven in another state or country. The double meanings were evident in the language of the oppressed: the water was deep, the water was broad, rolling, and dangerous. The water separated a people from Africa, from a new religious promise of a place prepared, and from freedom. Deep was the desire to enter the water and cross over:

Take me to the water . . . to be baptized . . .

I'm going to lay down my sword and shield, down by the river-
side.

Deep River, my home is way over yonder . . . I want to cross
over into camp ground.

Although white Western Christianity brought the concept of heaven into the black religious experience, black
religion nonetheless interpreted judgment in eschatological
terms in order to get back at the white folk.

Everybody talking about heaven, ain't going there.

And thus did Europe and Africa become fused into the
black religious experience in America. Implicit in it are the
Africanisms that blended with the biblical and traditional
Western cultural influences.

There is yet another critical principle to be noted in
black religious music: God-consciousness in the black
people's struggle.

d. God-consciousness in the black people's struggle.

There is another deep stirring of dignity in the human
spirit, and it is very evidently in the souls of black folk:
God-consciousness. It is not the God-consciousness from the
baptism of water, but consciousness kindled with the fires
of anger and the visions of freedom, justice, and permanent
struggle. There was always black defiance to slavery and
oppression, and there were always some religious specialists
fomenting and leading the struggle against injustice; for
instance, Nat Turner and Denmark Vesey and others led
many revolts and rebellions in the struggle for black liberation. Militant black preachers during slavery sang the
following:

Steal away, steal away to Jesus . . . My Lawd calls me . . .
He calls me by the thunder . . . the lightning.

These were the summonses to escape by underground to
freedom; and they were sometimes signals for violent

struggle. These were the continuations of the "secret strain," discreet communication about activities or plans to engage in the black people's struggle.

Other songs obviously sought to raise new leaders—a Moses in every place where God's children were in bondage. Egypt was symbolic of slave conditions, and Pharaoh was symbolic of the hard-hearted system of oppression, of "the man." God called the black Moses to lead His people from the clutches of the oppressors and the dehumanizing conditions of slavery, whatever the place:

> Go down Moses, way down in Egypt land and [downtown, to the White House] and tell ole Pharaoh [boss or president] . . . let my people go.

In other songs, the faithful depicted the battles and the battlefield where the Joshuas would replace the Moseses and rise up, encircle the walls of slavery, segregation, racism, and poverty, and sing and shout (struggle) until the "walls come tumbling down":

> Joshua fit the battle of Jericho, Jericho, Jericho
> . . . and the walls came tumbling down.

In fact, all Christians were challenged to respond as warriors and follow the militant (faith) style of commitment to struggle. Of course there were different kinds of battlefields, but it was the same commitment to struggle:

> I'm on the battlefield for my Lawd . . .
> And I promised him that I would serve Him till I die . . .
> I'm on the battlefield for my Lawd.

The love of being free in spirit never left the center of the black religious consciousness. There were those whose bodies and minds were afflicted with many wounds and stripes of oppression; nevertheless, there was a deeper defiance, another stirring of dignity in the human spirit and in the SOULS OF BLACK FOLK. The revolutionary spiritual expressed in God-consciousness the extent of the intractable and permanent struggle:

O Freedom for me. . . . And before I'd be a slave, I'd be
buried in my grave, and go home to my God and be free.

Those are only some scattered glimpses of the religious
dimensions of spiritual anger, hope, and determination in the
struggle—expressed in black religious consciousness through
music. Black religion virtually preserved blacks from race
suicide, from succumbing to the shocking devices of brainwashing, domestication, and emasculation. The defiance has
always had a stern and solemn warning of a black people's
judgment pronounced against the oppressors and oppression
of this world. James Baldwin, the black author, expressed
the mood of an apocalyptic-eschatological judgment in
suspension:

God gave Noah the rainbow sign, no more water, fire next
time.[43]

There were no double meanings in the judgment pronounced and sung through the black spirituals about the
struggle against white oppression:

Satan your kingdom must come down, you've built up your
kingdom all over this land, but Satan your kingdom must
come down. God's gonna bring your kingdom down.

The Afro-American recovers or discovers the spiritual
treasures in the black experience of African religion, in
poetry,[44] in rhythmic configurations,[45] in the political and
religious side of dancing,[46] in philosophy,[47] in blacks' "temperament," [48] and in the "invisible institution" [49] (African religious residuals in black religion).
Therefore, inherent in the black religious experience are
many threads that were deeply and inextricably interwoven
into the fabric of the black religious consciousness. These
black religious resources in America were the Africanisms
that accommodated and merged with the biblical Christian
experience as the black church emerged in America.

IV THE THEOLOGY OF THE BLACK EXPERIENCE

a *Black theology: A new beginning of Pan-African religion in the black diaspora?*

As a particular theological formulation and system, black theology attempts to engage some religious descriptions, interpretations, and expressions of the life-styles and God-consciousness of black peoples, beginning in the African context and moving into the black diaspora. In black consciousness the revelation of God is experienced with special kinds of universal implications.

As *the* theology it is the relevant message (*kerygma*) of God's activity in the contemporary situation. God has called black people into the center of history (He has called and calls others, also). Salvation-history in terms of black experience, is for a divine purpose. Black history is not purposeless, and the black religious experience has become a reference point in the drama of human redemption. Black theology, whether *a* or *the* theology, is not the only theology, but it is the most relevant revelation of God-activity to accomplish a "Providential design"[50] in the contemporary world—certainly from the blacks' point of view. Probably it is the only theological enterprise in contemporary history that can serve the circumstantial will of God in moving the black experience on a historical and universal mission.

Because the situation of alienation has been offensive to God's will and purpose, the message of liberation has appeared in the flesh—functioning as God's offense in revolution and reconciliation in the world. The suffering and oppressed peoples of the black diaspora have come to a new self-consciousness under the God-spell (*kergyma*). Black liberation as a Pan-African priority intends to serve all oppressed peoples in that which concerns the life needs of all humans—the only logic of redemption. Statements by black people in America move in the direction of affirming both Africa and religion. "We are an African People" and "We are a religious people." The spiritual humanity is the most basic right of life of all people. Black Americans pursue clarification of black history cast on the background of the black diaspora. Black theology may be the contemporary offense of God's judgment and grace in salvation-history, stretching to bring man into the new land. The "New Land" "beyond chaos" [51] is the context of faith and freedom as the quality of life experienced across the space of human geography.

b *Black theology in the black experience*

Black theology is dogmatic in the sense that it affirms the reality of God-consciousness as a given—a reality as natural as air for the lungs to breathe. Black theology is human-centered in affirming the sustained activity of God's pressure toward the total redemption of the human experience. Black theology from the black experience does not make an end of focusing on the skills of particular theologians or cultural or rational systems. The historical revolutionary struggles of the alienated and exploited peoples, the fostering of compassionate rather than paternalistic relationships among peoples, and the nurturing of creative Godly feelings in supporting the life-sustaining systems are the priorities in the reflections of black theology. As the Incarnation comes and lives within the particular human condition, especially the most dehumanized of those suffering from inhumane treatment, redemption, in black theology, perceive God's utilization of the black experience as revolutionary. The black experience is one of those particular human conditions now set in a revolutionary motion.

c *Black theology from black religion*

Whereas black theology does attempt to interpret the black religious experience in the light of the whole truth, its presentation and proclamation have the struggles of black people as the religious agenda, with the unconditional smashing of the fetters of exploitation as essential. At such points where black theology attempts to sharpen and describe the concepts and beliefs of the Christian faith in the light of the whole truth, including liberation from oppression, the role of black hermeneutics assists in accomplishing this function. On the other hand, it is in black religion that the concern about the quality of the black religious experience is especially nurtured, appreciated, and expressed. The crucible of suffering has enabled black people to internalize religion as the spiritual force that binds people in obedience to God. Religion is a quality of reverence for life and living. Theology has interpreted these qualitative experiences and relationships as spiritual values. Black people have been bound together, undergirded and sustained by such a religious force in an alien land. Black theology is a reflection of and from that life of faith—in survival and liberation.

d *Black theology of the black church*

Black theology, by and large, comes out of the black church, especially the church that maintains the continuity and creativity of the black religious experience. African religious consciousness is nevertheless the substratum of the historical religious experience out of which the black church has come. The various movements that have spun out of black religion in America have provided a latitude of experiences in and through which the faith of black people has been maturing. All of the sects, cults, denominations, and expressions of religious culture in the black experience, represented in the struggles of an African people in the black diaspora, have made the religion of the Church a part of that survival and struggle.

In the revelations of the "spirits" breaking into the consciousness, communications brought unions with divine energy, erupting, as it were, through the word of God, Scripture, through worship, and through the Divine presence that came in the personality of Jesus, strengthened by the Holy Spirit. When black folk said, "Let's have church," there was a special meaning—spiritual vibrations in the black experience were set in motion. The African temperament has been deeply subtle and strong in the black religious experience in America. There are profound religious sentiments and ways of doing things that manifest black or Afro-American religiosity. Within black culture there are survivals or Africanisms inherent in both the substance and the style of blacks, affirming religious reality in personal and interpersonal feelings and relationships.

The black church has nurtured the precious experiences, traditions, and culture of black people in America. The black church has nurtured faith, reason, and revelation—presuppositions both as ways to Christian knowledge and as spiritual resources implicit in the black religious experience. Black theology, evolving out of religion in the black church, whether viewed as primitive or orthodox, radical or sectarian, evolves existentially from an African religious rootage. At the same time, it advances toward African Christianity as the vanguard of Pan-African theology—a Third World force. I will now look at some of the reflections of African religion on contemporary black theologies in the United States.

e *Black theology and reflections of black theologians*

Black Americans are just beginning to recognize what African religion has contributed to Christianity in America through the total black religious experience in personality and cultural creativity. God was a given consciousness in the universal affirmation in the black experience that was, and endured, in spite of white racism, which sought to destroy black God-consciousness. The profound inwardness of God and spiritual awareness existed before black people came to accept Christianity from Euro-American Christian sources. God-consciousness was a manifestation of an inner spirit ordained by God.

In black religion the universal reality of God-Spirit entered into the particular humanity of Jesus Christ and thence into the experiences of enslaved Africans in America. As Jesus Christ sought to liberate man from the false, provincial, and dogmatic controls of a narrow and individualistic type of religious idolatry, so Jesusology in the black experience engages a theology that reforms Western Christianity. Some of the history of Christianity in Western culture has been that which bound the revelation of God to the sanction and support of racial, sensual, and materialistic exploits of antihuman systems. The negative aspects in the history of the black experience and the history of white Christianity have ofttimes been two sides of the same coin.

f *Pan-African Christianity and Pan-African theology*

It is a Pan-African Christianity and theology that would disengage the black experience from the narrowness and provincialisms of religious, racial and geographical limitations. A slave Christianity is forever bound by these selfsame limitations. The mission of God through Christ sets the objectives of the liberation movement in the context of the world. The power of Christ in the form of Pan-African Christianity and Pan-African theology sets forth the new means and instruments of salvation-history. At this level salvation-history through Pan-African Christianity and theology sets in motion the liberation process as a redemption process—in revolution, in reconciliation, and in the reconstruction of the whole human experience in the context of the multiracial world. African religion is implicit in Pan African Christianity and theology.

Black theology is inexorably driven to be the vanguard of Pan-African Christianity, even in America. The universal validity of Christianity lies not in terms of its correct ideological formulation or proclamations as such, but in terms of its humaneness and mission in the humanization of the quality of life and of environment for all mankind.

Pan-Africanism was born out of African Christianity in the black diaspora during the period of colonial domination of Africa. Continuity and change in the levels of awareness of African identity have taken place among some descendants of Africa in the diaspora. The element of continuity has persisted in the distinctive traits of temperament, sociopolitical awareness, and black life-style (Africanisms in the diaspora) in the New World. The element of change has transpired in the transformation of that continuity into the new stages of consciousness and in the forming of the linkages that have embraced the larger identity of African peoples.

I have already attempted to outline some of the distinctive traits of African religion that have been the critical

center of the African-American and Afro-American religious
experience in the black diaspora. As the characteristics of
African religion persisted in the continuum of the black religious experience, it has been relevant to Christianity in
America in at least two significant ways. On the one hand,
the African residuals in the black religious experience remain
fundamental in the black church movements, even where
changes have occurred in the various mergings of Christian
influences imposed by non-African cultural forms and life-
styles. On the other hand, there has been a relentless pushing
for the establishment or re-creation of valid African spiritual
linkages.

The probings into the past are now underway in black
America. The pushings for linkages with black Christians
in other parts of the world is a parallel effort. In this process
Africans in America are attempting to identify and define a
genuine loyalty to the spiritual aspects of Pan -Africanism.
This is not a gesture of romanticism, but a quest for an
authentic kind of wholeness about the truth of the life and
personality of the black.

With regard to the kinds of probing into the blacks'
past, P. O. Esedebe has set forth several conclusions about
the search for complete understanding of Pan-Africanism:

> Any complete definition of Pan Africanism must include all
> of the major aspects.[52]

He has noted the major aspects as: (1) the humiliating
experiences of African peoples in the New World; (2) the
racialism that continued during and after the abolition
period; (3) the independent African church movements; and
(4) the nineteenth-century nationalism.[53] These may be regarded as some of the important watersheds in the rise of
Pan-Africanism. I might also add that they contributed to
enlarging political consciousness and the concept of African
unity.

St. Clair Drake has described the movement as a religious
one in terms of "God's hand in Black history." [54] Esedebe has
outlined the first three periods.[55]

In the first period there were men like Paul Cuffee, John Kizzell, Lott Cary, Daniel Coker, Elijah Johnson, and John Russwurm from America. Drake captures the radical religious aspirations of these black men under two religious motifs: (1) the doctrine of "Providential design," and (2) Ethiopianism. With Alexander Crumwell, in the perspective of the Providential design, he stated:

> the forced and cruel migration of our race from this continent, and the wondrous providence of God, by which the sons of Africa by hundreds and by thousands trained . . . are coming hither . . . for Christ and his Church.[56]

Also Henry M. Turner, as quoted by Drake, states:

> The Negro race has as much chance in United States . . . of being a man . . . as a frog has in a snake den. . . . Emigrate and gradually return to the land of our ancestors. . . . The Negro was brought here in the providence of God to learn . . . and then to return to Africa, the land of his fathers, and bring her his millions.[57]

On the doctrine of Ethiopianism, Drake states:

> This Biblical myth is the core of a thought style that might be called "Ethiopianism," and which became more complex and secularized as it developed during the 19th and 20th centuries.[58]

Edward Blyden kept before Africans in America the self-image of that larger identity that linked blacks in America with Africa, the ancestral home. He provided for Africans that larger identity of peoplehood:

> Besides promulgating the main ideas, Pan-Africanism of this period took the dominant form of Back-to-Africa, the Fatherland. Behind this impulse was the belief of New World Negroes that it was their manifest destiny to regenerate Africa.[59]

The second period of Pan-Africanism started with Henry S. Williams at a September 1897 meeting in London and continued in successive meetings in Brussels, Lisbon, Paris, and Manchester. The young black intellectuals of the Caribbeans, America, and Africa had gathered in Europe seeking to identify and define the political objectives of African peoples, the objectives of Pan-Africanism. Indirectly, all of them had been influenced by religious institutions.

The third period of Pan-Africanism [60] came after the liberation of Africa had begun in Ghana and the end of the European central influence was visible. Pan-Africanism came to an African base under the leadership of Nkrumah, Kenyatta, and others. Conferences created a permanent structure, a political-cultural mechanism, the Organization of African Unity (O.A.U.) in 1963. Although the O.A.U. works primarily for Pan-Africanism on the continent, the Pan-African movement continues to establish various kinds of linkages with African nationalities in various quarters of the black world.

The fourth period of Pan-Africanism is now taking place in the various types of cooperative programs and projects wherein Africans from the black diaspora are brought into the orbit of Pan-Africanism on the continent. From the Christian point of view, the emergence of the All-Africa Christian Youth Assembly, the All-Africa Church Conference in 1962–63, and the various dialogues that have taken place in Tanzania and Uganda in the matters of African church life and theology have helped toward this end. In America several Africa-oriented groups continue the thrust of Pan-Africanism, even as black nationalists—organizations such as the Congress of African Peoples, and the Africa Commission of the National Committee of Black Churchmen. Dialogue between black churchmen and theologians have taken place, for example, in summer 1971 [61] in Tanzania, where African theologians and churchmen came together. In January 1972, at Kampala, Uganda, dialogue continued.

In the light of these realities, black theology and African theology are moving along in space and time from the African homeland to the black diaspora and from the past into the present and future.

In the first dimension, black theology and African theology are engaging in those conversations and explorations that will discover and describe the link of traditional African religion to the Christian presence in black religion in America as well as to Christianity as an African religion in Africa. Thousands of independent Christian movements document the fact that there is a fermenting energy that will one day burst forth in the unity of strength of Pan-African Christianity.

In the second dimension, the brokenness in the historical experiences of African peoples, especially in the black diaspora, is artificial and unnatural, and the people perceive a sense of inevitability about the linking and healing of the relationships among all African peoples in space and time. Indeed, the future of Christianity as a world religion will be greatly shaped by African Christianity coming up from the Third World or the black world. (The work of John S. Mbiti and David Barrett on the subject, *The Future of Christianity in Africa,* should be considered insightful, informative, and prophetic.) Between the movement to discover and describe African religion uniting the present with the past and the movement to unite the religious experiences of African peoples in the future, there is another and pressing dimension: the present stirring of dialogues at Kampala and Dar es Salaam. James H. Cone and Gayraud S. Wilmore moved in this direction in the presentation "Black Theology and African Theology: Considerations for Dialogue, Critique and Integration." In Kampala the conference on African theology and church life continue the proliferation of discussion.

Beneath the umbrella of Pan-African theology is the proper place to effect the blends of black theology and African theology. Both are based on the main thrust of the Christian religion in the religious experiences of African peoples, regardless of the diversity. Nonetheless, under the pressures of black humanity, African history, and the will of God, blacks are experiencing signs of the past and future in the labor pains of the present:

What we are experiencing among Black people in the United States, the Caribbean and Africa is an outright rejection of both of these assumptions (the "inferior" residuals of African religion in the Black religious experience and the adage by American liberals that the "Negro is nothing more than a chocolate-covered white American") . . . and a new consciousness of racial, national and cultural identity which asserts a certain discontinuity with Euro-American values and perceives Black peoples to have, by virtue of historical circumstances if not innate characteristics, a distinctive and independent contribution to make to world civilization.[62]

Whether one now speaks of African theology or black theology or other forms of theology emerging from non-American quarters of the New World, he is still dealing with Pan-African Christianity, the source and resource of Pan-African theology. African religion in America exists in the form of Christianity and black religion. Christianity as an African religious experience, whether imposed or imported, has been indigenized in black folk religion.

Traditional African religious resources may well enrich African Christianity in America. The black church movements have been extensions from the folk interpretations of the black experience, in which African religion has been an influential and sometimes invisible link. Black theology and African theology are manifestations of African Christianity, out of which Pan-African theology will emerge. The true Pan-African theology will blend other religious forms so that religion functions and serves the black man and humanity—in belief and in practice—for the ultimate coming of the brave, new New World. To this end, African religion is indeed relevant to Christianity in America and beyond—in the religion of Man.

NOTES TO CHAPTER 3

1. John S. Mbiti, "Christianity and Traditional Religions in Africa," *International Review of Missions* 59, no. 236 (October 1970): 430–40.
2. *Black Religion* (Boston: Beacon Press, 1964) is the title of a book

by Joseph R. Washington, who failed to engage the African residuals in his work. Washington's scholarship is moving in this direction in his more recent work, *Black and White Power Subreption* (Boston: Beacon Press, 1971).

N.B.: a. The words *preparation, fulfillment,* and *enrichment* are indigenized intensively and extensively in the African-American and black experience in that which concerns their theological significance.

b. *Black* is a term self-affirming and indigenous in the consciousness of descendants of Africa in the New World, especially in America. It is broader than skin color as a symbol in the struggle for liberation from racism.

c. Black diaspora depicts the new situation of experience of the descendants of Africa now scattered in the far reaches of the New World. It is also the title of a book to be published—*Black Diaspora* by St. Clair Drake.

3. Max Weber, *The Protestant Ethic and the Spirit of Capitalism* (New York: Scribners, 1930), and Eric Williams, *Capitalism and Slavery* (Chapel Hill, N.C.: University of North Carolina Press, 1938) show the correlations between capitalism and slavery and capitalism and religion.

4. R. H. Tawney, *Religion and the Rise of Capitalism* (New York: Harcourt, Brace, 1926) also describes the symbiotic relationship between the religious and economic forces.

5. Stewart C. Easton, *The Twilight of European Colonialism* (New York: Holt, Reinhart and Winston, 1960) engages the political appraisal or analysis of modern colonialism in Africa during a particular historical period. The title appropriately interprets the period of transition and change in reaction to structures and values.

6. V. F. Calverton, *The Passing of the Gods* (New York: Scribners, 1934) is a Marxist presentation.

7. E. R. Embree, "Rebirth of Religion in Russia," *Int. Jour. Eth.* 45 (1935): 422–30.

8. Robertson Smith, *Religion of the Semites* (New York: Meridian Books, 1956).

9. Yosef ben-Jochannan, *African Origins of the Major Western Religions* (New York: Alkebu-Lan Books, 1970) (hereafter referred to as AOMWR), quotes a variety of sources to substantiate this point of view: Homer W. Smith, *Man and His Gods* (Boston: Little, Brown, 1952), states, ". . . European and Asian (Jewish, Christian or Moslem) peoples followed the Africans from whom they modeled their own religions" (AOMWR, p. 67). Count C. C. Volney, *Ruins of Empire* (Boston: J. P. Mendum, 1866), states that all religions originated in Africa. Dr. E. A. Wallis Budge, in the "Coffin" and "Pyramid" texts in *Book of the Dead* (London: P. L. Warner, 1911) and *Osiris,* shows the background for the African god Ra and Mysteries (AOMWR, pp. vi, vii). E.g., ". . . with respect to the origin of religion, that there would have been no

Egyptian civilization (high culture) had not the Africans, the so-called Negroes of the Upper Nile Valley and Central Africa, not migrated North along the more than 4 thousand-mile long Nile River . . . equally there could be no Judaism, Christianity or Islam. . . ." ". . . The Mysteries . . . from the ancient religious rites of the indigenous African peoples and their descendants . . . are in fact the forerunners of Nile Valley religions, therefore, they are the creators of the Mysteries of Sais, Ethiopian Nubia . . . ," (AOMWR, p. vii).

Dr. Albert Churchward, *Origin and Evolution of Free Masonry* (London: G. Allen & Co., 1913), indicates that "ancient religious rites of the indigenous Africans . . . around the major great lakes of Central Africa and along the head waters of the Nile River were the forerunners of ancient religious influences as the source 'common to th heritage' of religious practices in parts of West, Central, East and South Africa with that of the ancient indigenous Africans of Sais" (AOMWR, p. vii).

10. AOMWR, p. xii; also Exodus 20:13, 15; and in the "Hymn of Adoration of the God," *Osiris*, chap. 1, n55.

11. Albert B. Cleage, Jr., *The Black Messiah* (New York: Sheed and Ward, 1969), p. 3.

12. Janheinz Jahn, *Muntu* (New York: Grove Press, 1961), p. 101; see also pp. 96–120.

13. Jochannan, AOMWR, p. xii.

14. C. P. Groves, *The Planting of Christianity in Africa* (London: Lutterworth Press, 1948), p. 59; also in AOMWR.

15. Jochannan, AOMWR, p. 78.

16. Mrs. Stewart Erskine, *The Vanquished Cities of North Africa* (Boston: Houghton Mifflin & Co., 1927), p. 80; also in AOMWR.

17. Jane Soames, *Coast of the Barbary* (London: J. Cape, 1938), p. 20; also in AOMWR.

18. Jochannan, AOMWR, p. 98. His reference is George H. Sabine.

19. Ibid., p. 108.

20. Matt. 2:14–15.

21. Acts 8:27–39; see also 1 Kings 10:28f.; Num. 12:1.

22. David Barrett, *Schism and Renewal in Africa* (New York: Oxford University Press, 1968), p. 21.

23. Carter G. Woodson, *The African Background Outlined* (Washington, D.C.; Associated Press, 1936), p. 126. "The study of religious phenomena in the Negro Church of today will explain much observed among African tribes. Most writings on the Negro Church, however, are purely narrative or statistical and never touch these reactions which require scientific study."

24. Howard Thurman, *Deep River: An Interpretation of Negro Spirituals* (New York: Harper Bros., 1955), p. 1.

25. Miles Mark Fisher, *Negro Slave Songs in United States* (New York: Russell & Russell, 1953), p. 20.

26. Woodson, *African Background*, p. 117.

African Religion: A New Focus for Black Theology 113

27. John S. Mbiti, *African Religions and Philosophy* (New York: Praeger Publishers, 1969), p. 67.

28. Ibid., pp. 3–6.

29. Ps. 139:7–16.

30. Mbiti, *African Religions and Philosophy*, p. 14.

31. The transcendence of God is biblical. E.g., Isa. 55:9.

32. Mbiti, *African Religions and Philosophy*, p. 21.

33. Ibid., p. 23.

34. Job 11:7–9.

35. Mbiti, *African Religions and Philosophy*, p. 12.

36. Matt. 19:26.

37. Acts 7:6.

38. Ps. 137:1.

39. Mbiti, *African Religions and Philosophy*, p. 67.

40. Ibid., p. 58.

41. Jahn, *Muntu*, p. 220.

42. Fisher, *Negro Slave Songs*, p. 178.

43. James Baldwin, *Fire Next Time* (New York: Dial Press, 1963), an introductory quotation.

44. Fran Fanon, *Black Skin, White Mask* (New York: Grove Press, 1971).

45. Jahn, *Muntu*, p. 38.

46. Ibid., p. 26.

47. Ibid., pp. 100f.

48. Woodson, *African Background*, p. 214. Woodson notes that R. E. Park contends that the African retained nothing brought from Africa but his *temperament*. Woodson himself speaks of *sentiment* as playing a large part in the life of the Negro in Africa, and "this must be taken into account in understanding the background of the present-day Negro." He adds, "The spirituals were expressions of the reactions of Africans to his [sic] lot in the New World."

49. E. Franklin Frazier, *The Negro Church in America* (New York: Schocken Books, 1964), p. 291.

50. See Drake's analysis in "God's Hand in Black History," in St. Clair Drake, *The Redemption of Africa and Black Religion* (Chicago: Third World Press, 1970), pp. 44ff.

51. Albert B. Cleage, Jr, "The Black Messiah and the Black Revolution," in James J. Gardiner and J. Deotis Roberts, Sr., *Quest for a Black Theology* (Philadelphia: Pilgrim Press, 1971).

52. P. O. Esedebe, "Origins and Meaning of Pan-Africanism," in *Presence Africaine* (Sierre Leone: Institute of African Studies, University of Sierre Leone, 1970), p. 111.

53. Ibid., pp. 111–20.

54. Drake, *Redemption of Africa*, pp. 41–53.

55. Esedebe, "Origins and Meaning," p. 1.

56. Drake, *Redemption of Africa*, p. 51.

57. Ibid., p. 52.

58. Ibid., p. 50.

59. Esedebe, "Origins and Meaning," p. 125; see also Drake, *Redemption of Africa*, pp. 60–62.

60. Esedebe, "Origins and Meaning," pp. 126f.

61. James Cone and Gayraud Wilmore, "Black Theology and African Theology: Considerations for Dialogue, Critique and Integration," in Patricia Massie, ed., *Black Faith and Black Solidarity* (Washington, D.C.: Association Press, 1973).

62. Ibid.

4

The Theological Posits
of Black Christianity

HENRY H. MITCHELL

Black culture is undergirded by and filled with a strong world view, an impressive collection of de facto theological assumptions. I, along with a great many other blacks, made a huge error in assessment in this regard, and I was guilty of it for a long time. It is high time the error was looked at and corrected.

For instance, when I first read Paul Tillich's *The Courage to Be,* I quickly concurred with his three major kinds of human anxiety: (1) Fate and Death, or what I call survival; (2) Emptiness and Meaninglessness; and (3) Guilt, Condemnation, and Self-Rejection, or the self-declared failure to live up to one's destiny.[1] But when I applied this categorization to black existence, I quickly concluded that most blacks were so caught up in the crisis of simple survival that they had no time for the luxury of pondering the meaning of their lives. Such a theory was supported by the dearth of discussions and rap sessions on this terribly important subject. The one place it surfaced was in the black pulpit, and even there it was not tackled in Tillichian terms. Oppression was assumed to have forced us to concentrate on food and drink and clothing and rent. The "privilege" of pondering one's life's meaning produced a crisis reserved for the affluent few.

I have for some time now come to reject this analysis almost entirely. First of all, meaning—the way one makes sense of his existence—is the literal basis on which blacks have been able to survive an existence utterly absurd and unbelievably brutal. In the black culture, meaning is no rare luxury, it is abundantly provided and communicated; and we never would have made it without the rich support of our world view. Tillich's insistence that one cannot live without a way of making sense is thus confirmed, and my "black exception" is wiped out. When he further suggests that it is not the fear of *death* but the fear of spiritual *non-meaning* that produces the *death instinct*,[2] I suddenly see why suicide has until recently been so rare among blacks.

Where, then, had this meaning been hiding all the time? The answer tends to make one ashamed. It was not hiding at all, and I was using it myself every day of my life. It was my "gut-level" assumptions about God and providence and grace. And I had overlooked them because they had not been formally belabored and taught. I had not had to wrestle for them in stereotypical Western detachment. They had come to me in trust levels communicated more *outside* the rational consciousness than in it. It was not inherited physically, but it started with my mother's milk, and it permeated the culture of the believing black masses in which I was reared. When, in the midst of the sophomore syndrome, I had a few healthy doubts about some of the things I believed, the education that brought the doubts was not a luxury; it was a dire necessity for purposes of liberation. And the crisis of meaning was, for me, not a real one. It was simply a crisis of cultural shock, suffered because I was trying to legitimate my soul supports on new and alien grounds. Once the task of translation was accomplished, I was "home free."

This kind of black religious and intellectual pilgrimage is not at all unique. Contemporary blacks simply need to shorten the journey for oncoming generations of blacks by helping them to see and consciously embrace the posits they already use. If there is a gap between these gut-level assumptions and the intellectual propositions to which they are attracted, they must be helped to close it. In so doing it would be well to understand that the feeling-level, cultural assumptions of the black community are profoundly both humane and Christian, and that they constitute the more important aspect of the system of belief of any person or culture.

Theological posits are most authentically the postulates of actual faith when they are culturally assumed and axiomatically applied by whole societies, long before they are subjected to inevitable scrutiny and healthy analysis. The theological posits of black Americans must never become assumptions to which they have been driven in an intellectual storm, and to which they cling only because every system of thought must be based on a priori assumptions. Theology capable of sustaining life has to be theology of the *people*—the accumulated insights of the vast masses of an ethnoreligious body or other traditional grouping. The immanent death of the white church as we know it is perhaps due not so much to tensions created by feeble stands on prophetic issues as to its failure to keep the theological enterprise related to its masses—the now ugly and silent majority of the white backlash.

I hold, therefore, that the posits that I am to discuss must come from the black cultural and religious roots and from the black American experience. They cannot come from the intellectual drawing board of any scholar, black or otherwise. Real foundations of faith comes from the bowels of existence, where people must believe *some*thing or go crazy and die. Any future theological construction to be proposed by black academic theologians must flow from these foundations, and it must be capable of naturally flowing back into and enriching the folk theology. Both the integrity and folk character of black theology must be maintained throughout the very legitimate and necessary process of enrichment, refinement, and increase of its already impressive relevance.

I propose to comment on that experiential process and its cultural roots before I deal with the posits that I and millions more have believed and lived through the years. And even before that process is discussed, there must be some basic understandings.

For instance, it must be understood that I make no claim for an absolutely unique black theological position. Even the African roots of black-American belief are not unique. Virtually every idea in African traditional religion has well-known parallels in other modern and primitive religions, some as far away as Korea and Japan. And certainly no theological posit of modern black Christianity is unique. Only recently I had the experience of expounding at length African and black American concepts of predestination, as opposed to the caricatures of Calvinism current in conservative Christianity, only to have a group of reputable white theologians insist that what black folk believe is exactly what Calvin was saying.

The existence of a black theological style and content does not hang on its uniqueness. It hangs, rather, on whether or not there are an experience and an interpretation of it that (taken as a whole) is sufficiently different in its balance and emphases from other racial and class-group interpretations to be reasonably identified as belonging to at least a majority of black Christians, as opposed to a majority of Christians of another race and/or class.

The majorities and minorities of races and cultures and bodies of believers must be understood to be just that— majorities and minorities, not "representatives" of a monolithic culture or faith. However, constant attention to the total spectrum of blacks' belief would be cumbersome and dull. It is both easier and more accurate to deal with that body of believers which is, of all black believers, still in the vast numerical majority—the black masses. They are the believers who contrast most with white believers (also quite varied). At all times it must be understood that what is said here represents the black majority and implies a wide spectrum of blacks' belief and disbelief, in which the overlap with Western white thought is much greater. The use of this comparison and the disclaimer of black uniqueness have already signaled the fact that even the faith of the black masses in the USA is not by any means purely African, but is an adaptation of African roots to American experience and Christian exposure.

Thus far it is clearly implied that there is, also, a black theology. This understanding needs to be explicit. To the extent that persons have a world view and value system by which they live and make decisions, *all* men of *all* cultures have a theology. To the extent that the folk customs and beliefs of black Americans differ from those of whites and others, there has *always* been a black theology. The African-American cultural continuum combined with slavery to start blacks off here on an entirely different footing. The difference is perpetuated by reason of oppression. The two-way acculturation process toward a relatively similar American folk theology will *follow*, not precede, the erasure of the social, economic, political, educational, and other distinctives of the experience of the vast majority of blacks. And *no* black of any position is ever free of these arbitrary assaults on his personhood.

That black Americans survived slavery and the horrors of "emancipation" when many forecast their devastation (the newly freed died by the thousands),[3] is proof enough that the black world view and value system were and are functional and supportive. There are other oppressed minorities who have not fared nearly so well numerically, and whose spirits have not been nearly so resilient as those who were fed on the black interpretation of existence. Another understanding, then, is that it is ludicrous to ask if blacks ought to develop their own special brand of the "universal" (but really only white middle-class) version of the Gospel. Like all separate cultures, blacks have inevitably had a theology all along, and they have survived, in part, because of it. There may be very legitimate objections to "black" retreads of European theologies, but black Christianity in America is the folk religion of most of the masses of believers. It has been so for a long, long time. The black masses were not always "Christian," but they always had a folk religious unity of sorts. In the earlier stages, the enslaved reflected their African roots more obviously, but the faith continuum *still* starts in Africa. William R. Jones of Yale is quite correct in suggesting that black theology look at indigenous sources.[4] The survival of blacks is due more to the original African elements than to the "Christian" adoptions added, in time, to their folk faith.

Black theology is as alive and healthy as it is because it has not suffered the linguistic, cultural, and strategic blunders of schoolroom theological enterprises. The process of sifting black posits must continue this unpremeditated strength. The posits must be stated in the terms in which ordinary folk state them, when they are verbalized at all. This means that biblical phrases must loom large in this belated codification of their belief. I must not "fight their feeling" and style, in the interest of scholarly credibility. If a widely used phrase comes from a fundamentalist hymn dear to the black brethren, I must tell it like it is believed and felt, even though there is on my agenda an item about acculturating people away from some of the unfortunate lyrics that go along with the profoundly nourishing items.

A final methodological assumption, therefore, is that the task of black theology is radically different in source and method from the white counterpart. The black theologian must enter his work shorn of all need to please the vast majority of his white peers. This is not to suggest that he should commit professional suicide. While I distinctly am not a theologian, I would readily acknowledge the need for a black theologian to master the white systems, both for purposes of black apologetic and interpretation to the wider world, and for professional survival. But his task of theologizing-in-black is to deal with the black folk corpus intensely and coherently, offering the world at large a set of road tested posits for an existence in a society the massiveness and complexity of which dehumanizes whites as well as blacks. If the black theologian does less than this, he will deserve and receive flak from whites as well as blacks.

Black folk have used well the clay of early American revivalism and even sterile fundamentalism. Perhaps it is more accurate to say that they have brought their own clay, in many cases, from Africa, and it only *appeared* to imply the same meaning as that of the conservative white racist who used the same words. Blacks have made theological bricks without straw, and they have had to use English terms without being able or even anxious to distinguish black usage from white. With or without straw, they have built a black Christian world view and value system that have interpreted an absurdly cruel existence and supported black survival in a manner that commands the respect and admiration of religion's most cultured despisers. It has clearly inspired efforts for liberation as well, and the task for today is simply to increase this emphasis while losing none of the essential inputs for survival.

What, then, are the posits of this black folk theology? What is the irreducible minimum of foundational belief that is beyond both proof and disproof, in the Western sense, and on which all living, as well as further believing, depends?

The first posit of black theology is that human existence, the creation, and the Creator are very good. This originally West African affirmation of the ultimate benevolence of all reality has been encountered in the indigenous world view and commented upon by an impressive variety of professional scholars and other observers, but its origin is utterly obscure. Why and how the inhabitants of a continent from which it is hard to wring a living managed to acquire so profound a genius for positive thinking escapes easy hypothesis. Suffice it to say that the affirmation and celebration of a life never easy (by Western material standards) prevail

in most of black Africa, and that the survival of this affirmation and celebration has not been thwarted by the pressures
and oppression of the black American experience. This outlook may appear as wishful to the cynic, but it supports
lives and empowers being in its believers. It might be
clinically established that it is self-fulfilling prophecy about
life, but so is all generalization about life. The track record
of this tenet of folk faith outstrips that of all others, and
suicides never occur among those secure in this belief.

Black theologians tend to concur with this reading of
the culture and faith, but I think that I detect a failure to
sense its ultimate significance for theology among blacks. If
God and life are ultimately good, they are surely on the side
of liberation; but this does not subordinate the goodness of
God and life to "liberation" as an all-pervasive and exclusively normative consideration. That is to say, the importance of
liberation is undeniable, but the positive assessment of God
and life—the fundamental belief in the goodness of the
Creator and creation—is more inclusive and ultimate as a
category of faith. The significance of this seemingly petty
technicality is enormous. It is evident in the *power of
affirmation*, expressed in the numerous and clandestine
praise houses, *to support slave life even without liberation*,
in a cruel and demonic system of chattel slavery. Again, the
will of God that men be liberated is of paramount political
and social importance, but the catalogue of things contrary
to God's will and destructive of life's fulfillment is larger
than even slavery and oppression. The self, both alone and
in extended family, is crucially expressed and affirmed in the
exercise of self-determination, or power. But the soul's
capacities are not exhausted nor its longings satisfied at the
fountain of power alone. The contemporary strategy for the
black agenda has rightly included extreme emphasis on the
sin of enforced powerlessness, but the sweep of black
theology is broader and deeper than the concerns for power
and liberation of the kingdom, and it involves the total scope
of the will of God for the abundant life.

The existence of this good God is a posit buried so deep

in African religion and culture as never to be an issue. In black American folk theology there is virtually no agnosticism, and no atheism either. Whatever the case against churches and preachers, the dictum of the mother in the play *Raisin in the Sun* still holds in mass culture: "In my mother's house there is still God." The writer of the book of Hebrews declares that "he that cometh to God must believe that he is, and that he is a rewarder of them that diligently seek him" (11:6). The host of black American believers has been able to draw strength from God in a crisis because there has never been any serious, massive failure to live up to the requisites of this text.

The memorable line quoted above from Lorraine Hansberry's play accurately serves as a response to a young black college student's internalization of white Western material criteria and overestimations of the powers of the human mind. No pre-Christian African traditional religionist, and no fullfledged participant in the religious and cultural tradition of the black American majority, would seriously offer the question raised by Miss Hansberry's student. There is even the hint that this young lady is following fad more than independent inquiry. It is sometimes suggested that the most gifted black abolitionists raised intellectual questions about God.[5] But it is easy to see that these are all rhetorical, skillfully used for propagandistic purposes. Even so, God had to be or to exist to be asked such questions, and there was always a way to maintain faith after all the cries concerning God's existence and support of justice had been raised.

The immense importance of the posit of God lies not in its indispensability to a theology but in its implications for living. Our African and Afro-American forefathers have consistently assumed that life is good and that reality possesses the necessary order to maintain that good, as humanistically defined. This assumption has not been based on a rationalistic and inadequate method of the "analysis" of the human condition, but on the intuitive reading of reality as having an order-giving persona, High God, the Creator of all other deities and divinities, as well as of all that is. His power guarantees the ultimate existence and goodness of creation, so He needs must be.

This raises the role of God as Creator, a third posit. Black folk theology has no awareness of process or naturalistic theology per se, but it has always known that the universe was created and governed, ultimately, by God, the source of all power. It has been known, also, that spiritual beings inhabit material residences, and that the ineffable God is present in all nature, whether in lesser deities in Africa or in the sense of the Holy Spirit in black American Christianity.

This creation is held, therefore, in awe; and one never attempts completely to understand and manipulate the natural order in Western fashion. To seek too fully to comprehend it all would be to seek to know and judge the very mind of God. The black American Fathers knew better than to try such madness, and they found in Job a useful model of their old African reverence before the handiwork of God: "Where wast thou when I laid the foundations of the earth?" (38:4). The more learned descendants of the black Fathers have had no choice but to echo and enjoy the question and let their joy in an adequate Creator bring their own achievements down to proper scale. It was partly for its value in puttin' ol' Massa' in proper perspective that this Scripture was so popular in the first place.

No matter how much power or knowledge men have, the Creator and His ultimate order are past finding out. This has not, however, stopped the black believer from searching persistently and pragmatically for truth. It is simply that the limitations on man's grasp of truth have been so well understood by blacks in the root culture that they could be open-minded and adaptive. This was and is precisely because they are not silly enough to engage in the arrogant assumption that they had all truth for everywhere. One does not feel the need to make such claims when he knows and can celebrate the fact that God's "got the whole world in *His* hands."

It is obvious to the black believer that God possesses the

power to create and sustain the goodness of life. Long
before the black Fathers in Africa heard of Christ or the
Bible, their praise names for God clearly showed that God
was omnipotent and omniscient.⁶ The whole certainty of the
goodness of reality was guaranteed by God. His power was
celebrated, not as awe before brute force in the mechanical
and perhaps Western sense, but as subtle yet very realistic
awareness that power is essential to the maintenance of a life
so good. This power seems always to be in tandem with
wisdom, revealing another subtle but acute perception—
the need for power to be used in keeping with the intelligence so highly held in esteem in African and black
American culture and religion.

The idea of God's omniscience is no more open to question than His omnipotence. It is a foundational posit to all
of the world view. Whatever negative folk attitudes are
verbalized against education are directed against an alien
and dysfunctional system known to blacks, and are not
directed against wisdom. Limitless wisdom and understanding are assumed in and attributed to God, who uses them to
keep human existence abundant and to guide the steps of
those who are open to his leading. It is just good to know
that *He* knows. It begets joy and celebration. One of the
favorite pastimes of the faithful is to recount all the dangers,
toils, and snares that they have overcome because God has
exercised his wisdom and power to deliver.

As one gets into the feeling of the subject, it becomes
difficult to establish a line of demarcation between elemental
axioms of belief and the corollaries thereto. African and
Afro-American tradition tends to transmit so functional a
set of conscious and unconscious posits or assumptions that
a far larger proportion, if not all of the world view, is
axiomatic rather than deduced from a set of prior propositions. It may be argued that "true faith" cannot be so unconsciously transmitted as to require so little conscious and
decisive embrace. But black affirmation of God and life is
far less exclusively cerebral and, therefore, far less amenable
to exclusively rational communication. Black belief is *caught*

at unconscious levels even before it is *taught* by means of tales and proverbs and biblical passages. One will usually posit the black world view of trust and affirmation (as a child) long before he consciously and verbally unpacks all of that world view's profound Christian significance. On this functional as opposed to rational basis, the following posits are properly considered root assumptions of black folk theology. They are not "derived," as such, from the prior posits, but they arrive at a rational fit and form a coherent as well as supportive "system" or living corpus of belief.

We have already seen God as all-powerful and all-knowing, Creator and Sustainer of a universe and a human existence that are inextricably bound together and good. The posit of God as Judge and Redeemer commonly follows, and some treatment of the subject must therefore be attempted here.

As I perceive the prior or root African world view, a world organized as an extended family society and an individual life, both already affirmed as good, was not in the same desperate need of judgment and redemption as is assumed in Western theology. Black American forebearers, however, were quick to seize upon or adapt their thinking to judgment and hell, especially after they saw the unprecedented evils of slavery. Hell was the perfect place to believe in when one thought of the justice of God and the sins of ol' massa. It was not a rational theological transaction per se, but it was an extension, at the same time logical and visceral, of the posit of the goodness of God and life. "You got to give a 'count at the Judgement, you betta min.'" "Everybody talkin' 'bout heaven ain't goin' there," (Massa especially) but the singer planned to put on his shoes and "walk all over God's heaven." Whatever use the master made of such awareness, the fact is that judgment was accentuated in the world view for basically positive reasons. Accountability before God is unquestionably a posit of black belief or folk theology, and its implications for an oppressive society and its members (here *and* hereafter) are at least as important as its implications for the petty morals of the individual believer.

The most likely question to arise from the black agenda in connection with this judgment is how much of it a man may help God do. Just as I share the Cross with Christ, may I not also share personally in the judgment, for purposes of blacks' liberation? The answer from black folk theology is, at best, a mixed one. There are still some Nat Turner types around to say that the answer is yes. I suspect, however, that the vast majority of the black faithful would go with the biblical idea that "Vengeance is mine; I will repay, saith the Lord" (Rom. 12 : 19). There are even traditional African religious ideas that boil down to the same thing.[7] The legitimate problem raised is the likelihood that black men will be docile and quiescent, while the judgment wheels of God grind slow, if indeed exceedingly fine—and meanwhile black men are ground to death.

I find no common tendency to a neat answer or a conscious posit. I do detect, rather, an unverbalized willingness to let God be God and give the sinner his wages in due course, but with it goes a firm and resolute position in the emerging black consciousness : "Let God *repay* the oppressor, but I accept my responsibility meanwhile, to *restrain* him. I must protect the sheep from the wolves of all colors. I keep trying to tell these white policemen that you can stop a man from stealing without stopping him from breathing." This position is illustrated by the large number of slaves who, with physical power, resisted the brutal and unjust beatings of their masters and yet never descended to the level of a relationship characterized by hate. I know of several powerful slave women who snatched whips from the hands of their masters and threatened, on the spot, to kill them if they ever tried to whip them again. Such slaves were sometimes sold by poor excuses for men, but many a master knew well that these people had both labor power and defensive powers, and that if he could keep himself from "acting a fool," he could count on both their labor and their love. Such love was not childishly ignorant. It was the logical if often unverbalized outgrowth of a world view that celebrated and *enjoyed* knowing about the judgment of God.

In a book I have written (*Black Belief*, 1975) there is quoted a slave narrative that illustrates the point. Solomon, a white slave driver or overseer, had a habit of knocking on a cabin wall with the stock of his whip and crying out threats to take the hides off the backs of the slaves if they didn't stop that praying and singing. The narrator said, "I *know* that Solomon is burnin' in hell today, and it *pleasures* me. . . ." [8]

The concept of God as Redeemer or, more accurately, the mercy of God, is even more at home in the originally African world view. An impressive collection of proverbs from Africa, also quoted by me in the above-mentioned book, declares the literal providence of God in beautiful and moving figures of speech. The imagery includes God pounding fufu (like mashing hard potatoes) for the man who has no arms, or fanning flies for the cow who has no tail, or seeing to it that when the Gonja leper's sandal breaks, he is near a camelfoot bush, which provides fibers for sandal repair.[9] In the Gonja world view, the providence of God acted universally, even as the belief in it was shared by all members of the culture.

It is not hard to understand how the black American world view quickly appropriated terminology such as "His mercy endureth forever." But the idea, as such—the posit— was not taught by representatives of the system of slavery. Black folk had known that truth for years, and much of their festivity in Africa had been based on it.

The literal idea of Redeemer assumes a more complicated and legalistic frame of reference, but the hymns and biblical rhetoric of blacks' worship reflect it often enough. The question is whether or not it is a posit of the gut-level black world view. While I hold the concept to be personally meaningful, I cannot honestly say that so complicated a concept as redemption shares the same elemental position in the blacks' psyche as the concept of the mercy of God.

Before concluding this essay, I expect that I should say

something about posits in reference to the other two persons of the trinity. Here again, to use the terminology of a Pope, I perceive Christian "grafts" on the original African world view.[10]

Traditional African religion assumes a system of intermediaries between man and an ineffable God. When carried from their native soil and into so hostile an environment as America, black slaves felt even farther from God. There is little wonder that they welcomed and so quickly embraced the Christ figure. He was swiftly (for a cultural movement) escalated as person to the level of a very pervasive and personal posit. One talks to Jesus, and uses his name in the address and mention of God to an extent that clearly constitutes the most fundamental change to take place in the American adaptation of the African corpus of folk belief. The goodness of God and the world and human life was advanced or expressed and implemented immeasurably by the introduction of the Christ figure, who suffers with man and yet is God. Life after death was the meat of the early Christian Gospel's fresh input, but it was "old hat" in the African world view. Black Americans took it for granted. The *Incarnation* was the "new" and vitally important addition.

White folklorists have greatly exaggerated the importance of superstition and magic in black folk belief. But if there had not been at least some of this strata of religion, there would never have been any of it to survive. The most significant factor in the fairly complete disappearance of spiritistic fear among confessing black Christians is, I believe, the introduction of the person of Christ, or Jesus, as we intimately refer to him.

The Holy Spirit or Holy Ghost is a similarly arrived at and now-posited person in the Godhead of blacks' belief. Traditional African religion assumed a vast array of deities. These beings possessed people on occasion, often in a very healing way.[11] The culture of Africa is still called upon by even the most sophisticated of psychiatrists to heal men's personhood by means of this ritualized response to spiritual

presences.[12] The healing character of the experience is
medically traceable, at least in part, to the fact that one does
not have to verbalize his problem to a single person. Rather,
he can dramatize it in the context of a supportive community
of faith, utilizing his total being in the process. That is, he
expresses his fears as well as his joys with body, mind, and
spirit. It is a de facto affirmation of the whole man by the
expression of all of his emotions in the presence of what
he considers to be the being he was born to serve.[13]

In the African tradition, one never lived in the presence
of another culture, whether as conquered or conqueror,
without coming to terms with the god of the other people.
Slaves were wide open to Christianity because they would
have been to any religion in any area under any circumstances. In America they came to know, sometimes by just
eavesdropping, that there was a Holy Spirit. They also knew
that they were most healed and fulfilled in the ecstatic experience of the spirit they had known in Africa, whose cult
they still precticed. It was almost inevitable that they should
make the connection and decide that there was not a host
of possessors but a single one of higher and in fact ultimate
divinity, and that this Spirit was the One possessing them.
As a black believer, I hold the connection to have been
providential, God having employed African religiocultural
expectations for healing access to Himself as Holy Spirit.

Today the masses of black American believers do not
feel that they have truly worshiped until they have sensed
the presence of and been possessed by the once inaccessible
but now approachable High God, in His manifestation as
Holy Spirit.

The strength to survive and to strive for liberation can
come in one blinding flash of light—one brief period of being
overwhelmed by a warming presence that tells a person that
God is indeed with him, even though a cruel world may
deny his fitness as abode for the divine presence. Whether
the brother or sister expresses that presence dramatically or
not, it is the climax and ultimate goal of all black worship.
Any qualifications to such an assertion would have to be

very limited. Religious ecstasy has every reason to be as important as it is in black religious life, but it is taken for granted and posited as the presence of God prior to the exercise of reason, in the nourishing world of the beliefs of blacks.

I could go on. There are hundreds of Western theological concepts for which there is some rough black equivalent. Even among the most basic ideas the surface has hardly been scratched here. For instance, I recently heard a black alumnus of Yale Divinity School expound an African-American black doctrine of man that included some brilliant posits. It was rewarding to see how well his work meshed with this. May this mere beginning be continued and refined, and may the black family and the world at large be the believing benefactors. It is not mere chauvinism when I say that what is so dear to me is, at this level of posits, capable of being shared across all lines of denomination and race.

NOTES TO CHAPTER 4

1. Paul Tillich, *The Courage to Be* (New Haven, Conn.: Yale University Press, 1952), pp. 42–54.

2. Tillich, *The Courage to Be*, p. 51.

3. George P. Rawick, ed., *The American Slave: A Composite Autobiography* (Westport, Conn.: Greenwood Publishing Co., 1972), 10:182.

4. See William R. Jones's essay, "The Case for Black Humanism," in this anthology.

5. Example: ". . . why . . . didst [thou, God] look on with the calm indifference of an unconcerned spectator, when . . . [one of] thine own creatures [was] reduced to a state of mere vassalage and misery?" Nathaniel Paul, *Negro Protest Pamphlets*, ed. Dorothy Porter (New York: Arno Press and the New York Times, 1969), p. 11.

6. J. B. Danquah, *The Akan Doctrine of God* (London: Frank Cass & Co., Ltd., 1968), pp. 55, 198–206; see also E. Bolaji Idowu, *Olodumare God in Yoruba Belief* (London: Longman Group Limited, 1962), pp. ix–xxv; and R. Sutherland Rattray, *Ashanti Proverbs* (Oxford: Oxford University Press, Clarendon Press, 1914), pp. 19–20.

7. Isaac O. Delano, *Owe L'Esin Oro: Yoruba Proverbs* (Ibadan, Nigeria: Oxford University Press, 1966), p. 22. "It is best to allow God to revenge, and stand aside."

8. Rawick, *The American Slave*, 5:240.

9. C. S. Kponkpogori, C. J. Natomaj, and O. Rytz, *Gonja Proverbs*, ed. O. Rytz, Local Studies Series No. 3 (Legon, Ghana: Institute of African Studies, 1966), p. 16.

10. Stephan N. Ezeanya, "God, Spirits and the Spirit World," in *Biblical Revelation and African Beliefs*, ed. Kwesi A. Dickson and Paul Ellingworth (Maryknoll, N.Y.: Orbis Books, 1969), p. 33.

11. Sheila S. Walker, *Ceremonial Spirit Possession in Africa and Afro-America* (Leiden, Netherlands: E. J. Brill, 1972), pp. 81–115.

12. Carol Tavris, "Magic & Medicine, A Sketch of Thomas Lambo," *Psychology Today* 5, no. 9 (February, 1972): 65.

13. Walker, *Ceremonial Spirit Possession*, p. 82.

5
Theological Methodology and the Black Experience

DAVID T. SHANNON

Liberation is thus a childbirth, and a painful one. The man who emerges is a new man, viable only as the oppressor-oppressed contradiction is superseded by the humanization of all men.

—Paulo Freire

The purpose of this discussion is to present a methodological approach to the theology of the black experience. My basic intention is to present the theological methodology of "horizon" as it relates to the black experience and then to analyze the two foci of this methodology. The basic components of black theology are: (1) the ambiguities of the black experience: (a) novelty-historical uprootedness, (b) complexity-ontological denial, and (c) insolubility-existential rejection; and (2) the Bible, the source book of the Christian faith. The praxis of the experience and the record of the faith constitute the core of this approach to doing theology.

There are many ways of "doing theology," of reflecting upon the relationship between God and man: (1) Creedal: this is one of the earliest methods (e.g., The Apostles' Creed). The basic Christian affirmations are presented in terms of statements of faith. John Calvin used this method in *Institutes of the Christian Religion*. (2) Apologetic: this is the presentation of the Christian faith as defense against heretics and antagonists. The Church Fathers Justin the martyr, Tertullian, Irenaeus, and Augustine followed this method. (3) Systematic: here the basic components of the creed are treated in a thematic and systematic way (e.g., Thomas Acquinas's *Summa Theologia*). (4) Dialectical: the arguments of the Christian faith are presented in dialogue with reason. The basic attempt is to establish the relationship between faith and reason (e.g., Friedrich Schleiermacher, Karl Barth, and Paul Tillich). (5) "Horizon": the emphasis is on man's *experience, understanding, judgment,* and *decision.* These four components constitute man's horizon, which determines his way of looking at the world and at God and becomes the foundation of his theology. Bernard Lonergan, the Jesuit scholar, has developed a diagram (*Begrifflichkeit*) that illustrates this methodology (see Appendix A).

First, there are the traditional divisions in Lonergan's analysis of the intellect: (1) experience, (2) understanding, (3) judgment, and (4) decision. Second, there are those disciplines which relate to history as the representation of fact. They form the basis for hermeneutics: (1) research is parallel to experience and involves the critical examination of the text; (2) next, one moves into hermeneutics, which is correct interpretation of the text, and which is parallel to understanding and provides the basis of critical history; (3) critical history is parallel to judgment and seeks to arrive at whether judgment "is" or "is not." It leads into dialectic; (4) dialectic, which involves conversion and personal decision, is parallel to decision and seeks to answer the question, "What do I think about these facts in terms of my rational self-consciousness?"

The dialectic brings one to the disciplines that relate to history as the interpretation of human existence: (1) the self-appropriation that takes place at the level of dialectic leads one into the foundation of one's theology; (2) one moves into thematization at this point, and this is also parallel to decision and dialectic; (3) foundation becomes the basis for doctrinal theology, is parallel to the judgment-critical history levels, and is a minimal judgment of the "it is-is not" syndrome; (4) elaboration takes place and develops into systematic theology—the attempt to understand the meaning of doctrinal decision. This corresponds to the levels of hermeneutics and understanding: (5) this brings one back to the level of experience—communication, the attempt to mediate reality and integrate understanding on the level of experience.

On this basis the individual is prepared to relate his experience to the problems he faces. Thus on the one hand, he has an awareness of the problem, and, on the other hand, he has a theological methodology that undergirds his work (see Appendix B). This methodology is helpful as one seeks to understand the black experience. There are two points of focus: (1) the black experience: (a) historical uprootedness, (b) ontological denial, and (c) existential rejection; and (2) the Bible, the source book of Christian revelation.

This approach to theology bases its foundations on man's situation and is allied to the phenomenological methodology and to the philosophy of existence. It rejects the type of theology that is called *Konklusionstheologie* and seeks to relate theology to life. The questions that emerge for the black man are: What is the nature of the Christian faith? What does it say to my situation? Does this faith assist me or deter me as I seek to overcome white racism?

i The Black Experience

The theology of the black experience has been the focus of much discussion since it was popularized by James Cone in his book *Black Theology and Black Power*. However, the roots of the black man's reflection upon his experience go back to the singer among the Wolofs in the Sudan who sang about the experiences of the national history of the Sudanese people.[1] As the roots of Hebrew theology go back to the poets of Israel, so black theology's roots go back to Africa's singers. Their songs were reflections on their lives, and out of them emerged the Negro spirituals. Other scholars have preceded James Cone in an attempt to understand black religious experience. An early study in this area is Benjamin Mays's *The Negro Idea of God*. In this doctoral dissertation he argues that many of the black religious beliefs in America were an adaptation of the Christian beliefs of the slaveholders. This same evaluation is seen in other works such as Carter G. Woodson's *The Story of the Negro Church*, James Weldon Johnson's *God's Trombones*, and James Washington's *Black Folk Religion*.

These studies place emphasis upon black acceptance of the religious beliefs of American Christianity, and they use these beliefs to make sense of the historical situation of the black man in America. All of these studies were concerned about freedom, but the actual formulation of a theology of liberation was to come much later. Little attention was given to the question of liberation as an important aspect of the Christian message.

A significant departure from the adaptionist approach was made by Howard Thurman in his *Jesus in the Disinherited*. He argues that Jesus' mission was addressed particularly to the disinherited, the outcasts. He spoke of liberation here and now. Thurman took seriously the studies of Albert Schweitzer and C. H. Dodd and made their understanding of realized eschatology applicable to the oppressed peoples of today. Today is liberation! This book set the tone for a new approach to Christian thinking. It is the precursor of black theology. What Thurman does is call attention to a significant motif in the study of Jesus that had peculiar and significant relevance for the black man but that had escaped serious attention.

A more recent study is concerned with the role of religion in the black experience and argues for its salutary effect upon the sanity of black people. William H. Grier and P. M. Cobbs, authors of *Black Rage*, have written a second book, *The Jesus Bag*. The religion of the master was converted to a survival mechanism and later to liberation:

We submit that if America is to discover that new experience, it must look to those who have survived its cruelty and must learn from them. The black capacity for converting weakness into strength needed for survival is nowhere more evident than in religion. It was thrust upon us to make us docile and it focused on the life hereafter. It gave little spiritual sustenance for life on earth and it left an unyielding conscience which is yet a barrier containing our rage.[2]

The black experience in America is aptly described by the titles of two recent broadway shows: *To Be Young, Gifted and Black,* and *No Place to be Somebody.* The stirring story of a young, gifted, black woman who died at an early age is depicted under the title *To Be Young, Gifted and Black.* This play, based on the life of Lorraine Hansberry, the author of the famous play *Raisin in the Sun,* drives one to tears as he shares the agony, trauma, and ambitions of a brilliant young woman who happens to be black. These cries express the plaintive groans and hopes of many black men and women; her struggle is that of many people who suffer oppression.

No Place to be Somebody is another illustration of this struggle for human dignity and respect. This play demonstrates the difficulty that many black persons encounter in seeking to be somebody. Both of these plays accurately portray the predicament of black men and women in America. Both speak to the struggle of black men and women to overcome the attempt of America to make black people invisible.

These plays are indicative of a new mood among black Americans. They are rejecting the role of the "invisible man." [3] The phrases "Black is Beautiful!" and "Black Power!" reflect this new awareness.[4] These are not empty phrases: they reflect a protest against years of conditioning in which the black man accepted white America's value system. Similarly, they exemplify a rejection of the powerlessness of black people, a powerlessness systematically imposed by the dominant culture.

Just as the black community has begun to reject the value systems and the power structure of white America, it has begun to reject the simple category of Jesus as the white "superstar"—a brainwashing mechanism used by whites to justify their oppression of blacks. Blacks, striving for some form of harmony, now accept Christianity as an integrating factor in their lives.

Gayraud S. Wilmore, in his recent book *Black Religion and Black Radicalism*, makes his readers aware of the fact that the Christianity that was taught to the slaves was radicalized, especially through Gabriel Prosser, Denmark Vesey, and Nat Turner. It was transformed to meet the needs of the black people in their plight here in America. Wilmore states:

> White commentators who write so glibly about the "other-worldliness" of the Black church fail to understand what is really going on. The Black preacher was most relevant to this world when he was telling his people what to expect in the next one, because he was whetting appetites for what everyone knew white people were undeservedly enjoying in the here and now, and because he was talking about a just God from whom everyone gets his due—including Black folks. White preachers have never made as rich and elaborate a use of religion as Black preachers. The disestablishment of white Christianity soon after Independence removed the church from the center of public life, even though it continued to exercise a certain authority in manners and morals well into the twentieth century. But for the slaves and their descendants, a religion that could unveil the reality of another world beyond "this vale of tears," and at the same time interpret what God was doing in history to redress the wrongs perpetrated against Black people, was an absolute necessity for survival. It has never really been disestablished in the Black community. It was precisely its mystique and "other-worldliness" which gave it license to speak authoritatively to Black people about daily life, about white oppression and Black liberation. For Blacks, "going to church" was never as much a matter of social custom and convention as it has been for white people. It was a necessity. The church has been the one impregnable corner of the world where consolation, solidarity and mutual aid could be found and from which the master and the boss-man—at least in the North—could be effectively barred." [5]

The radical thrust of Martin Luther King and others developed out of this heritage. He and others have led the black communities to new sensitivities.

Today the black community's sensibility comprises powerful negatives. Its questioning and skeptical attitude indicate destruction of the old form of synthesis in the lives of black people and, consequently, a destruction of the origin of the myth of black inferiority. That is, the black community has begun to redefine the role of theology and its meaning for the black community.

Questioning involves the individual's response to his or her situation. It is through the process of internalization and objectification that the black person says yes to blackness and no to white racism. Therefore, black people are forced to question a theology that grew out of white racism. The theology that is called *classical* was developed in a horizon different from the ambiguous situation of the black community. The historical situation was quite different for the so-called Fathers of theology. Thus, "classical theology" has suffered from a "Teutonic pervasiveness" that is foreign to the experience of black Americans.

Frederick Herzog speaks of the need to overcome this "Teutonic pervasiveness." He states:

> Theology today must begin with an identification with the wretched of the earth, the marginals, the marginal figures of life who are still struggling for personhood and dignity. Whether "God" immediately plays a role here is not the primary question. The first decision a man must make is how he wants to regard himself as a human being. Is he ready to discount his status, privilege and success, and to identify with the wretched ,the lost, the damned?

> I am trying to say two things: (1) We have to learn to think black theologically. To "think white" is to turn in upon the Cartesian self, to engage in "navel-gazing." The black self over against the white self is the compassionate self ("compatior, ergo sum"). It is the corporate self in which the "I" shares.

> I believe this is a more adequate corrective (from the Christian perspective) of the cogito ergo sum, than the "I rebel there-

fore I exist" (Camus). To "think black" means to be able to think from the perspective of the underdog. We could also suggest "thinking Indian"—the underdog has many colors in this country and the world over; (2) To think from the perspective of the oppressed, however, is not as yet to think theologically. "Thinking black" (thinking Indian) has to be radically tied to the originating event of the Christian faith in order to be theological. In fact, ultimately we can "think black" only if we are bound to the originating event. This does not mean leaving reason out of the picture. While the theoligian cannot be the man "who is led by reason alone" (qui sola ratione ducitur), he is a man who is also led by reason, a "black reason" that has been tied to the Incarnation. But reason as an agent here is not primary. It does not control the theological endeavor. To speak of this theology as liberation theology is to imply that the identification of Jesus Christ with the wretched of the earth not merely brought freedom of the individual, but also gave him public space for freedom to become operative.[6]

There is a great need to examine the history of black people in this country and to understand the ambiguity of their situation.

An ambiguous situation may be characterized in the following ways : (a) novelty—historical uprootedness, (b) complexity—ontological denial, and (c) insolubility—existential rejection.

Carole Taylor, in a Ph.D. dissertation at the University of Pittsburgh, has treated the subject of tolerance/intolerance of ambiguity in relation to educational supervisors.[7] She raises to visibility the role that ambiguity plays in many other areas of human relations, and I find her study suggestive for my examination of the black situation in America. She bases her study on the works of Else Frenkel-Brunswik and Stanley Budner. Although the basic thrust of Frenkel-Brunswik's work was the concept of intolerance of ambiguity, Budner refined the concept to focus upon cues available. This led him to define an ambiguous situation as "one in which usuable cues are not present." He goes further to identify three types of situation in which this occurs : a completely new situation in which there are no available cues; a complex situation to which there are a great number of cues to be taken into account; and a contradictory situation in which different elements or cues suggest different meanings. These are further characterized as *novelty, complexity,* and *insolubility.*

These types of ambiguous situation aptly apply to the American experience of black people. I suggest that the characterization *novelty* describes their historical uprootedness. They were brought to America, a country with a different kind of land, a different culture, and a different language. The cues for adjustment were not available.

Complexity characterized their existence in that, although they possessed all the earmarks of being human, their personhood, their being, was denied. They were referred to as "chattel property." They were also victimized by contradictory cues: although the Founding Fathers" cried freedom, blacks were in bondage; although the country extended the words of the Statue of Liberty to those from across the sea, they were denied elementary courtesies in eating, housing, schooling, and so on. Their existence was rejected. Let us look more closely at these ambiguities.

Novelty-Historical Uprootedness

As we look at the persons who came to America, the one group that did not ask to come was the Negro. He was forced to come. He was uprooted from his homeland and ruthlessly transported to a foreign land. Lerone Bennett, Jr., describes this uprooting in his book *Before the Mayflower:*

> The slave trade was not a statistic, however astronomical. The slave trade was people living, lying, stealing, murdering and dying. The slave trade was a black man who stepped out of his hut for a breath of fresh air and ended up ten months later in Georgia with bruises on his back and a brand on his chest.

> The slave trade was a black mother suffocating her newborn baby because she didn't want him to grow up a slave.

The slave trade was a kind captain forcing his suicide-minded passengers to eat by breaking their teeth, though, as he said, he was "naturally compassionate."

The slave trade was a bishop sitting on an ivory chair on a wharf in the Congo and extending his fat hand in wholesale baptism of slaves who were rowed beneath him, going in chains to the slave ships.

The slave trade was a greedy king raiding his own villages to get slaves to buy brandy.

The slave trade was a pious captain holding prayer services twice a day on his slave ship and writing the famous hymn, "How Sweet the Name of Jesus Sounds."

The slave trade was deserted villages, bleached bones on slave trails and people with no last names.[8]

This is historical uprootedness. The black man was taken out of his native land and thrust into a foreign country. This was an ambiguous situation.

Complexity-Ontological Denial

After the black man arrived here he was further victimized by ontological denial: he was denied personhood. As E. Franklin Frazier puts it, the black man was treated as an "animate tool."[9] He was thought to be not truly human. Very early in our history the black man was reckoned as 3/5 of a man for political reasons. Many years later, in 1859, Justice Taney said that the Negro was chattel property, a nonperson. He argued in the famous Dred Scott decision that the black man had no right to sue in the federal courts, and he stated furthermore: "The Negro has no right that the white man is bound to respect." This legally defined the black man as a nonperson, thereby denying him an ontology, a being.

This ontological rejection is attacked by W. E. B. DuBois in his book *The Souls of Black Folk,* wherein he sought to validate the black man's claim to personhood. The black man does have soul. Much of the debate about making slaves Christians emerged from this question of whether the black was a person.[10]

Howard Thurman related an experience that illustrates ontological denial even in the twentieth century. He was sweeping the yard of a white family in Daytona Beach, Florida, when the little girl of the family, about three or four years old, decided to scatter the leaves back after he had piled them up for burning. After she scattered his neat pile several times, he warned her, saying: "If you do this again I will tell your mother to spank you." She responded by kicking his leg. He cried out: "ouch!" He said that she really seemed surprised that he hollered. She looked at him in utter amazement and said: "I didn't know you hurt." Such has been the adult's, as well as the child's, response to the black man; his existence has been denied.[11] This is complex in that the cues that define personhood are not applicable to blacks.

Insolubility-Existential Rejection

The third factor involves existential rejection. Although the personhood of the black was affirmed, he has been put in second-class status. Existence follows being. One has to be able to actualize his being in terms of his everyday experiences. The whole career of "Jim Crow" and segregation point out this fact. To be black is never knowing when a clerk will refuse to wait on one or at least finish leisurely her conversation about the weather; or never knowing when a cabdriver will refuse to pick one up. It is to experience 1,000 daily insults because one is black. One's existence is constantly rejected. The extent of this denial is expressed in the report of the U.S. Advisory Committee on Civil Disorders.[12] The response to these ambiguities has been varied, and Budner helps to clarify these responses.

II THE BIBLE

Budner feels that response to ambiguity is contingent upon the perception of the threat involved in the situation. He suggests that there are at least four generic responses to ambiguous situations : (a) operative denial—actions aimed at eliminating threat; (b) operative submission—actions aimed at adjusting to a given environment; (c) phenomenological denial—perceptual restructuring (i.e., repression and denial); and (d) phenomenological submission—reaction in terms of inner stress.

Black response to the ambiguities of the American situation has reflected all four categories. Men and women like Sojourner Truth, Nat Turner, and Denmark Vesey sought to eliminate the threat (operative denial); others like Booker T. Washington sought to adjust to the situation (operative submission); many sought perceptual restructuring (phenomenological denial), for example, W. E. B. DuBois; and others yielded and succumbed to inner stress (phenomenological submission).

The purpose of this discussion has been to treat one point of focus of the horizon of the black experience, that is, the ambiguity of the American situation.

Another critical factor in the horizon of the black man is the Bible. Many black people have appropriated the Bible as a way to deal with ambiguity. In a way this response is closer to phenomenological denial than to any of the other three responses suggested by Budner. Both the experience of ambiguity and the Bible constitute the basis of the black man's horizon. An examination of the Bible as a component of the black man's horizon is in order.

As one reviews the way in which the Bible contributes to the black experience, it becomes evident that it speaks clearly to the ambiguity of the black situation in America. This situation seems to parallel in many ways the experience of the Hebrew people, and many of the spirituals reflect this kinship. The Hebrew people's experience has become a paradigmatic—that is, a pattern of living in ambiguity. It is at this decisive point that the Bible functions as a critical part of the black man's horizon.

There are three biblical motifs that speak to the three characterizations of ambiguous situations. In the experience of novelty-historical uprootedness, the biblical story of divine visitation has a powerful thrust. Likewise, the biblical account of creation speaks to complex-ontological denial, and the biblical emphasis on liberation addresses the question of insolubility-existential rejection. Let us examine these motifs.

Divine Visitation

One of the significant motifs in the Bible is divine visitation. However, in order to understand the full import of this concept, one has to see it in relation to the Hebrew meaning of the word *revelation*. The Hebrew word גלה (*gala*), which is usually translated "revelation," is often misunderstood. It does not mean intellectual enlightenment. *Gala* is a process in which something is given to a person so that he or she may know it, that is, experience its full reality. Whenever the Bible uses this word, it refers to God's self-giving and God's self-disclosure. Revelation, גלה is God's giving Himself and thereby making Himself known. The clear import of this concept is seen in the Incarnation. God revealed Himself in Jesus Christ; He gave Himself and thereby made Himself known: ". . . and the Word became flesh" (John 1 : 14). Another aspect of this concept of revelation is the recipient of the revelatory act. God gave Himself to the Hebrew people—He made Himself known to them in their culturally historical and social condition. The record of their understanding of this revelation is the Bible.

It is in this context of God's self-disclosure in a cultural, historical, and social context that the concept of visitation is made evident. In His visitation to the Hebrew people in a strange land, in an ambiguous situation, He makes Himself known. The concept of visitation is presented in Genesis 50 : 24 :

And Joseph said: "I am about to die; but God will visit you and bring you up out of this land to the land which he swore to Abraham, to Isaac and to Jacob."

The key word here is *visit*, פקד (*pagarh*). The basic meaning of this word is "to take care of." The original meaning was "to miss, to worry about." Here God is promising, through Joseph, that He will care for them. There is a mood of anticipation, of expectancy, as this book closes, and one finds himself anticipating the fulfillment of this promise. God is one who visits His people. This idea of visitation is also found in Psalm 8:4:

What is man that thou art mindful of him, and the son of man that thou dost care for him?

Here God's visitation is pictured as a part of God's way of authenticating man. Man's importance is seen in the fact that God visits, פקד him. Thus, His visitation (His caring) is a part of His relationship with man. The fulfillment of His original promise is found in Exodus 2:24–25:

And God heard their groaning and God remembered his covenant with Abraham, with Isaac and with Jacob. And God saw the people of Israel and God knew their condition.

And in Exodus 3:7, 8 as well:

Then the Lord said, "I have seen the affliction of my people who are in Egypt and have heard their cry because of their taskmasters; I know their sufferings and I have come down to deliver them out of the hand of the Egyptians, and to bring them up out of that land to a good and broad land, a land flowing with milk and honey."

These passages are pivotal for one's understanding the meaning of visitation. They make it clear that this is how God relates to His people. First God assures them that He has not been unaware of their struggles. Four words indicate God's awareness: (a) God *heard,* (b) God *remembered,* (c) God *saw,* and (d) God *knew.* God was aware.

Thus God assures: I have seen, I have heard, I know. In Exodus 3:8 God shares with Moses His response to the predicament of the Hebrew people. In a real way the burning-bush experience can be called a confirmation of awareness. Moses knew the condition of his people, and the people knew their own condition, but the question was: Is God aware, or is He secluded in the confines of Mt. Horeb? If He is aware, what is He going to do about it? God's call to Moses through the burning bush answered those questions. Here God identifies Himself as the deliverer. He said: "I have come down to deliver them" (Exodus 3:8). I (God) am already engaged in the process of liberation, of deliverance.

Before I discuss more fully the concept of liberation, let us look at the second biblical motif that speaks to the ambiguity of the black situation.

Creation

The Bible begins by enunciating the relationship between God and his creation. God is the "creator," mankind is the creature. And mankind does not come into being by some cosmic accident—mankind comes from the design of God himself.

The significant point of the Genesis story is the unity of mankind. In chapter 1 of Genesis this unity is clearly depicted and is a part of man's unique relationship with God. Three passages illustrate this relationship:

Genesis 1:26—Let us make man in our image.
Genesis 1:27—God created man in his own image.
Genesis 1:31—God saw everything that he had made, and behold, it was very good. (Cf. Psalm 8)

These verses suggest that God took the question of mankind seriously.

Verse 26 suggests forethought; it suggests meditation. However, I deal with the question of the sons of God alluded to here in the "let us" reference; the significant point is that God made man as a result of a deliberate thought, a deliberate choice, a deliberate plan.

The second verse argues for the unique relationship between God and mankind. Mankind was not made in opposition to God, or as coequal with Him, but in direct relationship with God. Although the original emphasis may have been on physical relationship, the latter understanding emphasizes a filial relationship. The Imago Dei in Christian theology emphasized this interpretation; another way of stating it is to say that God made man like Himself in love, intelligence, and truth. He made mankind capable of a relationship in an I-Thou continuum.

The third verse is a part of the continuous refrain that we read over and over again in this chapter: "and God saw that it was good" (Gen. 1 : 10, 12, 18, 25). This writer affirms the goodness of God's creation. The creation of mankind is seen as good. Mankind is a unity in unique relationship to God.

In chapter 2 of Genesis the unity of mankind is illustrated in the idea of the name *Adam*. Adam is not a proper name, that is, like Willie, Joe, Shug, Claude, or David. A proper name in Hebrew is never preceded by an article, for example, the David. The Hebrew *adam* is, in fact, preceded by an article; thus, it is not a proper name. Hence, exegesis reveals that *adam* is a symbol, standing for the whole of mankind. Further, all human characteristics referred to in chapter 2 of Genesis are representative of mankind and not of a particular couple named Adam and Eve. A fundamentalistic approach of viewing Adam and Eve as individual people is linguistically and exegetically wrong. This understanding of creation overcomes any attempt to deny the innate humanity, the being of any individual. This belief undergirds the biblical motifs of divine visitation and liberation.

Liberation

A study of the key words in the motif of liberation is very revealing. They are listed as follows :

1. *deror.*   The root meaning is "to release"; see Leviticus 25:10; Jeremiah 34:8, 15, 17; Ezekiel 46:17; Isaiah 61:1.
2. *anoyim.* Means "poor"—"oppressed" or "afflicted."
3. *mishgab.* Means "protecting wall"; see Psalm 9:9; this is the concept of God who protects the oppressed.
4. *dak.*   Comes from the root *dakah,* and it also means "oppressed"; see Psalms 103:6 and 146:7.
5. *ashaq.*   Means "poor" or "oppressed"; see Ecclesiastes 4:1; Jeremiah 50:33.
6. *dal.*   Means "poor"; see Genesis 41:19; Exodus 30:15; Leviticus 14:21 and 19:15; 1 Samuel 12:8; Jeremiah 10:2, 11:4, 14:30, 25:4, 26:6, 12:27, 5:11 and 8:6; Amos 2:7, 4:1, 5:11, and 8:6. Cf. Psalm 72:1, 3.

GOD, in response to the condition of the oppressed/poor/afflicted, is referred to as the *goel.* This sense of *goel* is used restrictively in the Old Testament to mean the claim for one's own, namely, God's claim of Israel as His own:

a) in delivering her out of Egypt; see Exodus 6:6 and 15:13.

b) in delivering her out of the exile; see Isaiah 41:14; 43:1, 14; 44:6, 22–24; 47:4; 48:17, 20; 49:7; 54:5, 8; 60:16; Psalms 74:2; 77:16; 78:35; 106:1; and 107:2; Jeremiah 31:11 and 50:34; Micah 4:10.

It is significant that the root of the word *deliver,* גאל (*goel*), means to snatch away. God is saying to Moses, "I have come down to snatch you away from Egypt and to place you in the Promised Land." Note here that the leadership and initiative come from God.

In these passages God is seen as deliverer. The psalmist expresses this same motif in Psalm 103:6:

The Lord executeth righteousness and judgment for all who are oppressed.

The New Testament continues the emphasis on visitation by referring to liberation. The key passage that relates to the theology of the black experience comes from Luke 4:18–19:

> The spirit of the Lord is upon me because he has anointed me; He has sent me to announce good news to the poor, to proclaim release for prisoners and recovery of sight for the blind; to let the broken victims go free, to proclaim the year of the Lord's favour.

The basic message of this theology is liberation. It is significant that Jesus spoke these words in his hometown of Nazareth. He volunteered to read the Scripture for that day, and, in traditional fashion, he proceeded to interpret the meaning of this passage. The new interpretation was the unexpected, the radically new thing that happened.

Jesus chose this passage from Isaiah deliberately. It suggested hope and liberation. He spoke of the coming of the new day, a new state of affairs. In Isaiah 61 : 1–2, the words are little different:

> The spirit of the Lord God is upon me because the Lord has anointed me; he has sent me to bring good news to the humble, to bind up the broken-hearted, to proclaim liberty to captives and release to those in prison; to proclaim a year of the Lord's favour and a day of the vengeance of our God; to comfort all who mourn, to give them garlands instead of ashes.

They describe the mission of the prophet. In both passages the emphasis is upon God's action, and the prophetic vocation is in obedience to God's choice. He has been anointed, he has been sent, and the authority comes from God. The key words in both verses are *anointed* and *sent*.

Next, the passage points out that this is good news (*euangelion*). What is unique is the recipients of the news. They are not the mighty, the proud, but the people who feel that they are left out. The author uses the poetic structure of synonmous parallelism, that is, two lines that are structurally parallel are ones that mean the same thing. The "poor" and the "broken-hearted" are identical in meaning. Then he adds:

> To proclaim liberty to captives and release to those in prison.

It is significant that the Greek word here is *kerux,* which comes from the word that signifies a herald from the King, the one who brings royal tidings. Here the prophet brings tidings (*euangelion*) from the King (God). In the sense of the parallel, news of liberation is the news of freedom!

The final section deals with the context of this message and announces the arrival of a new order, a new era. This indicates God's mercy, His care, His love, and His immanent participation in history. As one compares this passage in Isaiah with what Jesus reads in Nazareth, we find that he omitted the parallelism: he reads directly. He has good news for the poor and liberty for the captives, and he adds to these two groups the blind and the downtrodden.

This is similar to giving a catalogue of the low, or bottom, echelon of society, that is, the nobodies. Jesus begins with the top of the bottom and proceeds downward: (1) the poor, (2) the captives, (3) the blind, and (4) the downtrodden. Listen to the direct words of Jesus to these groups:

Poor	Good News
Captives	Liberty
Blind	New Sight
Downtrodden	Freedom

These are the words that speak to oppressed people. These are the words that characterize the theology of the black experience—good news! liberty! new sight! freedom!

Now look ot how Jesus summarizes this passage. He adds:

This day is this passage fulfilled in your hearing.

Jesus makes liberation synonymous with his speaking. The Sermon on the Plain in Luke 6:20–22 stresses this same motif:

And he lifted up his eyes on his disciples and said: Blessed are you poor, for yours is the kingdom of God. Blessed are you that hunger now, for you shall be satisfied. Blessed are you that weep now, for you shall laugh.

The emphasis here is on realized eschatology, or what C. H. Dodd refers to as "eschatology in the state of being realized." This is in contrast to the spiritualizing interpretation in Matthew 5. Jesus is saying to the poor, the hungry, the mourner—today your liberation has come, today you have become an heir to the kingly rule of God. This motif of liberation it at the foundation of the understanding of the Bible. This motif combines the black man's experience in an indissoluble union with the Bible. Out of this union emerges black theology. Black theology or the theology of the black experience is his way of seeking to understand the Christian faith in the context of historical uprootedness, ontological denial, and existential denial.

This emphasis upon theology-as-liberation enables the black to deal with the ambiguities of the American situation.

Gustavo Gutierrez accentuates this emphasis on the meaning of liberation as a key aspect of the Christian faith. He argues that the focus of the Christian message is liberation. First he distinguishes between development and liberation. He rejects development because of its pejorative sense:

> Developmentalism thus came to be synonymous with reformism and modernization, that is to say, synonymous with timid measures, really ineffective in the long run and counterproductive to achieving a real transformation. The poor countries are becoming ever more clearly aware that their underdevelopment is only the by-product of the development of other countries, because of the kind of relationship which exists between the rich and the poor countries.[13]

On the other hand, he defines liberation as follows:

> Liberation in fact expresses the inescapable moment of radical change which is foreign to the ordinary use of the term development. Only in the context of such a process can a policy of development be effectively implemented, have any real meaning, and avoid misleading formulations.[14]

One of the key chapters is his treatment of liberation and salvation. He concludes:

salvation embraces all men and the whole man; the liberating action of Christ—made man in this history and not in a history marginal to the real life of man—is at the heart of the historical current of humanity; the struggle for a just society is in its own right very much a part of salvation history.[15]

He maintains that the biblical focus upon liberation is on three levels: (a) political liberation, (b) the liberation of man throughout history, and (c) liberation from sin and admission to communion with God. He avers:

These three levels mutually affect each other, but they are not the same. One is not present without the others, but they are distinct: they are all part of a single, all-encompassing salvific process, but they are to be found at different levels. Not only is the growth of the Kingdom not reduced to temporal progress; because of the Word accepted in faith, we see that the fundamental obstacle to the Kingdom, which is sin, is also the root of all misery and injustice; we see that the very meaning of the growth of the Kingdom is also the ultimate precondition for a just society and a new man. One reaches this root and this ultimate precondition only through the acceptance of the liberating gift of Christ, which surpasses all expectations. But, inversely, all struggle against exploitation and alienation, in a history which is fundamentally one, is an attempt to vanquish selfishness, the negation of love. This is the reason why any effort to build a just society is liberating, And it has an indirect but effective impact on the fundamental alienation. It is a salvific work, although it is not all of salvation. As a human work it is not exempt from ambiguities, any more than what is considered to be strictly "religious" work.[16]

Gutierrez and Cone concur on the need for a reexamination of the content of theology. Both insist that theology must focus on the meaning of liberation and the implications of this thought for all men.

Thus far I have presented the component parts of the black man's horizon. Now the final task is to see how this relates to the Lonergerian methodology suggested above (see Appendix A).

The methodology of horizon provides a descriptive and analytical tool for the theology of the black man's experience. It focuses upon the uniqueness of the black situation and relevancy of the biblical message.

Experience.   I began with the ambiguity of the black situation in America: novelty—historical uprootedness; complexity—ontological denial; and insolubility—existential rejection.

Understanding. The participants in this experience become aware of the ambiguity. They apply the critical and analytical levels to seek the meaning that this experience has for them.

Judgment.   The next step involves evaluation of the normative judgments of black experience. Are they good or bad?

Decision.   This involves actions that one performs on the basis of his or her reflection. This involves operative denial, operative submission, phenomenological denial, and phenomenological submission.

In the application of these components to the two divisions, history as representative of facts (Lection) and history as interpretation (quaestio), one discovers the implications of this methodology for the black experience.

Lectio

(Experience) *Research.* This is critical for the black approach to theology. What are the actual data? Critical texts of the Bible must be examined.

(Understanding) *Hermeneutics.* This involves the correct interpretation of the texts. Two basic questions are asked: (1) what did the text mean to the author? (2) what does the text say to the black individual?

(Judgment) *Critical history.* This involves judgment of whether one accepts or rejects the interpretation of the texts. Does the text enable one to deal with ambiguity or does it suggest passive acceptance? "Is it" or "is it not" relevant to the black situation?

(Decision) *Conversion.* This is the level of dialectic. How do
I personally appropriate this text in my individual situation? How do I as a black
person respond?

Quaestio

(Decision) *Speculative theology.* Conversion—my stand regarding my judgment—leads to the founda-
tion of one's theology. It is the basis for
speculative theology and the enunciation of
specific issues, i.e., visitation, creation, and
liberation, etc. Research, hermeneutics, and
critical history also play significant roles in
forming foundational themations.

(Judgment) *Doctrinal theology.* Out of these themations
minimal judgment arises. Visitation, creation, and liberation are accepted as key
elements in the biblical message.

(Understanding) *Systematic theology.* At this level elaboration and explication of doctrinal decisions
are made. Basic concepts are created in
terms of systems rather than mere concepts.
Creation becomes the system of divine affirmation. Visitation becomes the system of
divine transformation.

(Experience) *Communication.* From this horizon one is ready
to mediate reality and integrate understand-
ing on the level of experience. Thus, the
theology of the black experience makes
a significant contribution to American
thought.

Black theology serves as a corrective of the basic thrust
of white, Protestant America. It accentuates the fact of the
black presence. It points to the fact that we are no longer
invisible brothers, the sleeping giants; it points to the awareness of black men that the day of our castration is over; that
our dungeons have shaken and chains have fallen off.

Black theology is symbolic in that it participates in what
it points to. In this sense the medium becomes the message.

Black theology is a way by which the Christianization of America takes place. As man hears of the work of black theology, the process of liberation takes place for the oppressed and the oppressor. Jesus said, "This day is this Scripture fulfilled in your hearing." Black theology opens us to the realities that are often closed to us. The very existence of black theology forces America to address black Americans in terms that are cognitive rather than instinctive. Black theology, because it is a rational enterprise, moves to the reality beyond the sense, to the "God beyond Gods." It asserts that man participates in the Ultimate Being and that faith is man's concern with the Ultimate. Black theology releases the barriers between men and opens them to the understanding that reality is not color, but God (See appendix C).

APPLICATION OF THE SELF-STRUCTURING OF THE INTELLECT TO THEOLOGY

Two Traditional Divisions:	Lectio—History as representation of facts.	Quaestio—History as Interpretation.
Analysis Experience— (a) Historical uprootedness, (b) Ontological rejection, (c) Existential denial.	Research—Black history, O.T.N.T., church history, contemporary History.	Communication—Proclamation in terms of ACT and BEING, that the work of God in history is liberation—celebration of awareness.
of Understanding—Black ordained to be inferior? Truly human? Result of exploitation?	Hermeneutics—Correct interpretation. Do the facts argue for liberation as a major theme?	Systematic Theology—An explication of doctrine through elaboration and analysis; reinterpretation of doctrines from vantage point of liberation.
Intellect Judgment—To be black is to be beautiful.	Critical History—Is this or is this not true? Is the Bible a book of liberation?	Doctrinal Theology—God, man, Jesus, are all understood from the question of liberation (Heilsgeschichte).°
Decision—Act as liberated man.	Dialectic-Conversion—Why is this important? What are the implications of this new self-awareness of the meaning of blackness?	Foundation of Theology—Speculative theology; black theology is a theology of liberation.

° Black becomes symbolic of oppression.

SOURCE: same as Appendix 1.

A SCHEMA ON HUMAN GOOD: This schema deals with the concrete meaning man finds in his life, what this good is on certain levels, and how he relates to it—the basic pattern of the meanings open to any man.

| | PROCESS OF MEDIATION | | | |
POTENCY	ACT	ITS SOCIAL MEDIATION	OBJECT MEDIATED	LEVEL OF GROWTH
Basic potentiality (basic needs)	Differentiated operation (e.g., Robinson Crusoe)	Cooperation (Crusoe and Friday)	Particular good (food)	Level of Immediacy
Capacity for development of basic potentials (esp. thinking and willing.)	Habits—a group of differentiated operations. (Intellectual habits—science; Will habits—vices or virtues.)	Institutions—(This expresses more than basic needs. It recognizes the possibility of thinking things out.) All meaning for society becomes institutional.	Goods, esp. the good of order. This good collapses when the society collapses.	Level of Mediation of Meaning
Freedom—man's highest capacity. A dissatisfaction with living on the level of the good of Order leads to an exigence for personal freedom.	Orientation—as opposed to habit. Habit is developed and then used. Orientation flows basically but freely from oneself as one is. E.g., love as an orientation is a total giving, a personal response of oneself at one's highest level. To make love a habit is to destroy it.	Interpersonal Relations—one's personal freedom awakens one to the respect demanded by other persons, other free beings. It is also a critical recognition of this relationship.	Values, esp. honesty, truth, love. Order is still a value but no longer the only value, for now values have meaning, a personal	Level of Constitutive Meaning—one recognizes, one makes his own world as a free person, by personal decision.

LEVELS OF MAN'S DEVELOPMENT (OF MEANING)

APPLICATION OF THE SELF-STRUCTURING OF THE INTELLECT TO THEOLOGY

TWO TRADITIONAL DIVISIONS:		LECTIO—History as representation of facts.	QUAESTIO—History as interpretation of human existence.
	EXPERIENCE	Research—the data. Can we achieve the actual data? Examination of critical texts.	Communication—an attempt to mediate reality and integrate understanding on the level of experience (n. 3).
ANALYSIS OF	UNDERSTANDING	Hermeneutics—Correct interpretation based on the best texts. What is the meaning of the texts?	Systematic Theology—the level of elaboration, the effort to understand the meaning of doctrinal decisions. Effort to understand carried on in terms of systems—Eastern, Western, Scholastic, Existential, etc. Understanding in one system leads to communication.
INTELLECT	JUDGMENT	Once the meaning has been determined, one must make the judgment of "is" or "is not". This is the level of Critical History.	Doctrinal Theology (it is, it is not). Gives the theologian a real assertion, a minimal judgment. Doctrine provokes questions and developments (n. 2).
	DECISION	Thence follows the question: "What do I think about these facts (about this judgment in terms of my rational self-consciousness)? What is my stand in regard to this judgment?" Level of dialectic, Conversion, and personal decision (n. 1). Geschicte	The foundations of one's theology. The horizon of theology proper begins—Speculative Theology becomes possible. Beginning to deal with specific issues. Speculation presumes the basic preliminary work of positive (historical) theology, the Lectio. The thematizations of the basic conversions.

SOURCE: David Tracy, "God: One and Three" (lecture notes on the oneness and trinity of God, Catholic University of America School of Theology, Spring 1968).

NOTES TO CHAPTER 5

1. Cf. Miles Mark Fisher, *Negro Slave Songs* (Ithaca, N.Y.: Cornell University Press, 1953), p. 1.

2. William Grier and Price Cobbs, *The Jesus Bag* (New York: McGraw-Hill Book Company, 1971), p. 167.

3. Ralph Ellison, *Invisible Man* (New York: New American Library, 1952).

4. Stokely Carmichael and Charles Hamilton, *Black Power* (New York: Random House, 1967).

5. Gayraud S. Wilmore, *Black Religion and Black Radicalism* (Garden City, N.Y.: Doubleday, 1972), p. 106.

6. Frederick Herzog, *Liberation Theology* (New York: Seabury Press, 1972), pp. 2, 3, 15.

7. Carole Taylor, "Tolerance of Ambiguity Among Graduate Students in Supervision" (Ph.D. diss., University of Pittsburgh, 1973).

8. Lerone Bennett, *Before the Mayflower* (Baltimore, Md.: Penguin Books, 1966), pp. 30f.

9. E. Franklin Frazier, *The Negro Family in the United States* (Chicago: University of Chicago Press, 1966), p. 359.

10. W. E. B. DuBois, *The Soul of Black Folk* (New York: American Library, 1969), pp. 42–53.

11. Howard Thurman, unpublished lecture, Virginia Union University, Richmond, Va., 1967.

12. *Report of National Advisory Committee on Civil Disorders* (New York: E. P. Dutton, 1968).

13. Gustavo Gutierrez, *A Theology of Liberation* (Maryknoll, N.Y.: Orbis Books, 1972), p. 26.

14. Ibid., p. 27.

15. Ibid., p. 168.

16. Ibid., p. 176.

PART II

Black Theology in Outreach

6
Black Evangelical Christianity and Black Theology

CALVIN E. BRUCE

For several reasons it is both necessary and desirable for black religionists who are constructing liberation theologies to retrench the communication gap between those theologizing within academia and those on the far right of the black Protestant spectrum, who know less about the study of God than they do about the God that theologians study.

Specifically, if it is the constructive task of black theology to foster genuine dialogue among black persons of all religious persuasions, then it is needful for black theologians to broaden their "liberationist" appeals to attract the widest black audience possible, including blacks of strongly evangelical backgrounds. Moreover, it is highly desirable for black theologians to tap the evangelical roots of contemporary black religion. For black evangelical Christianity exhibits a notable vitality that can be a wholesome resource for black theology as it attempts to win the allegiance of "grass roots" congregations to a theopolitical agenda aimed at the liberation of all black peoples from all forms of racist and sexist oppression.

I propose that black evangelical Christianity favors black liberation, insofar as it is the morally autonomous person who is free to serve God, to minister to the needs of humanity, and, yet, to seize the existential freedom to become his or her true moral and religious self. Furthermore, I am persuaded that most black persons undergo a profound quest for "authentic religious personhood"—which the black theologian should not ignore.

These two points relate to the overall concern of how the black theologian can most suitably shape his message of liberation and personal wholeness. Several specific assignments need to be undertaken.

A chief task for black theologians is to delineate the theological contours for promoting genuine *religious community*. This occurs wherever free moral selves can freely respond to the Gospel appeals to share the good news that in Christ is liberty from all forms of psychic oppression and debilitative threats to authentic personhood. Such a worshiping community is predicated on the strength of black Christian love. This love covers a multitude of personal and interpersonal sins. And it fosters moral character development and religioethical responsibility that serve to inspire all black persons to join hearts and hands in the betterment of life for those who merely endure in such troublesome times as these.

Another goal for black theologians is to demonstrate convincingly that black religion can be personally meaningful to blacks who daily face the forces of culturological despair that tend to make life meaningless and uninspiring. Even though black theologians who formulate experimental and radical theologies are tempted to expound the *newness* of their thought, they should not overlook the old virtues and values that have made black religion endearing and a wholesome part of growing up black in an alien, antiblack society.

Certain themes and emphases within black evangelical Christianity support the notion that if religion means anything, it means everything; and before religion can elicit any ethical commitment from the community at large, it must exhibit personal worth to the individuals who constitute that community. Many black Christians resonate to these themes and accept the personalist functionality of black religion.

A good number of black believers look to religion both to provide inspiration for shaping the moral self and to offer the biblical guidelines by which the church can act as informed moral decision-maker.[1] Such persons generally find attractive and wholesome the evangelical principles that underscore the personal appropriation of biblical truths that speak of spiritual completion in Christ. Black theology minus these emphases is less than fully liberative for the black spiritual community. But the point can be made positively.

What this essay contributes to the forum of discussion on the constructive redirection of black theology is the thesis that black evangelical Christianity offers a model for religious community growth, nurturance, and dialogical fellowship that the black-liberation community should prize and emulate. Liberation thus includes the grace and love that only Christ freely gives us.

My concern is not to advance a model for doing black-liberation theology, but to sketch the theological contours for community-building in keeping with the theopolitical goals of the black movement, while respecting the demand of many black people for personally fulfilling religious individualism.

These stipulated contours are spelled out under four headings: the meaningfulness of "black dialogue," the warrant of religious personalism, the contemporaneous relevance of the Bible, and the centrality of black worship for the liberated religious community.

I THE STRENGTH OF BLACK DIALOGUE

One can best appreciate the responsibility of the black theologian to facilitate wholesome religious dialogue among black autonomous selves by considering (a) a phenomenological explication of interpersonal dialogue and (b) a functional, multifaceted definition of black theology in terms of what is incumbent upon the black theologian to promote as educator-facilitator of religious values and aspirations.

Dialogue connotes something other than mere questioning and answering, and something more than mere sequential ordering of verbal pronouncements. Dialogue between human beings ought to include a *sharing* of one another's innermost being, a communion of souls in such a manner that the personhood of one individual reaches out to embrace that of another. Dialogue is the interpersonal fellowship of kindred spirits. It is the *élan vital* of human souls, pointing to the worth of the other person as an inherently valuable human being and underscoring the creative potentialities of shared experiences.

The essentials of dialogue begin with *presence* and *availability.* Obviously, a person-to-person dialogue cannot occur if one's thoughts, feelings, ideas, and reflections are not accessible to others. Actual physical presence may not be so important ultimately as one's being present in the willingness to overcome the barriers of distance and detachment that separate persons who would otherwise benefit significantly from mutual concern. When the barriers are overcome, the other person is accepted for what he is, not for what he should be in the eyes of the beholder. As such, interpersonal dialogue is based on an "I-Ens" relationship, not just an "I-Thou" encounter, which depends on each person's perceiving an eternal Thou above and beyond their relationship.[2]

Dialogue cannot proceed unless participants evince a notable degree of *mutual respect,* which inevitably leads to a consignment of *expectancy* for what each brings into the sharing experience. If X feels that Y has nothing of value to say, why should X waste his time listening to Y? Such truth is transparent to the point of being truistic. Only when both X and Y agree that they both can profit from extended interchange, can they actually benefit from what each has to offer. A sense of respect for what one can learn from

ion into intrapsychic rapport, dialogue pro-
vides the occasion for each party to acquire an *acquaintance*
with the perspective from which the other views himself,
the world, and all reality. In such a circumstance, the person
ought to acquire a heightened understanding of his own
vantage. That is to say, each person is initiated into a learning experience that is not unilinear. Neither person is object;
both become subjects actively contributing to the edifying
exchange. In knowing more of oneself, what the other person
becomes acquainted with increases in substance and significance. That is why a genuine dialogical relationship is truly
one of mutual revelatory insight.

The end result of dialogue is the achievement and sustenance of a sense of *community*. Out of mutual respect
bolstering a sense of sharing-expectation, the parties involved become acquainted with the best that each has to
offer. The resultant respectful understanding that each gains
serves as the foundation for transcendental communal fellowship. As Martin Buber taught, "Community is where
community happens." [3] And community happens where
meaningful communication promotes real communion.
Those who are at polar extremes cannot communicate. But
those who forgo ideological fixations can come together in
the kind of communicative exchange that may result in
a new reality: a dialogical communion of soul with soul.

What is true concerning the phenomenon of dialogue
between two persons has ramifications on a larger scale,
particularly in the academic world.

Perhaps more so than with other academicians, black
scholars in general and black religionists in particular ought
to be able to enter into a dialogical relationship with those
whose spirits have been crushed by the psychosocial oppressiveness of an unjust society. However one may define the
concept of *soul,* there seems to be a soulful quality to black

existence by which a sensitive black person can empathize with the suffering of all oppressed people. Soul especially facilitates understanding of the conditions and needs of black humanity. Speaking to the conditions and addressing the needs of black folk are a prime duty of the black scholar. Having benefited from acquiring the scholarly tools of analysis and synthesis, the black academician ought to relate the intellectualization of the problems implicit in "the black experience" to the "real facts," which may never find their way between the covers of a textbook. The reality of spiritual ambition is one important component of that collective experience, and a prime fact of life that the black scholar cannot ignore.

In particular, the black relgious scholar is obliged to approach his task with the foregone conclusion that whatever insights he has acquired concerning black religion as an academic discipline can be shared with all black peoples. This assumes that the black religionist is acquainted with, and respectful of, the actual religious sensitivities and *needs* of blacks who may never attend a seminary or understand black theology with any degree of sophisticated expertise.

Many such persons have embarked upon a quest for authentic religious personhood and appreciate the inculcation of spiritual and ethical values, which make religion something more than a datum for scientific scrutiny and make the quest worth sustaining. The dialogue that the black scholar promotes with these persons must touch the heart as well as edify the mind.

Initiating and facilitating dialogue serves broader purposes than ministering to the spiritual needs of individual worshipers. The strength of black dialogue is multidimensional. Its influences touch many persons (black and white) within the academy and within the black church at large. The black theologian, most often scholar *and* minister, must recognize the possibilities for enlarging the potentials for dialogue among all persons seriously concerned about black liberation. To make those possibilities reality, the black theologian faces several assignments.

As academician, the black theologian is in a pivotal position of teaching both black and white communities of the possible valuable contributions that black-liberation theologies can make within the spectrum of the larger theological enterprise. This entails raising the consciousness of an academic community to accept the legitimacy of doing theology in ways that are different from traditional brands of Christian theologizing and in ways that are meaningful for students from ethnic and oppressed backgrounds. Thus, upholding the "black ways" of doing theology is a preliminary and indispensable duty of the informed black theologian.

Similarly, it is incumbent upon the black theologian, through his psychological presence, to act as a sounding board for the concerns of all segments of the theological community. Mutual respect as part of dialogical interchange implies that professors can learn something from students and that the "oppressor" can equally learn from the "oppressed." Above all, the black theologian's presence in the academy draws attention to an insight crucial for all members of the academic community: "Ordinary experiences are often the basis for theological beliefs or at least confirmations of such." [4]

Undoubtedly, racism and sexism will proliferate in our society as long as Christian theologies can be invoked in justification of the schizophrenic mind-sets that condone the ontological devaluation of an entire sex or of entire races. The black theologian, present and available as a source of liberative enlightenment, is challenged to demonstrate how the vitality of interracial and intersexual dialogue helps obviate those mind-sets by promoting mutual respect for the personhood of all. He must teach that lesson—learned from ordinary experience—to those who do not want to learn it, as well as to those who welcome its inclusion in the curriculum.

Something more is called for, however. Attending to these tasks within academia should not induce the black theologian to shortchange his educational ministry to the

entire black community, especially the black church at
large. As a black religionist, the theologian ought to facilitate
liberative education, which convinces black clergymen and
laity that the goals of liberation are not incongruent with
the ordinary concerns of the black church. What is desper-
ately needed is to make the liberation message appealing to
grass roots constituencies.

A far-ranging black revolution outside the church is in-
conceivable. Revolutionizing the black community from
within the most enduring structure it knows (the church) is
feasible, though. And the possibility for this accomplishment
lies with how imaginatively black theologians positively
influence the religious, political, and vocational aspirations
of the strong arm of the black church: its talented youth.

Others may disagree, but I contend that the best way
to win black youth to the theological liberation movement
is by evangelizing them to adopt a firm commitment to a
higher cause, rather than by merely parroting support for a
goal that seems rather abstract and remote: establishing an
autonomous black subnation in America. Elsewhere I have
suggested briefly three imperatives that are instructive for
the refocusing of black religious education, in accord with
certain positive features of the demands of black consciousness.[5]

Suffice it to say in this space that the black religious
community expects its theological spokesmen to recognize
that religious education is esteemed primarily because it
fosters values and qualities of leadership essential for
edifying young minds and for building up the community
at large. Acting on this recognition, they are urged to extend
the outreach of theological dialogue in additional ways.

The black theologian should engage black pastors and
lay leaders and educators in other fields in joint responsibility for training leaders to advance the cause of black humanity in the years to come. Living responsibly for God and
toward fellow human beings should be the goal of every
black Christian. This is the task to which black evangelical
Christianity has been devoted: engendering a sense of moral

responsibility among those who take religion seriously and value living for and serving God above all. Black theologians would do well to support this goal explicitly and wholeheartedly. For present and future black leaders need to look to God for the will and strength to guide blacks to a higher plane of spiritual and temporal excellence.

One final assignment for the professional black theologian deserves note. In that black theology is meaningful dialogue among black religious personalities of all persuasions, it must surmount barriers of class affiliation. As facilitator-educator par excellence, the black theologian must be sensitive to the concerns of students as well as fellow colleagues, laity as well as clergy, the "disinherited" poor as well as the dispirited rich, and the moderately educated as well as the highly educated. Most important, he must dispatch insightful modes of theological communication throughout all segments of the black community. This includes blacks who do not hold a degree and may never have set foot inside a college classroom.

Whatever the black religionist has to offer the black community as a result of extended research, teaching, and reflection ought to be as meaningful to the scrubwoman who cannot even spell t-h-e-o-l-o-g-y as to the colleague in the Society for the Study of Black Religion. The black theologian should be especially indebted to those who choose to remain part of the black church and thus challenge theological spokesmen to make theology as enriching a dimension of day-to-day living as black religion tends to be. To a large extent, this constituency of prochurch blacks includes persons of lower-class status. If they are to comprehend black-liberation theology, it must resonate to their daily concerns as pilgrims in a strange and alien land who are journeying homeward.

On this score one could criticize Black Theology I for an apparent shortcoming. Certain academic interests seem to have resulted in black religionists' doing theology more for the benefit (or admiration) of white scholars than for the enlightenment of the black lower classes, particularly the disinherited sectarians. My disenchantment with the general tenor of black theology as colored by white-seminary, higher-critical scholarship is that the essence of what black religion can mean for the individual is phased out of the picture.

Not as a categorical denunciation, but as a general hypothesis to be tested by the evidence at hand, I suggest an attitudinal shortcoming of much of contemporary black theology. In point: many writings in black religion/black theology tend to ignore the crucial existential needs of the many black masses who savor something more than the sociopolitical ideology expressive of some utopian dream for establishing the long-awaited Black Nation.

With due respect to those who would passionately argue to the contrary, I cannot see where a black messiah has appeared or that a *black* Kingdom of God is imminent, proleptically or otherwise. I *do* see the pressing need for black theology to attend to the spiritual needs of a religious community hungering and thirsting for more of God's righteousness, and for a closer relationship to the Lord of faith.

The demand for black theology to be "something-more-than" theopolitical ethics finds full expression in the quest for authentic personhood, which tends to include an important religious dimension. The following section elaborates, in suggesting why a liberation theology for the community should fully respect religious personlism.

II THE DEMANDS OF RELIGIOUS PERSONALISM

The ideal religious community that black theology ought to endorse should be predicated on individuals' acting upon the demands of existential freedom in order to be their true religious and moral selves. Before I discuss the implications of freedom for the moral self, the reader may profit from a brief explication of what constitutes the demands of religious personalism.

As Paulo Friere has noted in another context, liberation is impossible to achieve outside the parameters of a certain value-judgmental education.[6] The kind of liberative education that can be of crucial concern to the black religious community is that which teaches blacks to avail themselves of the enriching religious experiences that lead, hopefully, to a sense of individuality that is conducive to psychological and religious well-being. If black persons are not free to respect the integrity of their spiritual ambitions and to translate this integrity into achieved authentic personhood, blacks can just as easily become prisoners in a black nation as bondsmen in a white one.

More specifically, to a vast number of black Christians, being saved from the bondage of political servitude is no more important than being liberated from the shackles of spiritual servitude to sin. To those engaged in the legitimate quest for personal salvation, for example, it appears that black theology is irrelevant and less than liberative.[7]

Generally speaking, the main thrust of black theology to date has succeeded in relating theology to the need for the black community to adopt a corporate social politic commensurate with the imperatives of Black Power. However, it appears that contemporary black theology has not dealt seriously with the concerns of spiritual individuals desirous of a deeper relationship with God, as instrumental for the achievement of viable religious personhood. Such unconcern has weakened the dialogical possibilities for black theologians to relate to a major sector of black Christianity: persons of staunch evangelical upbringing.

Granted, black theology cannot be everything to everybody. Yet I would think it infelicitous for its proponents to ignore, deliberately or otherwise, communication with such a large division of black Christendom. The following section will draw focused attention to the specific contributions that black evangelicalism can make to the enterprise of black dialogue. At this point it should merely be underscored that the *sharing* presupposition of black theological dialogue would allow the black evangelical to offer his personal religious experiences as something inherently credible and worth sharing.

Black theology must surely recognize that black religion is at heart a soteriological enterprise. Thus, theology-in-black draws for its historic sources a variety of testimonies of salvific experiences, documented dramatizations of God's power in the lives of believers, and attestations of the ongoing revelation of the Christ of faith. This is the stuff of actual black religious experience to which a black theology should relate practically.

A broader normative claim can be made.

Although one cannot so easily prove an axiom of faith, it is worth considering that religion has meant a great deal to blacks because it expresses a dimension of life that other concerns leave unaddressed. For blacks, religion itself is not the ultimate concern that gives meaning to existence. Rather, knowledge of and deeply felt faith in the God of "Abraham, Isaac, and Jacob" accord a supramundane ultimacy to the religious life of black Christians.

For individuals who value personal fellowship with God (the *majority* of black Christians), theology is practical insofar as it heightens the possibility of such a relationship's being nurtured and deepened. As one moves further to the right on the scale of religious conservatism, of course, more and more does it become necessary for the black theologian to relate his theological pronouncements to the demands of the Gospel incumbent upon those who tend to equate salvation with a very definite conversion experience. The point to stress is that religious personalism is a normative part of black faith and is what makes demands upon black theology's reformulation of its outreach dimensions.

Several implications can be drawn. The demands of religious personalism warrant a new *content* for black-liberation theology. As much as black theological dialogue speaks to all expressions of black religious experience, it must somehow appreciate the concerns of the "far-right" religious masses—as the fulcrum for a balanced intercharge of ideals and aspirations. Inasmuch as many blacks look to religion to meet fundamental existential and spiritual needs expressive of a yearning for a personal relationship with

Jesus Christ, the Lord of life, black theology must be strongly kerygmatic as well as "experimental-political."

Further, since dialogue centers on sharing, the black theologian should expect to teach all segments of black Christianity, and especially to *learn from* all sectors of the black religious community. In so doing, black theology can broaden its appeal to conservatives and neo-fundamentalists, such that black theologians can say that they have entered into meaningful social intercourse with persons who view Christ as normative for the liberated black community.

As a third implication, any theological system for the black church that debilitates personal religious expressions of the Christian faith is blatantly *immoral.* This point is stressed, primarily because at least one black theological manifesto appears to foster a sense of political impersonalism.[8] If individualism as a part of personalistic appropriation of the Christian faith is not encouraged by the black community, the risk of conformity may lead to some type of state-religion totalitarianism. If black Christian (or Muslim) nationalism categorically prescribes what ultimate political allegiance must shape the actual moral and religious self, individual religious personhood is demeaned, in favor of politically robotized subservience.

Theologizing is one thing. Propagandizing is quite something else. Against the backdrop of current political oppression, spokesmen for the black religious community should engage in the former and shun the latter. The freedom of the moral self to enlarge and mature is at stake.

The moral self requires a sense of self-definition, a source of guidance and nurture, and a locus of ambition that draws the becoming self beyond itself toward greater moral aspiration. The maturing moral self must be inspired to develop, in a relational setting, along the guidelines of deep religious conviction and commitment.

By this analysis, autonomy to become is not nondirectional. The self-in-becoming is strengthened by a definite course of growth. This potential growth is both moral and spiritual. As long as this autonomy is safeguarded, the freedom of the self to advance is insured. That which debilitates this freedom is oppressive and sinful. When oppressive forces assail, the black community is threatened, because individuals are restricted from becoming what they could become : sons and daughters of God.

The following section provides some suggestions as to how the Bible can serve as a useful tool in the construction of a prophetic social ethic as part of the black-liberation community's witness against the sins that encroach on moral and religious autonomy.

III The Relevance of the Bible

As unlikely as it is to conceive of a black social revolution outside the black church, it is implausible to presume that a black liberative theology can ignore the profound significance of the Bible for the edification and enlightenment of the black Christian community of faith. Abundant informal evidence indicates that most Afro-Americans have been reared on a diet of "bibliocentric" faith and are not easily convinced that theology minus God or his Word can meet their spiritual needs for existence.

What is crucial is the hermeneutical interpretation of the spiritual application to modern life of the Bible's chief tenets. Those who have been bred on the Bible as the living "heavenly manna" will probably not find some other substitute palatable or desirable. This body of hungry souls includes countless numbers of black Christians of all denominations who have understood the meaningfulness of religion in terms of the applicability of Scripture to the concerns of everyday existence in a world of heartache and suffering.

The majority of black Christians are not aware that there has been a post-Christian theological revolution. For them God is neither "dead" nor secularized into nonentity. He is very much alive in their own lives and in their understanding of religious faith.

Thus I question the suggestion made by some Black Power spokesmen (within and without academic circles) that

the Bible has justified oppression historically and that, in
fact, a bona fide liberation enterprise must discard Judeo-
Christian Scripture for distorting our view of reality. This
mode of thinking runs contrary to the affirmations of faith
that sustain the moral and spiritual ambitions of most black
folk, and it ignores the testimony of black historical theology.

The tradition of black faith has underscored this theological posit: black Christians see themselves as part of an
ongoing, saving history of Christian engagement in the
world. Blacks are not willing to acquiesce in a wholesale
discard of the principles of Christianity, including its ethic
of personal response to the agapeic demands of the Gospel.
Nor are we eager to abandon personal belief in God as a
result of reading Benjamin Mays's thesis that Judeo-Chris-
tianity's "white God" is generally nonfunctional for black
peoples.[9]

For the black community, religion is viable, God is functional, and faith is endearing when the biblical message
speaks to the current situation, which demands a revelatory
"word from the Lord." When one speaks of black preaching
as a strong point of black religion, the assumption is that
within the canonical Word of God exists a "Black Bible," [10]
which occasions a contemporaneous prophetic utterance that
speaks directly to black existential despair.

The despairing black community needs a vivid hope
to animate the aspiring religio-moral self. The ingredients
for this hope are found in religious personalism, a fundamental building block of a transcendent community of faith.
And they are discoverable in the biblical theme of eschatological hopefulness (a vital part of evangelic doctrine).

This theme serves as an appropriate leitmotif for noting
the relevance of the black Bible for the establishment of a
theological-ethical critique that considers spiritual nurturance of the responsible Christian self as a timely theological
concern.

To begin with, it is hope, notes theologian Jürgen Moltmann, that serves as the central Christian theological category that counters culturological despair. Christian hope

can rightly be viewed as the "foundation and mainspring of [Christian] theological thinking. . . ." [11] It points to a reality beyond the immediacy of present adverse situations. It bolsters faith when it is subject to the most gruesome tests.

A theological ethic for the black religious community is called upon to be an ethic of hope. It needs to be based on biblical assurance that God will establish His kingdom in the hearts of those who set their minds and affections on things beyond the temporal, the mundane, and the transitory. And it should fortify black faith when it is threatened by oppressive forces that dehumanize.

By this reading, liberation occurs when minds and hearts heretofore bound by weights of oppression and distress are freed by the redemptive love of God acting in Christ. Persons set free from sin are at liberty to become creative religious personalities as well as responsible moral selves. Those who become fellow workmen with Christ live as "sons of God" in the present, but are yet aware that the completion of God's agency-in-the-world rests on a vantage in the future.

By becoming an eschatological community of hopefulness, the black church would understand the central principle of spiritual freedom. "Man is only free when his life is shaped according to 'the image of God,' that is, when he knows that he is living on the power of God, on the gift of God." [12] When individuals are freed *from* all sins that result in ontologic-psychological oppression, they are free *to* dutifully serve humankind and worship God in the beauty of His holiness. I see this as the essence of achieved authentic religious personhood.

Alternatively, I would refer to this as "the politics of spiritual advancement." I am convinced that black belief and dialogue have provided the nurture for the Christian soul that is drawn more closely to God's beauty and love. It is eschatological hopefulness that backs up the spiritual politic by which the nurtured soul is inspired to mature. Two main points deserve attention.

a. Biblical eschatology informs us that in the "fulness of time," the re-created order will be established, in which old things have passed away and all things have indeed become new. The paradox of the present moment is that it never remains the present, but pulls the past into the future. One cannot look to the here and now for the completion of God's work, precisely because God knows the end from the beginning and such knowledge is not completely available to humankind.

For liberation theologians, history must very definitely be open-ended. If there is no reason to postulate the possibility of change, there is no motive for constructing a hopeful theological mandate that encourages the oppressed to believe that something better than oppression lies ahead. Accordingly, it is incumbent upon the liberation strategist to imagine a decisive goal toward which the liberated community may channel its thought and action. Since history is neither static nor one-dimensionally linear, the liberation theologian must extract from the past usable ingredients for postulating a more amenable future.

This is fine and dandy, the evangelical would say, but one important thing is missing. Not only does man have a part to play in the destiny of humankind, but God himself has something to do with the course of events in the world and among all peoples of the world. As much as humans may carry out their own agendas for a radically new world of peace, brotherhood, sisterhood, and full humanity, God operates by a plan that must find ultimate fulfillment by his design. Coincidentally, what God intends for humankind may not be altogether disparate from what the radical theologians posit as a more wholesome, livable future for the world.[13]

However one may square away on the issue of relevance of apocalyptic literalism to contemporary understandings of the Christian faith, one must be convinced that the Old and New Covenants of the Bible are unified by an eschatological hopefulness centering on the inauguration of a radically new era of unprecedented peace and worldwide fellowship. Evangelicals can draw heavily on both Old Testament and New Testament millenarian themes to extract assurance that one day the "lion will lie down with the lamb" and there will be the occasion to "study war no more."

To date, black theology's concern for achieving dramatic sociopolitical ends has tilted the fulcrum of a balanced Christian theology away from apocalyptic eschatology toward practical ethics-for-the-present. What needs to find fuller elaboration in black theological thought is the biblical message that any "interim ethic" must point toward fuller realization in the future, of humanizing concerns of the present. The whole creation groans and lies in wait for the cosmic rejuvenation yet to come.

Black Theology II cannot afford to ignore this prophetic theme, and it must attend to incorporating into itself an ecological-theological critque prescriptive of a more humane society for all. If technocracy continually perpetuates the wastage of resources and threatens ecological harmony of the species, there may not be a world to live in for blacks or anyone else.

On this issue of making black theology more conducive to the humaneness of human existence, I have elsewhere suggested that black theology learn a few lessons from feminist theologies.[14] In this context, I can only reemphasize that black theology should more sensitively promote appreciation for the created order as it now is, along with interpreting the eschatological themes of re-creation in terms directly meaningful to the black religious community.

The black community is in dire need of restoration, regeneration, and a radical "rebirth." And its spiritually ambitious members need to be assured, through a seasoned and informed theology, that taking a stand for the sanctity of life and joining all creation in praise of the Creator are noble endeavors.

b. Within the biblical canon, the New Testament more completely unfolds what the Old Testament foreshadows: hope in the ultimate resurrection of humanity. This theme has become linked with judgment and an imminent coming of God's Anointed. The Good News is that Christ has come, has sent back the Comforter following the Ascension, and is coming again. Black theologians should not overlook or underestimate the significance for black congregations of this kerygmatic proclamation: Jesus the Christ cometh! In light of the many "signs of the time" foretelling Christ's Second Coming, the black religious community should strengthen its faith that complete deliverance (salvation) is at hand.

By and large, black religion has preserved some tint of the strong doctrinal emphasis on personal judgment that has colored Christian theology since the days when men like Edwards, Finney, and others boldly preached the evangelical message that "all must stand before the judgment seat of Christ and give an account of the deeds done in his body." Though modern theological theorists of secularization would look askance at teaching that is concerned with actual bodily resurrection and a "White Throne" judgment, black Christians of most denominations retain a measure of fearfulness at the thought that this life is not the end and a final accounting is in store.

The black church is generally geared toward an otherworldly outlook and should not be ashamed that such is the case. The black laity have been made aware that "the end of all things it at hand." Accordingly, they need direction from the clergy as how best "to redeem the time, for the days are evil." In course, the black *professional* theologians can strengthen the theological affirmation that the black community ultimately stands beneath the mantle of God's judgment,[15] and that as much as the black church needs political ethics for the here and now, it needs judgmental warning regarding the there and then.

Existential philosophers inform us that death is the "most possible of possibilities." Theologians cannot stay the hand of death; but they can point to a hope for resurrection that can animate the body of Christian believers not to despair at the thought of dying. The same Jesus who "tasted death for all men" is the central figure in John's Apocalypse, who could claim, "I am he that liveth, and was dead; and, behold, I am alive for evermore . . . and have the keys of hell and of death."

The hopeful eschatological community is necessarily a *repentant* community.[16] Because the community recognizes that this age is not the last age and that God's Kingdom is only partially realized in the present, a spirit of repentance should capture the hearts of those who intend to be prepared for the fullness of time and the consummation of Christ's kingdom.

Regardless of when death may come, Christians need to be prepared spiritually for all consequences and inevitabilities of this life and for personal judgment after this life is over. The dutiful Christian theologian (black or white) is obliged to teach the faithful how they can live life to the fullest until they die, and await, hopefully, the promise of something more.

Black theologians should nurture the Christian conviction that the trial of one's faith is "much more precious than of gold that perisheth," for which one may rejoice "with joy unspeakable and full of glory." In contradistinction to the "doom-and-gloom" prophecies made by post-Christian, God-is-dead theorists, those who theologize for the black church are encouraged to point to a ray of brilliant hope for those who share in Christ's suffering. "At the appearing of Jesus Christ," the elect can receive the end of their faith, even the salvation of their souls.

IV The Importance of Black Worship

As seen above, the essence of black theology is the promulgation of genuine black dialogue that unites autonomous moral and religious selves into a service of love and mutual concern. Accordingly, the black theologian is duty bound to heighten the sense of religious dialogue that adds cohesion to the black community.

As was stressed, the black-liberation community can profitably learn from its theologians how black religion in general and the "Black Bible" in particular can offer suitable inspiration for the achievement of a religious community concerned as much with spiritual liberty in Christ as with political liberation from societal "antichrists." [17] Given the factor of experiential verification of liberation theology for the black church, a central normative characteristic of black theology emerges from black dialogue. In a word: contemporary black theology can best address the spiritual needs of the black church by becoming, in part, a theology of black worship.

Worship promotes spiritual wholeness. The diabolical nature of evil within society and within personal relationships tends to affect adversely personal wholeness. The invidious nature of "spiritual wickedness in high places" and the preponderance of "principalities and powers" at work in every domain of human endeavor leads to psychological alienation from one's self and spiritual alienation from God. On this score, the psychoanalyst and the evangelical clergy agree: sin separates persons from that which fosters emotional stability and psychological well-being.

The neurological disturbances associated with blackness[18] suggest that blacks need something to counter feelings of isolation, alienation, self-hatred, ressentiment, and futility. It is religion that touches the inner core of being in such a way that the roots of the problem are exposed. Religion does not guarantee spiritual and psychological wholesomeness. But religious worship does bring the worshiper into the presence of the divine—and such an encounter may be therapeutic. A worshipful attitude among black believers should engender a more wholesome spirit of dialogical exchange within the larger community.

Worship fosters personal creativity. Because black religion is emotive as well as intellectual, the worship experience is highly valued for lending itself to spontaneous, creative ways of enjoying the faith. There is a richness to black spirituality that is appreciated fully only when one *participates* in the worship encounter. In many black congregations everyone is expected to join in the service and make it an occasion of exultation.

The preacher contributes, by way of a flexible hermeneutic, an impromptu revelatory exegesis and a preaching style that is so *non*structured that the channels for prophetic immediacy are always open. Contributing more than just a robust and invigorating delivery of his sermon, the black preacher lends a personal charismatic *presence* that makes the worship experience dramatic and "ecstatic." Captivating the hearts and minds of the congregation, the artful black preacher takes the believers to God's throne, where they feel the presence of the Almighty Himself.

Not everyone is called to preach. But everyone can have a song, psalm, praise, or testimony to contribute religious inspiration to the worship service. Above all, it is crucial to "let the Spirit have its way." When everyone adds to the worship event, the Holy Spirit pours out a blessing for all. Creative participation in worship stimulates a sense of joy that animates all those who are "of one mind and one accord." No one leaves empty.

Creative participatory worship also promotes a dramatic sense of expectancy on part of the congregation. Worship fuses hands and hearts into the corporate enterprise of "touching heaven," so that drops of divine favor and goodness fall on those who await the "showers of blessings." The sense of expectancy leads to a special rapport between congregation and preacher: a dialogical sharing of enthusiasm for God's honoring the concerns and addressing the needs of all gathered to hear the Word of the Lord. This kind of intimacy of feeling exemplifies "black dialogue" at its best. For when a consecrated congregation and preacher allow the Word to address them, a genuine and lasting "Gospel encounter" takes place.[19]

The importance of black worship for theological liberation deserves special mention. Worship, as an everyday dialogical encounter with the divine, means that God makes a difference in the lives of believers. Thus, a worship attitude that is respectful of the personal significance of black religion to most black Christians should be endorsed by all black theologians who join the poets, the minstrels, and the

clergy in telling the story of Afro-American liberation.
Black Americans have a story to tell of religious liberation. It is a religious story of fundamental existence, survival, and ontologic self-worth as human beings. It traces the roots of black human freedom from Africa through the course of American history, in which there has been evidence of a perpetuation of black courage to "tell the story," even though slave masters and ecclesiastical authorities did not wish to hear it.

It was in the era of developing independent black churches that paramount importance was placed on the legitimacy of instituting structural forms for enabling our forefathers to continue to relate the "old, old story" of God's grace and love. I suggest that contemporary black theology not bypass the spirit of spontaneity and "irrational creativeness" that have made individual appropriation of the story personally enriching and enlivening.

This is the point at which black evangelical Christianity can best make a contribution to the enterprise of black religion/black theology. Black evangelicalism supports theological investigation of black spirituality, which—hewn from the stone of hope-in-suffering—stands as a timeless monument to the fortitude of a people who refused to be crushed by the weight of demonic oppression. Further, black evangelical teaching wholeheartedly advocates the sharing of the positive qualities of black religion—as an educative, nurturing experience that is *lived,* not discussed over coffee or mapped out on the blackboard.

Yet, those doing black-liberation theology in the classroom are urged to remember: the creative vitality of black evangelicalism offers many themes that can be easily appropriated into a black theology of worship for the black regious community of liberation.

Such a theology would reflect genuine black dialogue as that which has historically embraced constituents of the black community into a fellowship of believers who are fully cognizant of the strength of black religious faith. This faith is the soul of black existence, the backbone of black rectitude, and the spirit of black love.

Notes to Chapter 6

1. Ethical theory on this matter is offered by James M. Gustafson, *The Church As Moral Decision-Maker* (Philadelphia: Pilgrim Press, 1970).

2. To note the distinction, see H. Paul Santmire, "I-Thou, I-It, I-Ens," *Journal of Religion* 48 (1968): 260–73.

3. Martin Buber, *Between Man and Man* (New York: Macmillan, 1965), p. 31.

4. Eulalio R. Baltazar, *The Dark Center* (New York: Paulist Press, 1973), p. 109.

5. See my article "Refocusing Black Religious Education: Three Imperatives," *Religious Education* 69, no. 4 (July-August 1974): 421–32.

6. See the section "Education As The Practice Of Freedom," in Paulo Freire's *Education for Critical Consciousness* (New York: Seabury Press, 1973).

7. This is not to suggest that liberation as a theopolitical category is to be equated with the Christian doctrine of soteriology. My point is that liberation is a multidimensional reality that is incompletely captured in the rhetoric of theopolitics. For many black Christians, the language of "sin and salvation" better expresses this reality, which is at base "spiritual."

8. N.B.: "The Black Nationalist Creed" in Albert B. Cleage, Jr., *Black Christian Nationalism* (New York: William Morrow & Co., 1972), p. xiii.

9. N.B.: Benjamin E. Mays, *The Negro's God* (New York: Atheneum, 1969).

10. See Henry H. Mitchell, *Black Preaching* (Philadelphia: Lippincott, 1970), chap. 5: "The Black Bible."

11. Jürgen Moltmann, *Theology of Hope* (New York: Harper & Row, 1967), p. 19.

12. Emil Brunner, *The Divine Imperative*, trans. Olive Wyon (New York: Macmillan, 1942), p. 170.

13. E.g., Eric Mount, *The Feminine Factor* (Richmond, Va.: John Knox Press, 1973), chap. 4: "Toward a more 'Feminine' Future." Mount is not so radical, though.

14. Calvin E. Bruce, "Toward a *Feminist* Black Theology?", unpublished ms., 1974.

15. As the prophetic canonical literature so boldly attests, all humankind will face this indictment. E.g., Isaiah 34, Jeremiah 18, 25.

16. See Paul S. Minear, *Commands of Christ* (Nashville, Tenn.: Abingdon, 1972), pp. 26, 28.

17. By contrast, feminist Mary Daly would stress that liberation theologies favor those who are antichurch, or antichrist. See her *Beyond the Father* (Boston: Beacon Press, 1973). This doctrine would never hold for mainstream black Christianity.

18. See Abraham Kardiner and Lionel Ovesey, eds., *The Mark of Oppression* (New York: World Publishing Co., 1951), esp. chaps. 8 and 9.

19. Mitchell, *Black Preaching*, p. 106.

7
Black and White Theologies: Possibilities for Dialogue

CLYDE A. HOLBROOK

INTRODUCTION

In undertaking to discuss the possibilities of a dialogue between black and "white" theology, an author immediately lays himself open to criticism from both sides.[1] Either too much bias will be shown, or not enough, depending on the side the reader chooses. The pitfalls of misunderstanding and passion will compete for one's attention with the goals of frankness and sensitivity. Yet without the latter, and the overcoming of the former, it would be futile to expect that sufficient ground could be laid for a fruitful dialogue between the proponents of black and white theology.

Protestant theology in America was shocked in the 1960s by a movement that unabashedly and uncompromisingly announced itself as *black theology*. With puzzlement bordering on consternation, white theologians viewed the notion of employing the term *black* as a justifiable theological category as blatant "racism." The widely held assumption of Christian theology had been that theology was done either specifically for the Christian community or more

189

generally in reference to mankind at large. Now that assumption was being ruthlessly denied and even characterized as white racist in nature. Thus William Jones, a black theologian, could refer to the established theologians as "racist." [2] What appeared to white theologians as racism in black theology was now reversed as a term of opprobrium upon themselves. Regardless of the predominantly liberal social tendencies of white theologians, they found themselves castigated for carrying on thoughts and defending actions of an oppressive type. Certainly some of those who, from the earliest days of the republic to the present, had protested the treatment of blacks would find it difficult to accept the terms *white* or *racist* as synonymous expressions used in the contemporary situation. From George Keith and Samuel Sewall, through Anthony Benezet, Samuel Hopkins, William Ellery Channing, Theodore Parker, Theodore Weld, and Charles Finney, to Buell Gallagher, Liston Pope, the Niebuhrs, Kyle Haselden, Joseph Hough, and many others, the charges did not seem to fit.

However, an issue hitherto unsuspected, deep and ominous, had suddenly appeared within the theological world. The possibility of dialogue between the white theologians and the black theologians was jeopardized. The terms themselves used by the black theologians had ruptured the relatively placid surface of theology. The elasticity with which *white, black, black experience,* and *racism* were used made them appear as sloganeering instruments of strife rather than means of mutual comprehension. *White* could mean that a person's skin was light or, more pejoratively, as used by James H. Cone, that "God's revelation on earth has always been black, red, or some other shocking shade, but never white. Whiteness is a symbol of man's depravity." [3] Nestled in the word *white* was concentrated all that was wrong with white-skinned people and all that had been done to oppress black-skinned people. Hence God was construed as black, as was Christ (Albert Cleage). More ambiguously, whites were instructed to become black. This was to be done by identifying themselves with the sufferings of black and other oppressed peoples. "To be black means that your heart, your soul, your mind, and your body are where the dispossessed are." In sum, the color of one's skin would seem to have little to do with either whiteness or blackness, as Cone pointed out: "Being black in America has very little to do with skin color." [4] But the ambiguity remained as to the meaning of *color*, as when it was stated that black people must "bring color to a sterile and depraved white people." [5] Is the meaning symbolic, as in Cone's effort to write of blackness as "an ontological symbol," or is it literally a reference to skin pigmentation? The answer is seldom clearly put.

When one turns to the meaning of the term *black*, again the ambiguity presents itself even more emphatically. It refers to the dark-skinned people, but it also refers to the condition of oppression under which dark-skinned people have been forced to live. But its ambience extends even further to embrace any oppressed people, including, whether intentionally or not, a very large group of middle-class whites who, in other circumstances, could as well be labeled oppressors and therefore white in the worst sense. Such people, like blacks, suffer, but less intensely because they cannot shed their white skin, which is their badge of dishonor no matter how often they have felt the sting of political, social, and economic injustice.

The *black experience* also confronted the white theologian with a puzzle. Sometimes it signified a heritage of slavery now extended into systematic oppressiveness that reduced the dark-skinned to powerlessness. But it also referred to an atmosphere of exalted joyfulness that presumably was uniquely connected with black religion and a black outlook on life. With a variety of meanings, the *black experience*—incorporating the spirituals, the yearning for release from injustice, the dance, the joyfulness of almost ecstatic form, and much else—came to be called *soul*. This attribute, it has often been suggested, is something that the white cannot, or at least does not, possess. Again, even the term *black experience* is not monolithic; there are economic,

political, and cultural class distinctions within it that shatter
its announced uniformity. How to relate to this multiform
phenomenon has remained a vexing and confusing problem
for the white. Then there remains the oft-repeated charge
that the white theologian cannot penetrate or understand
black theology because he does not share the black experience. Yet, as we have seen, he is challenged to think and
feel and act black. It would seem that black experience is
a citadel whose doors may be opened or shut at the behest
of the black theologian when he wants to make points
against white theology. When that door is closed, one discovers that recourse to the uniqueness of the black experience turns out to be, to change the figure, a two-edged
sword. Just as the white has no access to the heritage of
slavery or soul," by parity of logic, neither does the black
theologian have access to the white experience as it is understood by whites. Only when the black becomes, even in a
small way, an oppressor does he fit the picture of the white
man offered by some black thinkers. Otherwise, according
to the black definitions of whiteness, he remains as solidly
an outsider to the white experience as does the white man
and theologian to the black experience.

  Racism offers as much ambiguity as the other terms, but
its use has a bite on the conscience of whites and has a
more universal scope than even the word *white*. It has come
to be loosely used to refer to any act, policy, or sentiment
that is viewed as injurious to a minority, and especially to
black people. The purposes or intentions of those who promote such policies, or of those who hold certain views, have
become matters of relative indifference to the black thinker
who recognizes in these actions what works to the dis-
advantage of the black community. However, the term
racism (or *racist*) can be so lavishly used that it can identify
practically any act or sentiment, and hence define nothing
in particular that distinguishes one kind of act or sentiment
from another. Therefore one finds a mixed collection of
policies and actions that is identified as racist: law and
order; building freeways into cities; gun-control legislation;

family planning; examinations for sickle-cell anemia; desegregation, segregation, or integration; requests for clear and uniform use of words in theology; absence of soul, or overt expressions of contempt for blacks—all can be counted as examples of oppression by racist whites. The white at last finds that whichever way he turns, he is branded racist, first by virtue of his color and then by virtue of his heritage. His ethnic history has condemned him to the role of oppressor, regardless of what he has done on behalf of blacks. He is forced onto the defensive about a heritage that, to be sure, is his, but that he would only selectively defend. It is a case of guilt passed on by ethnic origin, from which, presumably, he cannot disentangle himself.

One of the most difficult meanings to be appropriated by whites is that of the phrase *institutional racism*. Apparently, hatred of or condescension toward the blacks in this case is not important. What is important is that blacks should have power and representation in the major institutions of the country, in government at all levels, in economic matters, and in educational institutions. There is a neat twist to institutional racism, in connection with its apparent lack of concern about motives. As a contemporary sociologist has pointed out in redefining *racism* in institutional terms, it has become by definition impossible to apply the term to blacks. "Racism had, by redefinition, become an impossibility for an underprivileged group; by the same redefinition, all members of the racially dominant group, irrespective of individual attitudes, are collectively guilty of racism." [6] The casting of *racism* in institutional terms has found considerable support in judicial decisions that concern employment, where lack of minority employees is automatically assessed as discrimination, if not as outright racism. Since racism has thus become a white, not a black, problem, it appears as mere nitpicking for whites to be suspicious of a definition that a priori exempts one group from the charge while it totally transfers the burden to another group, regardless of those groups' attitudes. In any case, whites, including theologians, soon become aware that the term *racism* can be hurled whenever disagreements break out.

The terms here reviewed might be thought to cast up insurmountable barriers to any civilized theological discourse, and put an end to dialogue. However, it is the thesis of this chapter that dialogue between white and black theology not only remains a possibility, but is imperative. As Major J. Jones put it, "History has set the two, black and white, on a confrontation course, and the point of contact will be either one of violent conflict or one of dialogue and mutual agreement." [7] Theology may not be able to avert violent conflict, but its task of mutual understanding cannot be underestimated. Not all black and white theologians may be sanguine in their hopes for such a dialogue, but the effort must be made within the framework of Christian thought and faith. In the present situation it is especially incumbent on white theology to recognize that its insights have often been deeply affected by social, political, and economic factors as much as by intellectual ones. As Claude Welch has remarked in another context, "We do well to be on guard against the bias which assumes that the fundamental determinants of theology are always to be sought in philosophical presuppositions or influences or secularly in conflicts with science." [8] Black theology certainly has taken the sense of this dictum far more seriously than has traditional theology. The impact of slavery, the apparent loss of cultural antecedents, and the devastating influence of prejudice and brutality have all been woven into the texture of its thought. Not a little of the reason for calling traditional theology *white* stems from this lack of awareness among white theologians of how cultural forces have molded their theology. Themes that have pungently surfaced in black theology have been muted in white theology because white theologians, often without conscious intent, have been blinded to them by the kinds of experience they have had.

Let us see then how black theology interprets itself, how it regards white theology, and then turn to see what possible responses white theology makes to black theology, as well as the critical points of disagreement. Finally, with utmost tentativeness, I will attempt to point out some broad areas of agreement on which black and white theology can begin to do business with each other beyond what looks like the present impasse.

I

Among black theologians, the common ground from which Christian theology must originate is everything that might be classed as oppression of blacks by white people. There is a history of cruel uprooting of blacks from Africa, of their enslavement abroad and in America, of prejudice, of disbarment from the advantages and goods of American society, and of political and educational deprivation. Since blacks are stereotyped and caricatured by whites as shiftless, sex-hungry, stupid, smelly, and lazy, it is understandable that those who speak for the blacks should feel outraged. To be sure, some blacks have been both systematically and unsystematically dehumanized to the extent that they have adopted images of themselves, perpetrated by whites, as being a subbreed of person and a nonparticipant in American citizenry. The history is undebatable: it stands for all to see, if they have the will. In the face of the staggering burden imposed on blacks throughout this history, it is inevitable and natural that the key word to parallel *oppression* will be *liberation*. Black theology, for the most part, has therefore centered on these two terms.

James H. Cone, one of the most intransigent advocates of black theology, interprets theology as having the sole purpose of applying the "freeing power of the gospel to black people under white oppression." Therefore, each doctrine of Christian theology must be related to the emancipation of black people. In fact, "God has chosen black people." [9] The struggle for liberation is pronounced as of divine character, and the attendant theology is aimed at assisting the oppressed in this struggle for liberation. As such, black theology may possibly be the "only expression reactions there are, are often muted. Impressions are the best assessments we have, although, of these impressions, one stands out quite clearly. No white theologian of consequence has mounted a frontal assault on black theology like the attacks made on white by black thinkers. This may be due to a variety of reasons. Perhaps no theologian sees himself as a white theologian or ethicist; perhaps it is because black theology is such an extreme and disorganized bundle of claims that it is unworthy of serious attention; perhaps it is because a sense of guilt forbids a white theologian to "pick on" representatives of a long-subjugated people whose cause is just; or perhaps the reluctance to meet black theology head-on is caused by the inescapable horror of being called a "racist." After all, white theologians have been warned off repeatedly from trying to penetrate and understand the black experience. Consequently, it appears that it is fruitless for them to try to come to terms with black theology, since whatever is said or written can be counted out of court because of the speaker's or writer's ignorance of the black experience. Certainly, hard things have been charged against white theology. It would be strange if some hard things had not at least passed through the minds of those counted as white theologians.

Although allowance must be made for the speculative quality of the three tendencies I offer below, they do exemplify a possible range of attitudes toward black theology that are conceivable, if not publicly stated. How typical or representative these views are, it would be difficult to ascertain at this stage of discussion.

First in the group of impressions are the decidedly negative evaluations of black theology. If the word *racist* has any identifiable meaning left in it, black theology is an example of racist thinking. It takes as a primary category not suffering and oppression as such, but blackness. In spite of such efforts as Cone's convoluted attempts to fasten the term *racism* only on whites, no white theologian at least has ever taken color as the premise of this thought. Furthermore, the attempt to turn the phrase *ontological symbol* into a broadly conceived way of talking about all oppressed people always fails because, in the last analysis, only black-skinned people are the models of true oppression. It is they who actually are the focus of attention, and the white oppressed have never entered into the depths of degradation that has been visited upon the blacks. The result of this kind of thinking in black theology is to ghettoize theology by making skin color the primary and only context in which theology can properly be carried on.[24] When it is asserted that God has identified Himself with black people, too large a segment of humanity has been left out of account, and the Deity has been shrunk to the dimension of a tribal deity.[25] Of course, it has been repeatedly stated that black theology is not racist, although it is admitted that "blacks hate whites." [26] So when J. Deotis Roberts criticizes whites "who think in racist terms" about black theology, he concludes that "blacks, for the most part, have no racist intention." Major Jones, however, is more frank about the existence of a "black racism current within much of the black community." However, he also thinks that some "counter-racism" may be needed, although "black theology should not extend justification for it." [27]

Other negative evaluations may also be current. Black theology castigates a whole race of white people, thus dealing in unjustified and undiscriminating generalities concerning individual whites. It is filled with strident, hyperbolic rhetoric that understandably arises from the experience of subjugation, but nevertheless hinders communication between concerned whites and blacks. Black theology may serve as a "shout" for liberation, and a tactic adapted for freedom, but it answers the offers of assistance from whites with insults. In fact, the threat of violence is never far off in the writings of some black theologians.[28] Although white theologians have done the principal theological and liberal scholarship on which black theology largely depends, white theologians have been excoriated for their failure to meet the demands of black theology. In its interpretations of the Deity and Christ, black theology has reduced the Christian faith in scope, and prostituted it into a social and political tool in keeping with the predominantly utilitarian ethos of American culture, which on other grounds it professes to abhor. It refuses to acknowledge that the doctrine of suffering has always been a theme in the white theology that it disdains. It charges whites, and white theologians in particular, with hypocrisy for not living up to their professions of faith, without consideration of the common human failure to live up to the best one knows. Christian faith has for centuries identified this failure as one aspect of sin, and has not exempted its theologians from the charge.

These negative appraisals of black theology may sometimes melt into an attitude of patronizing tolerance of the aberrations found in that form of theology. It may assume an attitude of relative indifference that awaits a certain measure of moderation yet to appear in black thinking. Time will at last quiet the more passionate utterances continually heard from the most radical of the black theologians. In the meantime, white theologians and churchmen should refrain from negative judgments and absorb as gracefully as possible the slurs and criticisms hurled at them. After all, black people have undergone so much deprivation in the past that it ill behooves whites to resent their claims and charges. Therefore, white theology should not enter into controversy with black theology during this transitional period.

The possibilities for dialogue are indeed bleak if the only perspectives available to white theology are those of negation, tolerance, or indifference. But a far more positive reaction to black theology has also appeared. Black theology has been increasingly accepted as a legitimate enterprise. It arises out of a history, as well as a contemporary situation, in which those who are disadvantaged by virtue of their color have been trodden on and refused the elemental conditions of human life. It is no wonder that spokesmen have arisen in protest against that condition and have seized upon some of the most crucial features of the Christian faith in order to make their case. They have called to the attention of white theology in a challenging manner the of Christian theology in America." [10] It serves as a survival technique against extermination, and provides a rallying point for black identity. Its sources and norms lie in the black experience, which includes a history and a culture that are to be seen from the centrality of Jesus Christ. But it is to be understood that as Jesus Christ reveals God, he thereby makes revelation a black event, as attested by Scripture and tradition. Christ is the liberator; he is the one identified with the oppressed. He is the black Christ "who provides the necessary soul for black liberation." He is "only for the oppressed of the land." [11] The symbol *God,* if it does not help to lead to freedom for blacks, may need to be cast aside. Or even more strongly put, "Black theology cannot accept a view of God which does not represent him as being for blacks and thus against whites." There can be no use "for a God who loves whites the same as blacks." [12] The revelation of God in Jesus Christ has made it clear that the blackness of Christ is the "decisive factor" about his person, and any attempt to bypass that fact is a denial of the New Testament message. But having stated this, Cone goes on to say that Christ's actual color is irrelevant so long as we acknowledge that "he was not white in any sense of the word, literally or theologically." [13]

Without surrendering the emphasis upon oppression and liberation, other black theologians point their endeavors in a slightly different direction. Major J. Jones, under the influence of Jürgen Moltmann, argues for the importance of the dimension of hope. He also criticizes Cleage and Cone for their interpretations of Christ and God, because he fears that at last God will become "the idol God of a folk religion." He also affirms, against Cone, that the blessings of God "cannot be only for God's chosen people; they must be for the whole human family." [14] J. Deotis Roberts brings into clearer focus than does Cone the theme of reconciliation. Liberation and reconciliation must be considered at the same time and in relation to each other, while he finds the more violent language about victory or death in the struggle to contain "more rhetoric than reality." [15] Furthermore, he claims that

Cone has attempted to impose a narrowness on black theology that must be rejected. Like Major J. Jones, Roberts affirms that the goal of a worthy black theology must be an authentic Christian existence for both blacks and whites.[16] William Jones, while admitting that no special or privileged criteria should be employed in judging black theology, nevertheless claims certain exceptions for black theology on the grounds that it has not yet entered its established and constructive stage. Criteria for theological discourse appropriate to a fully developed theology, therefore, are inappropriately used in the present stage of the development of black theology. Criticism from outside the circle of black theologians themselves, Jones implies, amounts to a covert form of racism that presupposes the inherent superiority of nonblack theology. Black theology, on the other hand, feels free to raise questions about Christian faith, demanding a reconsideration of every major theological category.[17] Jones makes good on this programmatic intention by sharply raising the issue of theodicy. He sees the primary question to be "Is God a racist?" Unless a negative answer can be given to this question, black theology cannot get on with its work. It is a question that he believes has not been fully faced by the black theologians Joseph R. Washington Jr., James H. Cone, and Albert Cleage. Jones identifies white theology as racist and oppressive. "Black theology suspects that the norms of the Christian tradition are racist [so] it must proceed, as it were, *de novo.*" [18]

II

This comment of William Jones fittingly shows how some black theology regards white theology. The stage is set for two further comments by Jones. The black consciousness requires "a theological movement not simply beyond white theology, but in conscious opposition to it." And even more sharply put, "the class of authentic Christian theologians is without members." [19] Cone is prolific in his castigations of white theology: It is too abstract; it talks too much without translating its talk into the life situations of black people; writers of theology like Barth and Bonhoeffer may serve as examples of how to relate theology to life, but they cannot define the major issues; white theology is not Christian theology because it does not take its departure from God's activity in the situation of oppressed blacks. "The white God is an idol created by racist bastards . . . so it must be smashed." The theology taught in theological seminaries is the spouting of "garbage" and only reflects the oppressive posture of the lecturer. A doctrine such as sin has been perverted by white theologians; it is a concept that only blacks can properly understand. White theology has taken for granted that its norms of discourse are inherently superior to those of black theology.[20] Major J. Jones is less violent in his rhetoric, but he also charges that white theologians "have been producing systems in which the alien virtues of harmony, order and stability have been stressed." The church, he sees, has preached revolution "without meaning to do so. In fact, it has not known what it has been talking about." [21]

In a similar vein, it is argued that since all major theologians have been white, they have operated with metaphysical approaches that fail to come to grips with the condition of the black, no matter how compassionate may be their intent.[22] A reporter who reviewed a symposium on theology held at the World Council of Churches in Geneva remarked on the separate worlds of thought and experience that divide so-called First World theologians from Third World theologians of Africa and the United States. He concluded with relish, "It appears that as the hegemony of the West wanes, Western theologies once dominant now take their places alongside Third World theologies hammered out in the experience of oppression. The monolithic theological establishment is on the ropes." [23]

III

The response of white theology to black theology is difficult to assess. It forms no unified position, and what fact that life conditions do mold theological insights and thought. Too much theology has gone on in its own way without taking seriously the social and political situations that have either informed or failed to inform its conclusions. The blind spot in white theology, which has shielded many of its thinkers from the impact of the distressed conditions of blacks, has perhaps been less one of color than one of the caste orientation that has surreptitiously crept into its thought. Consequently, although it has been assumed that theological thinking has been based on a concern for all men, it has sheltered a less-than-universal perspective on the nature and possibilities of mankind, as well as on the nature of the Christian faith. Theologians and preachers have talked about the revolutionary implications of the Gospel, but their efforts to implement these implications, when tried, are clogged by the slow, lethargic movements of the churches. The theologian who believes that his task is to do his work on behalf of the Christian church soon finds that he is thwarted and condemned not only by those outside the church but by those within. Theologians have over the years unwittingly given hostages of themselves to the church's identification with the security of the society's status quo. It is not surprising, therefore, that a mode of theologizing has arisen that no longer takes its mandates from the church's unwillingness to disrupt the contemporary situation. The theological task is interpreted as being of wider scope than that which generations of theologians have taken for granted, and it calls for a more radical insistence upon action. Black theology has been a powerful agency in helping to bring about these effects in white theology.

Christian ethics, as an essential part of theology, has been called upon to reinterpret the love ethic in relation to power and justice, without a hint of sentimentalism. White theology has begun to catch on to the fact that speculative ethics may have its place in the total theological enterprise, but that Christian ethics must also resituate itself. As one author puts it, "It is necessary for Christians, in response to the

God who is the 'liberator of peoples from oppression and neglect' to rethink their ethical categories from the standpoint of the poor, the oppressed, and the powerless, that is, through the eyes of 'those who are victimized by the present order.'" [29] This resituation has already begun to take place, and although there has been a long-standing theme of the importance of charity as a reflection of the love ethic in Christian theological thought, now it has become even clearer that charity bespeaks a patronizing and condescending attitude that jars with the present mood of a struggle by blacks for justice and freedom. When power and justice are the implementations of love, Christian ethics is called upon to assume a more radical and activistic role, including that of providing guidance and tactics for insuring these goals. By tradition, Christian theology has not overtly assumed this role, but there are evidences that it has begun to do so under the spur of black theology.

The theme of reconciliation, when heard in black theology, elicits a response from white theology. It is being recognized on all sides that this cannot be a superficial rapprochement between whites and blacks. In fact, some feel it to be premature to discuss the possibility. However, it is not too early for white theology to think of the conditions under which reconciliation between at least black and white theologians can occur, if not, for the present, between the bulk of whites and blacks. One of the most difficult roadblocks to such reconciliation lies in the suspicion that whites will attempt to set the conditions and limits for reconciliation. Preston N. Williams voices this suspicion while offering suggestions as to the directions in which reconciliation will have to move. "Reconciliation demands a new metaphor, one symbolizing the white's acceptance of the black's worth and dignity as well as solidarity with him." But whatever this metaphor turns out to be, it cannot be what Williams calls the "tarnished concepts" of human relations and integration. Rather, he wants to return to the idea of reconciliation, in its biblical sense of God's free gift, resulting in not simply individual acts of reconciliation, but in social structures of reconciliation as well. As a preface to such a reconciliation, whites must bear the "burden of their sins." That eventuality involves "the loss of status entailed in repairing the wounded self-esteem of the black American; the loss of power in structuring social institutions and the change in cultural perspective implied in opening themselves to new patterns of interaction, and adopting some black styles as the most adequate expression of the human." Promise-keeping, reparations beyond those of an economic type, and accountability are listed as necessary for both blacks and whites, and as the basis of hope for Americans to find a way "through conflict and cooperation to racial justice." [30] Obviously, whites and white theology have hereby had laid on them the task of removing not only the suspicions concerning their good will, but also those social actions that impede a coming together of blacks and whites. Probably white theology by itself cannot perform this herculean task, but it can open the way.

An impact that black theology has had, if not on white theology, at least on white religion, is its emphasis on and justification for the emotional component in the religious life. It has been noted that white Protestant services, except for certain Pentecostal groups, lack the spontaneous outpouring of religious ecstasy that has traditionally marked black religious services. Compared to the "cold," ritualistic, moralistic, or intellectualistic character of white religious services, the black service stimulates and affords opportunity for people to participate freely in the upsurge of spiritual power elicited by fervent preaching, singing, and bodily movement. It is not always clear that black people appreciate being stereotyped in their religious life in terms of their emotionality. To describe their religious life solely as one of shouting, clapping, oral ejaculations, and the repetitive, rhythmic cadences of the clergyman can easily turn into a patronizing evaluation of the peculiarities of "black folk." Furthermore, it is not even obvious that such behavior is uniquely black. Some aspects of these services are suspiciously close to the more extreme forms of behavior of

whites exhibited during the Great Awakening of the eight-
eenth century, and carried on in the revivals of the early
nineteenth century. Yet whatever the sources of this heightened emotional content, there has come to the foreground
in some white churches a fresh appreciation of festivity and
emotional involvement of congregations. How much this is
due to the influence of black religion is not easily decided.
It is manifest that black theology identifies such fervent
expressions with (and justifies them as) *soul,* which is recognized as an energizing and uniting feature of black people's
search for emancipation.

IV

As one considers the representative views of black
theologians and their impacts on white theology, it becomes
clear that dialogue will be difficult. There are certain focal
issues that will have to be faced, if not before dialogue can
take place, at least in the course of such dialogue. As long
as black theology assumes a monolithic black experience
that shuts out the proponent of theology who is white, of
course it is impossible to transact business. All talk of white
theologians "thinking black" does not do the job, because
at any time the realization that one is not dark skinned can
arise to confound understanding. In such a situation the
equality that is in every respect needed for full participation
in dialogue is jeopardized. If on one side, black theologians
can claim intimate knowledge of white theology while
denying to white theologians the possibility of penetrating
black theology and experience, and on the other side, white
theologians insist that they alone understand the proper
role of theology and disdain as amateurish the efforts of
blacks, dialogue will be a long way off. If this impasse is to
be no more than a rhetorical standoff, it will be necessary
to surmount it by efforts on both sides of far more percep-
tivity than has thus far been exercised.

Granted that this fundamental impasse can eventually
be overcome, a number of substantive issues, in which dis-

agreement may well appear, are to be reckoned with. Probably first among these is the question of the nature, shape, and purpose of theology itself. In one of the clearest statements on the nature and purpose of Christian theology, Cone states that it is "a rational study of the being of God in the world in light of the existential situation of an oppressed community, relating the forces of liberation to the essence of the gospel, which is Jesus Christ." [31] This definition may be taken as representative of the majority of black theologians, although, as we have seen, the theme of reconciliation has also been sounded by some of them. Certain questions arise concerning such a definition, and this writer is not attempting to answer them except by dealing with the implications in the questions themselves. Has black theology in any of its several forms narrowed the scope of the theological enterprise to the single theme of oppression and liberation? Must all theologizing find its footing in the reality of oppression and its purpose that of liberation of those oppressed? Are there not other themes that must be explored, such as God's relation to nature, the problems of genetic engineering, war and peace, or the problems of personal salvation, individual morality, guilt, and death? If the integrity of Christian theology can be placed at the disposal of liberation, can it not also be employed for other far less worthy goals, as it often has been? Must not theology be free to continue to speculate, even when the consequences of speculation are not immediately and recognizably useful to a specific cause? As Peter Berger has commented, "There are important segments of the theological enterprise that are validly irrelevant to the mundane concerns of the times." [32] Can theology be itself if the doctrine of God is treated only in terms of His attributes as judge, liberator, or savior, without reference to God as creator of all men? Can the Bible be honestly interpreted as representing God only as judge of whites and liberator of blacks? Can one pick and choose in the Bible only that which serves the purpose of liberation of blacks, without taking into account the years of careful biblical scholarship that, among other things, shows the universality of God's reign and action? Did not Christ have more than ethnic appeal, and has not Christian theology at its best offered Christ as a universal savior? [33] How many times must Christ be dragooned into the service of some cultural ambition and project? Even Christ as a symbol of a liberator remains a moot image. Whom did he liberate in respect to political, economic, and social structures?

These questions bring us to interpretations of God's nature as suggested above. Whereas white theologians have repeatedly affirmed that God is color-blind, black theologians seem determined to do away with this notion.[34] Some years ago Buell G. Gallagher stated what he regarded as a truism of Christian theology: "The Christian faith is color blind." [35] It follows then that the God to which Christian theology points is Himself color blind. This conviction is based less on the themes of God as judge and redeemer than upon the doctrine of universal creation. The question at stake then becomes: Can white and black theologians come to an understanding on this question? William Jones raises the question most pointedly when he states that theology "cannot proceed as if the goodness of God for *all* mankind were a theological axiom." [36] Another question closely connected with interpretations of God's nature is whether God is the kind of being whose nature does or does not have its own essential character that cannot be disposed of and subjected to human purposes. Thus Major Jones sees black theology searching for what he calls "a usable concept of God." [37] Not only does this statement do scant justice to the integrity and uniqueness of the Deity, it suggests the further question that Cone poses when he suggests that the oppressor and the oppressed do not even mean the same thing when they use the term *God*. He claims that the oppressors' God is a God of slavery, and that the God of the oppressed is one of revolution, one who breaks the chains of slavery.[38] Here, then, the questions for theology center on the nature of Deity, and these promise to be long and difficult of solution, although the task is not hopeless.

Several questions that refer to the atmosphere in which a dialogue may go forward are no less important than the questions already stated. As a high-priority item, it would seem important to pay attention to the language that has been used by some of the potential participants in dialogue. If clarity is necessary for communication, and communication in turn is necessary to understanding, then must not every effort be made to clarify and make consistent the usage of the words discussed at the beginning of this chapter? Must not also strenuous efforts be made to achieve the same ends in respect to the theological language and idioms in which dialogue will become possible? It may be that some terms are fated to be value-charged, but intensity of emotional power is not to be equated with value-weight. Certainly excessive, offensive rhetoric will do little to forward mutual understanding. But it may be at this point that white theology will show its vulnerablity. Can white theology hear the essence of black theology, yet screen out those too shrill voices of passion? Will white theology have the patience, without becoming blasé about these voices, to take the reconciling steps toward critical yet empathetic understanding of the blacks' awareness of their predicament? Can white theology confess its own shortcomings and yet maintain the authentic integrity and universal scope of the Christian Gospel? Can white theology shed the cultural accretions that divert it from its task of the exposition and defense of the Christian faith? Can it do so by understanding afresh doctrines that have been enshrined in certain world views and must now take on newer and deeper tonalities? Can it do these things without the defensiveness of condescending pretentiousness? Can honesty between white and black theologies come into its own? In short, can an atmosphere be produced in which at least its tone and the ground rules are such that the unresolved issues between the discussants may have some hope of resolution?

v

In pointing out some of the problems that lie in the way

of dialogue, I have certainly not covered all that endangers the prospects for an enriched, mutual understanding. Neither can I prophesy that, because dialogue is possible, all controverted issues can be resolved to the satisfaction of all parties. However, the identification of some of the difficulties suggested in the body of the chapter may be a first, tentative step in clearing the path to dialogue. What follows is an even more hazardous undertaking. If I have stressed what divides black and white theology, now I must turn to those grounds wherein what is common to both is briefly stated.

At the outset it is well to affirm that although two common bases may be appealed to, there are differences between blacks and whites that should not be overlooked. The two commonalities are the Christian faith and common humanity, but both have been so distorted for centuries as to give rise to the present tensions between black interpreters and white interpreters.[39] Thus, in proposing Christian faith and common humanity as the irreducible grounds for understanding between blacks and whites, one is stepping on fragile ground, although it should be the firmest of all. Yet both must be appealed to. The essential humanity of the black is one of the final resting places for the black defense. Even Cone asserts that "color is not the essence of man's humanity," a truism that Major J. Jones echoes when he writes "the humanity of man is much deeper than color." [40] All claims to special treatment on the basis of color, black or white, founder on this irreducible insight. As Kyle Haselden put it on behalf of white theology, "So long as we deal with the Negro as Negro, we skirt the central issue of his dignity and right as man." [41] Thus, in entering into dialogue, *humanitas* must not be surrendered to the claims of ethnicity.

Similarly, the appeal to a common Christian faith that affirms the common humanity of all men under God must not be given over, no matter how much it has been besmirched by injustices practiced in its name. There is a measure of agreement that Jesus Christ is central to Christian theology. He has revealed the nature of both man and

God. His kingdom message "strikes at the very center of man's desire to define his own existence in the light of his own existence at the price of his brother's enslavement."[42] The criticism of self-assured pride that is implicit in this teaching aims directly at the tendency to identify too readily one's own or class interest with divine purposes—a doctrine that finds acceptance in both black and white theology. The suffering of mankind or its oppression at human hands, both agree, is not a fit state in which God has placed the human family. Therefore, justice, akin to that affirmed by the Old Testament prophets, remains the unfulfilled goal of the Christian life. But so must there be a love, unsentimental and courageous, central to both motive and act. What one author claims as "justified self interest of the oppressed" may, as "the concrete expression of love in history," be a debatable dictum, but that black and white recognize love as the dynamic and direction of justice is not debatable.[43] The Christian faith has produced many theologians, black and white, and they agree that the use of the mind in biblical studies, upon which much theology depends, must be an essential part of the theological enterprise.[44] Without the critical use of reason, theology is bereft of any intelligible grounds on which to proceed, in the development of either biblical studies or theological doctrine. And certainly both white and black theologians agree with Roberts, as cited above, that the aim of theology is "to lead both blacks and whites to an authentic Christian existence."[45]

Of course such grounds of agreement as these must yet be worked through in the light of those aspects of the black experience which bear upon them. But it is a sign of hope that representative black theologians are already in dialogue with white theologians in seminaries. They have both been trained in the tools of theological and ethical speculation, and although their perspectives may differ, conversations and writings show that their differences do not hinder intelligible communication. Some courses in black theology have been offered in colleges where white and black faculty and students may come to closer understanding of the agreements and disagreements that infect such dialogues. The fissure in theology may yet be healed, not simply by dialogue, however, but by the action to which dialogue should properly lead.

NOTES TO CHAPTER 7

1. Although I do not accept the notion of *white theology* in the pejorative sense defined by some black theologians, I use the term to distinguish theology emanating from white thinkers from that offered by their black counterparts.

2. William Jones, "Toward an Interim Assessment of Black Theology," *The Christian Century*, May 3, 1972.

3. James H. Cone, *Black Theology and Black Power* (New York: Seabury Press, 1969), p. 150.

4. Ibid., p. 151.

5. Ibid., p. 148. The ambiguity of the word *color* is evident in this quotation.

6. Pierre L. Von den Berghe, "Academic Apartheid," *World View*, October 1972, p. 27. Radical white thinkers have also come to accept the idea that racism is to be understood primarily in institutional or social rather than personal terms. Thus Robert W. Terry, in an address to the American Society of Christian Ethics (Bergame Center, Dayton, Ohio, January 22, 1972), defines racism as "any societal activity in which one goup/society treats another group unjustly because of color/race and rationalizes that activity by ascribing undesirable biological, psychological, social, and/or cultural characteristics to the unjustly treated group." By the same token, Terry argues that talk of "black racism" only obfuscates race relations because power remains in the hands of whites. I know of no white theology that fits Terry's definition.

7. Major J. Jones, *Black Awareness: A Theology of Hope* (Nashville and New York: Abingdon Press, 1971), p. 138.

8. Claude Welch, *Protestant Thought in the Nineteenth Century, 1799–1870* (New Haven and London: Yale University Press) 1:21. Cf. H. Richard Niebuhr, *The Meaning of Revelation* (New York: Macmillan Co.), 1941, pp. 12, 21.

9. See Cone, *Black Theology and Black Power*, pp. 31, 121, 151.

10. Cone, *A Black Theology of Liberation* (Philadelphia and New York: J. B. Lippincott, 1970), pp. 11, 22–24.

11. Ibid., pp. 53ff., 65, 80, 91.

12. Ibid., pp. 111, 131–32. However, note Major J. Jones's comment on the idea of God in black theology. He observes that God is not the guaran-

tor of the status quo, but neither should God be interpreted as "the avenging God of the offdended," of which, he says, too much has been heard in black theology (M. J. Jones, *Black Awareness*, p. 119).

13. Cone, *A Black Theology of Liberation*, pp. 214, 218.

14. M. J. Jones, *Black Awareness*, pp. 114, 116, 119.

15. J. Deotis Roberts, *Liberation and Reconciliation: A Black Theology* (Philadelphia: Westminster Press, 1971), pp. 13, 14. Cone refers to reconciliation also, but slants it toward the becoming black of whites. See Cone, *Black Theology and Black Power*, p. 151.

16. Roberts, *Liberation and Reconciliation*, pp. 19, 24, 139.

17. W. Jones, in *Christian Century*.

18. W. Jones, "Theodicy and Methodology in Black Theology: A Critique of Washington, Cone and Cleage," *Harvard Theological Review* 64, no. 4 (1971): 541–44 ff., 549 ff., 553 ff.

19. Ibid., p. 543; see also W. Jones, in *Christian Century*. It is interesting that so-called white theologians are seldom mentioned by name.

20. These references can be found in Cone, *Black Theology and Black Power*, pp. 31, 43, 55, 83; and Cone, *A Black Theology of Liberation*, pp. 28–29, 114, 119.

21. M. J. Jones, *Black Awareness*, pp. 89, 92.

22. J. D. Roberts, Sr., "The Quest for Black Theology," *Quest for a Black Theology*, ed. James J. Gardiner and J. D. Roberts, Sr. (Philadelphia: Pilgrim Press, 1971), p. 65.

23. Rogers Cornish, "Oppressors and Oppressed: Theological Impasse," *Christian Century* 90, no. 21 (May 23, 1973): 588–89.

24. Cf. "The fact that I am black is my ultimate reality. . . . It is impossible for me to surrender this basic reality for a higher, more universal reality" (Cone, *Black Theology and Black Power*, pp. 32–33; see also pp. 15–16). "It is the task of the Christian theologian to do theology in the light of the concreteness of human oppression as expressed in color, and to interpret for the oppressed the meaning of God's liberation in their community" (Cone, *A Black Theology of Liberation*, p. 12; see also p. 27).

25. Cone, *A Black Thealogy of Liberation*, p. 26.

26. Cone, *Black Theology and Black Power*, p. 15.

27. Roberts, *Liberation and Reconciliation*, pp. 15–16; see also M. J. Jones, *Black Awareness*, p. 96.

28. So Cone, when he writes that in an extreme situation "we will take some honkies with us" (*A Black Theology of Liberation*, p. 42).

29. Verne H. Fletcher, "Social Change and Christian Ethics," *Theology Today* 29, no. 4 (January 1973): 388.

30. See Preston N. Williams, "The Price of Social Justice," *Christian Century* 90, no. 19 (1973): 529–33.

31. Cone, *A Black Theology of Liberation*, p. 17; see also pp. 20, 22.

32. Peter Berger, "On Not Exactly Reaping the Whirlwind," *Christian Century* 90, no. 4: 96.

33. Cf. "Jesus is not for all" (Cone, *A Black Theology of Liberation,* p. 25).

34. "In a racist society, God is never color blind" (Ibid., p. 25). God has made "an unqualified identification with black people (idem, p. 26). Terry claims that "color blind policies are racist. They perpetuate white power and privilege by passivity." See n6 above.

35. Buell G. Gallagher, *Color and Conscience* (New York: Harper and Brothers, 1946), p. 9. See also "The clear consensus of Christian theology is to affirm the doctrine of the unity and equality of social life in creation" (Waldo Beach, *Faith and Ethics* [New York: Harper and Brothers, 1957], p. 209).

36. W. Jones, "Theodicy and Methodology," p. 543.

37. M. J. Jones, *Black Awareness,* p. 123. Cf. Cone's interpretation of the symbol *God*: "If the symbol loses its power to point to the meaning of black liberation, then we must destroy it" (Cone, *A Black Theology of Liberation,* p. 111).

38. Cone, *A Black Theology of Liberation,* p. 112.

39. Terry, "The popular appeal to our common humanity is one of the most frequently used ploys to avoid the significance of whiteness", 16. "Asserting common religious heritage, especially Christian, as the basis for black/white unity is another way to avoid whiteness." See n6 above.

40. Cone, *Black Theology and Black Power,* p. 17. M. J. Jones, *Black Awareness,* p. 116.

41. Kyle Haselden, *The Racial Problem in Christian Perspective* (New York: Harper and Brothers, 1959), p. 168. Haselden used the term *Negro* before the more common contemporary usage of the term *black* had appeared.

42. Cone, *Black Theology and Black Power,* pp. 35–36.

43. Fletcher, "Social Change and Christian Ethics," p. 390.

44. See Cone, *A Black Theology of Liberation,* p. 212; Roberts, *Liberation and Reconciliation,* p. 57; Miles Jones, "Toward a Theology of Black Experience," *The Christian Century* 87, no. 37 (1970): 1090.

45. Roberts, *Liberation and Reconciliation,* p. 24.

8

The Case for Black Humanism

WILLIAM R. JONES

I APOLOGETICS OR THEOLOGICAL CONSTRUCTION

There are several ways to execute the assignment that is implied in the topic. On the one hand, the topic calls for the formulation of a systematic theology from an humanist [1] perspective. This reduces to an exercise in theological construction. On the other hand, the topic demands that I justify the possibility, the necessity, and the value of theologizing from a humanist viewpoint, and this reduces to an apologetic enterprise. No doubt the best apologetic in this context is the successful construction of a humanist theology, but for various reasons the approach of this essay must adopt the apologetic model.

Factors more crucial, however, dictate that the apologetic assignment must precede the constructive undertaking, and these relate to some commonly held, but questionable, presuppositions about the nature of theology, humanism, and black religion. More specifically, it appears that the current black theologians want to restrict the title of black theologian to theists and members of black Christian denominations.

Accordingly, the humanist theologian encounters several problems that his theist counterpart can avoid (this is even more pronounced if the humanist theologian is also black). At the outset, the humanist theologian must legitimate his perspective and approach as a *theological* enterprise. Other theologians may be pressured to validate the Christian character of their work, but their membership in the theological fraternity is not questioned. The response to the death-of-God theologians is a case in point. Though many types of humanism do not require the premise of God's death or nonexistence, they are not received into the theological community as the death-of-God theologians have been. It would appear that the different response to the death-of-God theologian and humanist theologian results because a strictly etymological definition of theology is operative. Consider, for instance, John Macquarrie's description of the boundaries of theology, where an etymological definition segregates theology from other disciplines in religion.

> Let us be quite clear at the outset that if anyone wants to construct a theology without God, he is pursuing a self-contradictory notion and is confusing both himself and other people. He may construct a philosophy of religion (and he may even do this brilliantly), or he may construct a doctrine of man (anthropology) or a doctrine of Jesus (Jesusology) or an ethic or a mixture of all of these, but whatever results from his endeavors, it will not be a theology.[2]

In addition to the objection of a John Macquarrie, the humanist theologian must also respond to the charge of a Charles Hartshorne, who affirms that humanism is a defective religion and incapable of supporting the minimal requirement of the religious life. "If religion, or any satisfactory philosophy of life, has as its goal the integration of the personality ('salvation'), then humanism is a very partial and inadequate religion. No matter from what angle the question is viewed, integration by humanism will show itself incomplete and unsatisfactory."[3]

But the most serious challenge to the black humanist theologian issues from the black theist theologians. They hurl the same charges advanced by Macquarrie and Hartshorne, but with a decidedly different force and sting. When the black theologians raise the issue of the religious and theological authenticity of humanism, the issue merges inevitably into another question: Is humanism alien to black religion? Joseph Washington asked in another context, "How Black is Black Religion?" [4] This, for him, is another way of asking: Is black religion authentically black or is it white religion in blackface?

The black humanist faces a similar interrogative: How black is humanism? And the black theologians insist that he must respond by establishing that humanism is rooted in the black *church* if he is to receive his theological credentials. The arrogant test of the black theologians here would seem to require that an orthodox rabbi be graduated from a Dominican seminary to be certified. This view must be challenged.

Clearly the black humanist is engaged in something other than a friendly debate when he throws his religious views into the black theological circle. Nevertheless, this is the agenda I must address here: to justify humanism as an authentic expression of black religion, to develop a concept of religion and theology that accommodates humanism, and to validate that a framework that is closer to the humanist pole of the theological spectrum is viable, if not required, for a black theology that defines itself as a theology of liberation.

II Humanism: Saint or Subversive?

One might think that a nontheist model for a theology of liberation would be highly attractive for contemporary blacks. It is generally agreed that white Christianity has in the main hindered the cause of black liberation. Nor does black Christianity have an unblemished record as a liberating agent. Therefore, because of the failure of white Christianity and because of the checkered success of black Christianity, it seems only reasonable to consider as candidate models for black-liberation theology other forms of theism or nontheism, if only to supplement black Christianity. A quick glance at the extant black theologies [5] presents a bleak picture for the black humanist, however. There are yet no acknowledged points of entry for his perspective, as theology, into the theological arena. The available black theologies constitute a rigid monolithic theism, and it is a theism of a specific variety. Each is a representative of Western biblical theism; each is mainline Protestant. To state the obvious, each spokesman is a black, Christian, Protestant theologian. It is worth noting that none has yet returned to indigenous African sources for his primary theological materials. To speak of a monolithic theism is not to disregard the real differences between Cone and Roberts, for instance; but they are of one voice in affirming theism to be normative.

If one emphasizes the fact that black theology is still a relatively new discipline, the prospects brighten for black humanism's acceptance as an essential part of black theology. Black theology has not been around long enough to spawn the theological pluralism that informs other traditions. With this understanding of the status of black theology, one would expect that its present theological monolithism would blossom into theological pluralism as it grows and matures.

The prodigious obstacle to black humanism that I perceive is, however, not temporal but theological. The evolutionary development of black theology will not guarantee a niche for black humanism. Rather, a radical shift in theological perspective must occur before humanism is admitted into the black theological circle.

I will now examine in detail the presuppositions that control the extant black theologies and thereby blackball humanism from the theological fraternity.

Major Jones epitomizes the theological monolithism I have in mind when he admonishes blacks not to "ignore the basic tenets of the Judeo-Christian faith. To do so would be merely to establish a folk religion that would not survive the test of history . . . and the black man will have lost the God who brought him over so many difficult places in the past." [6] Several claims that merit consideration are packed into this statement. Note the conclusion that only the Judeo-Christian perspective can provide a sound foundation for black religion; only biblical faith will "survive the test of history." From a pragmatic standpoint, anything else is futile.

A second presupposition demands equal attention, namely, that the God of Christian faith has been the black man's agent of salvation in the past. This conviction also has a pragmatic ring. What Major Jones is arguing is that black liberation will become a reality only through the activity of the God of our past. Thus the success of black liberation demands that we blacks make and maintain umbilical contact with the God of our fathers.

A similar spirit informs the thought of other black religionists who describe blacks as a religious or spiritual people. When one unpacks the meaning of *black spirituality*, it invariably collapses into a password for black theism. To say that blacks are a spiritual people means ultimately that they believe in and worship God, in particular the God of the Judeo-Christian faith.

Clearly this equation of authentic religion and Christian theism forces a theological straitjacket on black humanism at the outset.

A third presupposition segregates humanism from the black theological circle. All of the extant black theologies advance the thesis that the black church is to be the incomparable vanguard of black liberation. Joseph Washington has described this ecclesiological strategy as "The Politics of God." Reduced to its essentials, this category means that black liberation requires the creation of effective and community-based power structures in the black community to operate as agents of change at the political and economic frontiers. The black church, according to this strategy, is the logical and most promising institution to form this power base. "Negro churches are the only natural communities universal enough to command the loyalty and respect of the majority of the Negro masses. They alone are so extensive as to form unity in political power." [7] Add to this the conviction that the black church is "the institutional center" and "the dominant social institution" [8] of the black community, that the black church came into being as a vehicle for freedom and equality, that it is the single institution that is indigenous to blacks and owned and controlled by them, and the rationale is established for the church as the avantgarde of black liberation.

The connection between this ecclesiological strategy for the black church and the theological status of humanism may be obscure, but clearly this view of the church's status and mission automatically creates certain limits to what is theologically permissible. Theological continuity must be maintained between the masses in the pews and the black ministers engaged in the politics of God, at least at the level of rhetoric and symbolism. A program of black liberation based on the black church as the avant-garde cannot succeed if the theology from the pulpit is abrasive to its hearers.

At this point the second presupposition assumes control. Since blacks are inherently religious—substitute here *theists* —the "alien" perspective of humanism will only subvert the theological consensus that is the foundation for communal unity. Thus the black humanist finds his blackness under attack on two counts. Given the equation of black religion and theism, black humanism is an apostate who desecrates the heritage of his forefathers and blasphemes the sacred memory of all the black saints gone to glory. Given the understanding of the black church as the vanguard of black liberation, the black humanist is a stubborn obstacle to group unity and, thereby, black liberation. Politically speaking, black humanism is acutely counterrevolutionary.

Ins spite of these arguments, persuasive though they appear to be, the theistic monolithism of black theology must be challenged, and primarily for the same reason that

black theologians excommunicate humanism—the demands
of black liberation. Let it be clear at the outset that the
agenda of black humanism does not involve the destruction
of the black church. Neither does it value a wholesale deni-
gration of the black church, past or present. Nor is it concerned with denying the enormous potential of the black
church for the future cause of black liberation.

All that black humanism seeks is the admission that the
strategy of the black church as vanguard is based on the
potential of the black church as a liberating agent. The
black church, as Washington acknowledges, may be "the
natural" but is not yet "the real center" [9] of power in the
black community. Cone also confesses that the black church
has not always made liberation its reason for being. Rather,
the more secular agents of liberation—NAACP, the Urban
League, Core, and SNCC—"were created because of the
failure of the black church to plead the cause of black
people. . . . The current civil rights protest organizations,"
in sum, "are visible manifestations of the apostasy of the
black church" [10] from its divinely ordained mission to liberate
the oppressed.

Because the black church's history, as Cone and others
have indicated, is checkered relative to liberation, black
humanism wants to avoid the "all-the-eggs-in-one-basket"
strategy implied in the black church as avant-garde. The
enormous potential of the black church has been appropriately captured in its description as "a sleeping giant." [11]
Black humanism, however, thinks that it is unwise for the
fate of black liberation to depend upon whether the black
church awakens from its slumber or continues to snore, however piously and rhythmically. In this connection, the possibility must also be entertained that the emergence of black
humanism as a formidable opponent may successfully prod
the black church, as other secular movements have done,
"to be about its father's work."

Black humanism would also accent the fact that the
black church has never corralled the majority of blacks into
its pews. This is not to negate its real influence beyond its

altars and sanctuary walls. Nor should it be concluded that the unchurched are less religious than their church cousins. There appears to be a growing number of so-called secular blacks who find the theology of the black church hard to digest, and this unchurched flock can hardly be neglected if black liberation is to succeed.

The black church and black theology have not collided with the pervasive phenomenon of secularity; some affirm that the encounter need not and ought not to occur. One wonders, however, if the meeting and necessary dialogue can be delayed much longer. Secularism does not make *homo religiosus* extinct, but it does make problematical the traditional pillars of black theistic religion. And it does elevate some of the central themes of humanism to first rank.

The black church faces an agonizing dilemma in its quest to unify the black community by forging links with these prodigal sons. How can it capture this unchurched herd without sacrificing the symbols and the more fundamentalist theology that enchant the people in the pews and keep them loyal worshipers? Should the black church hunt for the bird in the bush or tightly clutch those already in hand? No matter how the dilemma is viewed, the imagination that pictures the black church as the organic center of the black community is teasingly utopian.

Black humanism seeks its constituency from this large unchurched group, this secular "congregation" that appears to be multiplying rapidly. Accordingly, black humanism should not be regarded as a replacement for the black church, but as its necessary complement for black liberation.

III HUMANISM: SON OR STRANGER?

Once the black humanist acknowledges his debt to the black church, honors its past labors in the cause of black freedom, but respectfully declines to further its theistic claims, he must address the charge that his position is alien to the black religious perspective. Behind the charge that black humanism is alien to black religion lies an insidious equation that must be exposed for critical examination: the equation of black *religion* and black *theism.* This shibboleth must be openly attacked in order to obtain a more accurate understanding of religion in general and black religion in particular.

It is often necessary for me to remind my colleagues in The Society for the Study of Black Religion that it is not The Society for the Study of Black *Theism.* Black religion cannot be reduced to black theism, nor can the chronicle of the black church encompass the full sweep of black religion in America. For this reason the following analysis of J. Deotis Roberts must be criticized.

> The question of existence in reference to God is not the real issue for blacks. This does not preclude the fact that many blacks are nonbelievers. This is often true of "cultured despisers" of Christianity, black intellectuals who equate status with a militant rejection of the Christian faith. . . . It is characteristic of many older black intellectuals who are humanistically oriented and are greatly influenced by the position of Auguste Comte. Add to this the lack of exposure to religious scholarship . . . the sentimental Jesusology of an ill-informed magico-religious upbringing, and one begins to understand why in their intellectual maturity, they have found their "God too small" and their religion inadequate. But the return to religion, often as blind faith in middle life, together with the spiritual strivings of their children, leads me to believe that religion is native to most blacks. Religion in some form or other appears to be an Africanism.[12]

Several points here merit special comment. First it should be noted that the final sentences make no sense without the equation of religion and theism. It is also characteristic of Christian despisers of black humanism that they invariably trace its roots to nonblack sources—here Comte. If this is an accurate description of the genesis of black humanism, the charge of alienation truly gains considerable support.

However, the error of this reading of black humanism is implicitly affirmed by some of the black theologians themselves, for they are forced to acknowledge the presence of a nontheistic strain in black religion. In this connection, one can cite Benjamin Mays's classic study, *The Negro God.* To provide a comprehensive picture of the Afro-American's "God-talk," he includes a chapter entitled "Ideas of God Involving Frustration, Doubt, God's Impotence and his Non-existence." The humanist element in these materials is easily identified.

James Cone's most recent work, *The Spirituals and the Blues,* tacitly admits the presence of a religious perspective among blacks that is not, to use his term, *God-centered.*[13] He cites the slave seculars, the nontheist counterpart of the slave spirituals, and the blues as examples of a tradition with a religious dimension outside the black church and black theism.

Admittedly, this nontheist tradition is a minority view-point in black religion, but it nonetheless establishes a firm link between black humanism and the black religious past. Black humanism need not draw upon traditions that are alien to the totality of the black religious experience. Human-ism is a legitimate part of black religion, though obviously not of the black church tradition. In this connection, Mays has correctly noted that black humanism has not developed primarily as a result of the studies of modern science—and one could also add positivism—or from a conviction about the cruelty and indifference of nature, but "because in the social situation, [it] finds [itself] hampered and restricted." [14] Mays's point is that black humanism emerges not from Comte, but from wrestling with the horror of black oppres-sion and the crimes of human history where blacks are the unwitting victim. Black humanism is not estranged from black theism because humanism is alien to black thought. Rather, the theist rationale for black suffering and oppression is thoroughly unconvincing. Indeed, I have argued that the black theologians' treatment of black suffering forces us to ask: Is God a white racist? [15]

The black humanist must also question the normative apparatus that decides the value of a theological perspective by gauging its conformity to the beliefs of past generations of blacks, especially if that past is narrowed to the black church. Continuity with the theological tradition of our forefathers is not the critical factor if one purports to formulate a theology of liberation. Because the overriding purpose of a theology of liberation is to exterminate oppression, it is obliged to establish certain guidelines and patterns that will take priority in theological construction. The theologian of liberation, for instance, must identify those tyrannical beliefs and attitudes, such as quietism, which smother the impulse toward liberation. Only after these inauthentic elements of the tradition have been isolated, sterilized, or neutralized, can the theologian of liberation entertain conformity to that tradition. Otherwise, he runs the risk of unknowingly endorsing and perpetuating ideas and concepts that undergird oppression and, consequently, contradict his explicit purpose.

The same point can be made from another perspective. Because black religionists are convinced that traditional interpretations of Christian faith are infected with the cancer of racism, again a thorough examination of both white and black Christianity must precede any advice to ally oneself with that tradition. Once the virus of racism or oppression is detected, the entire tradition must be quarantined, and each part forced to certify that its racist or oppressive quotient is immunized.

Black humanism contends that to emphasize allegiance to either black or white Christianity *prior* to a root-and-branch examination of both is to beg the question about the liberating character of each. First, we must know with some clarity where white Christianity ends and black Christianity begins. Moreover, God, the heart of black theism, has not been sufficiently cross-examined to determine the nature of His responsibility for black oppression. Black humanism asks whether making God's intrinsic justice and benevolence the cornerstone of black faith is a perpetuation of white Christianity. Black humanism suspects that blacks' convictions about God, especially His intrinsic goodness and justice, and traditional explanations of black suffering may be part and parcel of black oppression. In sum, blacks today should be asked to conform only to those aspects of the tradition whose proliberation impact has been clearly established.

Indeed, it is necessary to ask: Is this not in fact the operational methodology of the extant black theologians? It seems that they do not simply read off their theologies from the diaries of their forefathers. Black theology, at least in practice, has not been the recording of "a latent, unwritten Black Theology." Rather, a conscious process of selection and rejection is clearly evident in their approach to black Christianity. Certain of its features, for example, a "pie-in-the-sky eschatology," have been summarily dismissed because of their quietist implications. It can also be argued that such an approach to the tradition has been taken simply to affirm the freedom of man that Cone insists must be exercised relative to the deeds and words of Jesus himself.

> We cannot solve ethical questions of the twentieth century by looking at what Jesus did in the first. Our choices are not the same as his. Being Christian does not mean following "in his footsteps. . . ." His steps are not ours; and thus we are placed in an existential situation in which we are forced to decide without knowing what Jesus would do. . . . Each situation has its own problematic circumstances which force the believer to think through each act of obedience without an absolute ethical guide from Jesus. To look for such a guide is to deny the freedom of the Christian man.[16]

To affirm the freedom of man in this manner is not creeping idolatry; in fact, humanism would affirm that choosing without absolute guides is the given condition of humankind. Actually, I am guilty of a greater idolatry if I presuppose the intrinsic truth and demonstrated value of the tradition. Once racist and oppressive elements are uncovered, the greater idolatry is not to subject every jot and tittle of that tradition to the most unsparing cross-examination.

It can also be argued that I am convicted of idolatry if I do not bestow coequally both revelatory truth and theological significance on my own perspective. To assign to another human perspective, be it black or white, absolute or definitive importance is to confine God's revelation to a particular human context. The black theologian will inevitably tumble into inconsistency if, on the one hand, he denies absolute status to white God-talk on the grounds of the particularity of God's revelation, but in the next breath, leases absolute merit to a black past.

I cannot conclude this discussion of alienation without noting the harsh and unappreciative response of segments of the black church to black theology itself. The charge that black humanism is a prodigal son must be considered alongside the charge of a prominent black denominational leader, who regards black theology as racist and not suitable as a part of seminary training.

IV HUMANISM AND THEOLOGY: SOME SEMANTIC PROBLEMS

I have postponed until now a discussion of the possibility of a humanist theology. Two crucial questions constitute this issue: Is humanism an authentic *religious* perspective? If so, what does this entail for an understanding of the activity of theology?

The first question obliges the black humanist to formulate a definition of religion that can accommodate humanism. Of course, it is always possible in a situation of this type to advance a stipulative definition that establishes a niche for own's own pet position. But such a strategy is obviously a self-serving method. The humanist's position is strengthened if he can show that a more general analysis of religion incorporates his perspective. I suggest that the concept of *religion as soteriology* captures the essence of religion and furnishes room for the humanist position as well.

Religion, I contend, reduces ultimately to a way of salvation. Its basic purpose is soteriological: "to convince men that they need salvation and then to offer them a way to achieve it." [17] In this sense, religion is like the medical enterprise: its activity is always preventive or corrective. That is to say, the raison d'être for religion is the conviction that something is radically wrong with man; something essential to man or to his condition must be replaced or supplemented, or special precautions must be taken to prevent the occurrence of the unwanted condition that demands correction.

Religion differs from other preventive and corrective activities in that it advances its specific program as a matter of *ultimate concern,* necessary not merely for man's good, but for man's *highest* good. The religious enterprise, in short, is placed at the core of the ideal, what ought to be. Not to receive the enriching fruits of the religious life is to place man in jeopardy.

Put in other terms, salvation is defined as the ideal, the proper relation between (a) man and ultimate reality and/or (b) man and his fellowmen. Salvation can also be described as man in possession of his summum bonum. Obviously, how the proper relation is delineated and what the procedure is for reaching it will depend on the particular religion being analyzed.

It should be noted that this analysis of religion employs the category of ultimate reality instead of God; this is done to avoid a question-begging point of departure. The inner logic of Western monotheism makes God and ultimate reality one and the same, but other religions do not establish the same ontological equivalence. Buddhism, for instance, is often described as atheistic, because it does not have a prominent concept of *God;* although there is a vibrant doctrine of *ultimate reality.* Lucretius's ontology is another case in point. Gods are included as part of the metaphysical scaffolding, but the gods are not ultimate reality. This, for Lucretius, is reserved for the atoms and the void.

In summary: I submit that soteriology, not belief in God, is the sufficient and necessary condition for religion, and humanism easily fits under the umbrella of religion as soteriology.

With this understanding as background, I can now examine the category of theology. To make this understandable, it is necessary to call attention to an implication of religion as soteriology. Each religion emphasizes a (or more than one) specific *soteriological singular*(s), that is, that about which one must have accurate and adequate information and to which one must properly relate himself if the summum bonum is to be realized. For Western theism, God, *theos*, is the soteriological singular. Thus, God is crucial precisely because of his soteriological significance. In this sense, theology becomes a subclass of soteriology. The function of theology is to describe, reflect upon, draw implications from, and systematize information about the soteriological singular. Nontheist religions would obviously have a (or more than one) different soteriological singular(s), but the explication, analysis, and/or "talk" about the latter are functionally the same as theology.

The humanist faces an acute problem in semantics at this juncture. What is the appropriate term to identify the study of his soteriological singular; is it *anthropos?* If he follows the line of the theist and speaks of anthropology as the humanist equivalent of theology, the entire soteriological factor is lost. In speaking of himself as an anthropologist, a humanist would identify himself as a scientist rather than a religionist. Nor does philosophy of religion supply the necessary clarity, for it also does not connote the centrality of the soteriological component.

I can only point to the problem at this juncture. A term is needed to describe someone who advances a precise soteriological system without making God the soteriological singular. Should one burden the category of theology to encompass this position, which the strict etymology of the term *theology* negates? Or should we coin a new term, such as *anthropologian*, to describe the humanist theologian?

v The Coming Debate

In this concluding section the concern is to identify for discussion and for debate additional topics that bear on the issue of the possibility and character of a humanist theology.

These are issues that I have discussed elsewhere or that require separate and detailed treatment.

The first obligation of the humanist theologian is to nominate the prescriptive principle(s) of his variety of humanism. That principle for me is *the functional ultimacy of man*. This is another way of describing Protagoras's epigram, "Man is the measure of all things," and Kierkegaard's principle of truth as subjectivity. Humanism tends to affirm the functional ultimacy of man relative to values, history, and/or soteriology. This principle, I contend, is not absent from theism, though its import is limited to the sphere of values and/or history. For instance, Cone's analysis of the freedom of the Christian man relative to the ethical authority of Jesus' words and deeds presupposes the functional ultimacy of man. I have also isolated a variety of theism, which I term *humanocentric theism*, where the principle is elevated to a central position.[18]

The next item on the agenda of the humanist theologian is to demonstrate that the prescriptive principle of humanism is utilized by the extant black theologians. I submit that an analysis of their actual, in contrast to their stated, concept of authority will confirm this point.

Another line of analysis would show that the black theologians will be pushed toward the humanist pole of the spectrum as they are required to deal with some inescapable problems, most of which are raised by positions they have already adopted. I have argued that black theologians' own principles make theodicy the controlling category for theology, and that their resolution of the theodicy question, in light of their claims that theirs is a theology of liberation, will necessitate the adoption of the prescriptive principle of humanism.[19] The encounter of black theology and secularism, I suggest, will produce the identical theological movement.

Humanism, from my vantage, points to a verity that black religion, especially if it is to be a liberating agent, cannot escape. Whether the religious insights of humanism are accurate can be decided only when a black humanist theology takes its place alongside the now familiar texts in black theology. For the self-understanding of both black theism and black humanism, I trust that that day will soon dawn.

NOTES TO CHAPTER 8

1. This essay does not advance a precise definition of humanism; the determination of the defining properties of humanism requires further analysis and debate. It is the general meaning of secular humanism—in contrast to Christian humanism—that is intended.

2. John Macquarrie, *New Directions in Theology Today, Volume III, God and Secularity* (Philadelphia: The Westminster Press, 1967), p. 13.

3. This is the essential thread of his argument in Charles Hartshorne, *Beyond Humanism* (Lincoln: University of Nebraska Press, 1968), p. 12.

4. This is the title of an essay in James J. Gardiner and J. Deotis Roberts, eds., *Quest for a Black Theology* (Philadelphia: Pilgrim Press, 1971).

5. When I speak of black theologians I have in mind Albert Cleage, James Cone, Major Jones, J. Deotis Roberts, and Joseph Washington.

6. Major Jones, *Black Awareness: A Theology of Hope* (Nashville and New York: Abingdon Press, 1971), p. 118.

7. Joseph Washington, *The Politics of God* (Boston: Beacon Press, 1967), p. 201.

8. Ibid., p. 207.

9. Ibid., p. 193.

10. James Cone, *Black Theology and Black Power* (New York: Seabury Press, 1969), p. 110.

11. I am indebted for this graphic description to Lucius M. Tobin of Benedict College.

12. J. Deotis Roberts, *Liberation and Reconciliation: A Black Theology* (Philadelphia: Westminster Press, 1971), p. 82.

13. James Cone, *The Spirituals and the Blues* (New York: Seabury Press, 1972), p. 108.

14. Benjamin Mays, *The Negro's God as Reflected in His Literature* (New York: Atheneum, 1968), p. 255.

15. William R. Jones, *Is God a White Racist? A Preamble to Black Theology* (New York: Doubleday, 1973).

16. Cone, *Black Theology and Black Power*, pp. 139–40.

17. Winston King, *Introduction To Religion* (New York: Harper & Row, 1954), p. 286.

18. W. Jones, *Is God a White Racist?*, pt. 3.

19. William R. Jones, "Theodicy: The Controlling Category for Black Theology," *Journal of Religious Thought* (Summer 1973).

9

Liberation Theism

J. DEOTIS ROBERTS, SR.

Provisional definitions of *liberation* and *theism* are essential to this discussion. *Liberation* is now closely associated with a new consciousness that has arisen during the postcolonial period in the Third World. Black liberation is often viewed in the broader context of Pan-Africanism as a bold program of human liberation. *Liberation* is tied to a rapid, even a revolutionary social transformation. The setting free of the oppressed from various types of bondage is usually meant when the word is used.

Theism is related to an understanding of the god-idea. *Theism* can be treated in several ways, and philosophical as well as theological treatments of *theism* are common. Any treatment of theism should have a concern for a god as an "idea," if not as a personal reality. Theism may emerge from reflection upon a metaphysical or ethical ultimate just as it may develop in the context of revelation to faith. It may be manifest in *deism, polytheism, pantheism, monotheism, panentheism,* and in other such word combinations. In all cases, *theos* or *deus* is implied as the root word. That is to say, some personal or abstract understanding of a god in singular or plural form is implied. Whether we are concerned with atheism or deism, the key concept is "god." Without a god-idea, theism is not present. God is the presupposition of philosophical theism and the faith-claim of theological theism. My own position is somewhere between monotheism and panentheism in my understanding of God. I choose to stand in a theological circle that affirms faith in the God of the Bible Who is revealed supremely in the Incarnation. This is a convictional and not an evaluative statement vis-à-vis other expressions of theism or nontheism.

Among representative black theologians, one finds the Christocentric theism of James Cone, the humanocentric theism of William Jones, and the mediating theism of J. Deotis Roberts, Sr. The word *mediating* is being used here to describe my position, which is somewhat midway between Cone and Jones and, though independent and distinctive, bridges basic differences between them. In Jones one finds a religion of reason exalting the functional ultimacy of man for his own liberation. In Cone one encounters a leap of faith that places great weight upon God's commands and promises and has little to say about human ability and responsibility in bringing about the liberation of the oppressed.

I would like here to indicate how reason and revelation, faith and works, are united. These merge, not as men turn down God, but rather, as they discover "the human face of God," and when they encounter God's liberating work in their midst and join Him. Is it not possible to see God as concerned about human liberation without denying His transcendence and omnipotence? Is it necessary to minimize God in order to accept the dignity of what is human? The deification of man is as serious a problem as the "iconization" of God. Man without God is unable to save himself or redeem the social order. Man standing *before* God and laboring *with* God is ennobled and empowered to do the good and be a co-laborer in the greater humanization of man. Man, in relation to God and through His grace, is allowed to be a co-creator and co-laborer with God.

I The Point of View

What William Jones calls humanocentric theism seems limited to a select few among blacks in the middle class, many of whom cannot handle the razor-sharp logic in Jones's position. They have a rather affective grasp of a world view or a religious affirmation. Jones does not make contact with the mass religious or secular movements in the black community. He is *too* rational, and he presents a religion without revelation. Most mass movements are highly emotional and are often theocentric, though not necessarily Christian. William Jones's critique of existent programs in black theology does not radically change the present omissions in black theology. What is needed is an open door to non-Christian movements involved in black liberation, on the one hand, while on the other hand, what is needed is a way of entering into meaningful conversation with African traditional religionists as a part of blacks' quest for their Afro-American religious roots.*

What William Jones has set out to do is address a highly select group of black people who are secular in outlook, who are optimistic about man's self-sufficiency, and who are capable of serious abstract thought. He provides a program of philosophical reflection on the black religious experience. His is a philosophy of religion in "black perspective." Only when the God question becomes a matter of revelation to faith as well as an axiom of religion is there a theological concern for theism.

References to non-Western religions without a god-idea—like Theravada Buddhism, classical Confucianism, or those religions of the ancient Greeks—do not seriously alter the case. One can, of course, find all sorts of germinal concepts among the Greeks, depending on the men and periods being examined. The roots of religion, theism, humanism, and ethics were all explored by the Greeks.

The study of black religion must be pluralistic, allowing for programs in philosophy of religion as well as theology proper. William Jones is a philosopher of religion who is in

* Cf. the essays by Mitchell and Thomas in this volume.

conversation with black theologians on common concerns. He is alone, both in his perspective as a scholar and in the religious community he represents. This makes his contribution most valuable. It is not essential that he be called a "black theologian," or that his program be designated as "black theology." At the moment he wavers between a secular humanism and what he calls humanocentric theism. *Theology* does have a special meaning, whatever the character of the experience being reflected upon. *Theism* can be treated philosophically without reference to the community of faith or its faith-claims. *Theology* refers to reflection upon the faith of a believing community. When the term *theology* is used, there is not only the idea of God, there is faith in the God believed in. This is true whether we speak of Judaism, Islam, or Christianity. There is a need to distinguish between a black Jewish theology over against a black Christian theology. A black Protestant theology differs from a black Roman Catholic theology. My understanding of what William Jones provides is in the nature of black religious thought rather than a black theology.

A black theology may be biblical or philosophical as well as systematic. The biblical and philosophical theologies-in-black will still require that the idea of God center in faith in the revelation of God. More specifically, black theologians will need to decide first of all whether they are "church" theologians. If they are, it will be necessary for them to take very seriously the Bible, the tradition, and the total revelation of God as Christians have understood that concept. There will develop clearly a black Christian theology that will have its own distinctive character. On the other hand, there will be an openness to others who do not accept the fundamentals of the Christian faith-claim. There have always been Christian humanists, but for the most part they have accepted the doctrine of God. They have had problems with the Trinity, with the divinity of Christ, with the traditional doctrines of man and sin, and so on. They have stood for "the human face of God," and they have been strong on the goodness and responsibility of man. They have embraced activism as a very important ethical stance. The traditional "natural-theology" position has contributed much to both a universal understanding of religion and moral endeavor. This humanistic strand of Christian thought has permeated Protestantism and Roman Catholicism without giving up the revelation of God to faith.

Theology includes epistemology, but it is clearly more than that. It goes beyond a neat, abstract edifice, however neatly packaged. If it is only a rational structure, it is dry bones for faith. It has most to do with a reasonable understanding of what happens when a human being puts ultimate trust in the living God. While there are other theologies related to other religious systems, it is clear to me after some careful study of these other theologies, that there is something distinctive about the Christian understanding of God. My task is to treat this position from the "inside" of an affirmation of faith in the Christian creed. The God of the Christian faith cannot be found as the conclusion of a syllogism. While the "reasons of the head" may satisfy philosophy of religion, theology includes the "reasons of the heart" as well.

There is a need to engage that considerable audience of blacks who are non-Christian (secular and religious) and who are outside the black church. This includes a host of our finest black youth. Many of my close ministerial associates cut loose from me when I wrote my first volume on black theology. Some of these same pastors have invited me in later for workshop sessions. Their youth have been leaving in droves. It dawned upon them that a church without youth has a past but no future.

Many persons and groups are committed to the liberation of blacks, even though they claim to reject the Christian creed. Blacks need to understand the sects and cults and whatever religious movements are at work in their midst. This is where sociologists of religion and historians of religion can help us understand the nature of black religion. Black theology must develop within the context of black religious experience. Black religious experience is the "stuff" through which the Christian faith is sifted to provide a black theology. All theology is the reflection upon the faith-response for a religious ultimate. Black Christians, in their reflection upon their faith-response to the Christian God, experience His presence and power radiating through their own *Lebenswelt*—living world. Faith is expressed in the experience of black suffering, in the sorrow, joy, and hope they have carved out of a position of powerlessness in a society saturated with systemic racism.

There is a common black experience shared by all blacks, whether Christian, Muslim or Jew, or atheist. The sects and cults and even secular-minded blacks share the same experience. When James Cone asserts that to be black is to be blue, he reaches into the experience of all blacks. The black experience is the river from which all the tributaries of the black experience flow. The phenomenon of the black experience needs proper analysis and interpretation. This is the province of the history of religions. Those who study religion in its universal dimensions can contribute much to an understanding of black religious experience.

The real breakthrough will center in the bridge-making task of linking African traditional religions and black religion. This connection is of vital importance for black theologians, both in their constructive task and in their encounter with African churchmen and theologians. Black theologians will need to develop their program in such ways as to be open to dialogue in two directions beyond their faith-claim. On the one hand, they must be mindful of blacks who are non-Christians but religious and others who are avowedly secular-minded and are allies in the liberation struggle. And, on the other hand, they must be aware of the African roots of their heritage and the spiritual riches that can flow into their understanding of faith from this source. The encounter with African religions and the heritage undergirding it can contribute much to blacks' spirituality, their worship, and the sense of the unity and wholeness of their personal and corporate life.

The contribution of scholars like Leonard Barrett of Temple University and Charles Long of the University of North Carolina is beyond estimation. Theologians find Gayraud Wilmore's work invaluable. The influence of Long upon James Cone is now beginning to be strongly manifest. Unfortunately, Cone is writing on the subject matter known best by Long, who is a reluctant writer. This is not so helpful as it would be if Long were writing on such things as "spirituals" and "folklore." James Cone imposes ready-made theological structures on this material, and they do not fit. Cone does not have the skill or the investigative knowledge to do the necessary anthropological, phenomenological, literary, and historical interpretation. It would be best to allow the myths and symbols and their meanings to emerge from the phenomenon itself—black religious experience. If this were allowed to happen it would be possible to begin the process of indigenizing black theology.

At the moment, it seems that Cone is not ready to learn what he needs to learn from black sources. He quotes incessantly from the spirituals, blues, and folklore in our Afro-American past and ends up exactly where his major works in theology leave us. His works are too similar and are being produced too fast for any real indication of significant growth in what he produces. Until William Jones's work was published recently, Cone had not been carefully critcized in print by any black scholar, and white theologians had only aimed a few cautious broadsides at him. As it is hoped this volume will reveal, vigorous constructive criticism is essential for the development of any theological program.

Cone's Christocentric understanding of revelation does not allow him adequate room for growth, even after the research on the black sources has been done. Without a reexamination of the foundations of his program, I cannot see the possibility for an openness to black religious experience that is necessary to relate to non-Christians in the black community or to Africans. Once Cone limits his understanding of the revelation of God to God's revelation in Jesus Christ, he cuts off conversation with all those who do not accept this affirmation as normative. Add to this the dogmatic manner in which he asserts the finality of God's revelation in Jesus Christ and his insistence upon the identity of blackness and this revelation, and one becomes aware of the inadequacy of Cone's position to move blacks in the direction they need to move.

Blacks must expand their understanding of God's revelation to include nature and history. God is the author of nature, the Maker of heaven and earth. He is the Creator-Spirit. God is Lord of history. His benevolent providence unfolds as history's purpose finds its meandering way from Creation to Consummation. God unveils his purpose in all things, in all places, through all time, and among every people.

This position is not a problem for a black once he is aware that the God of creation is the God of re-creation. The Creator is the Redeemer. The Incarnation, the word made flesh, is the "materialization" and the "inhistorization" of God's saving purpose and activity in time and among men. Creation and history are the mediums through which God makes Himself known. To hold this more expansive view of revelation is not to reduce God's revelation in Christ, but it is really a robust affirmation that He is Lord of all. The author of nature is the giver of grace and the Lord of history. This is to emphasize the "Godness of God."

At the same time there is opened up to blacks the context in which black theologians may enter into a meaningful dialogue with non-Christian religionists, and the secular-minded as well. Black theologians, in asserting the liberating work of God, will need to hold out the possibility that this work can happen outside the black church as well as inside it. It is well for black theologians and churchmen to heed the summons of the theologians of revolution when they insist that blacks should seek to find out where God is at work making life more human and join Him. It may be that God's liberating work is happening where the Black Congressional Caucus is at work, or where a black mayor is pleading for laws to control handguns or deliver goods and services to the blacks, more than it is happening in blacks' feast days and solemn assemblies. One should not forget that the Lord of the Church was crucified not on an altar between two candlesticks, but in the marketplace between two thieves.

The Atlanta statment on black theology was forged out of a meeting of minds of black scholars in religion and churchmen. For some reason they have drifted apart. Black theology is becoming more and more abstract and is moving further and further away from the churches and their leadership. I am disturbed by this trend. This came home to me in a meeting with African scholars at Union Theological Seminary in New York in June 1973. In the meeting, as well as in correspondences between us and the All-Africa Conference of Churches, no such distinction was made. Again, as I met with the National Committee of Black Churchmen, I saw few scholars, and at the meeting of the Society for the Study of Black Religion I saw few churchmen. Furthermore, the leadership of the scholars seems to be gravitating toward those black professors who have plush professorships in Ivy League universities or ranking theological seminaries that are predominantly white in outlook and program. Could it be that while black scholars talk black, they really prize the fact that the white world has cast the mantle of respectability on them? Could this be similar to the problem of a black congregation that insists upon a white pastor, and no black minister is qualified, just because he is black? Whatever the reason may be behind this situation, there must be deep psychological wounds that need to be healed. The unfortunate fact is that black scholars and theologians are getting away from the mass experience of their people, who need to be liberated from all forms of oppression, and they are not being informed by those persons who are in touch with the black masses. If this trend continues, black theology will not be church theology—it will be ivory-tower theology, and its spokesmen will have joined the bandwagon of most American and European theologians who are addicted to an arid theological scholasticism that is dry bones for faith.

I am pleading for a theology of the black experience that grows out of the soil of the heritage and life of blacks. For the black man, faith and ethics must be wed. There can be no separation of the secular and the sacred. Jesus means freedom. He is the Lord of all life. His healing touch makes one whole in mind, soul, and body. The church is the agent of social change as well as the ark of salvation. Material goods and services are a part of the black man's quest for humanity. Black people are to be equally devout as leaders of prayers and precinct captains. Black churches must no longer be comfort stations that administer spiritual aspirins or hospitals that administer salves to wounds that require surgery. The black church, a sleeping giant, must become a household of power that supports those social, economic, and political programs that make life more human for blacks. To this end, blacks need a theology emerging out of our experience of the Christian faith that informs our worship, our life, and our witness in the world.

II THE CONSTRUCTIVE TASK

Black theology is to be *indigenized* theology. It is to make a careful study of the particular character of the black religious experience. It is rather morbid to characterize all black experience in the context of conscious suffering. This is to overlook the joy and hope that are writ large in the black experience. We blacks have the "gift of laughter," and we have been able to sing the Lord's song in a strange land. Gladness and celebration are so much a part of black religion that one cannot describe the phenomenon without these ingredients. More accurately, the black religious experience is a "sorrow-joy" experience. But the experience, when it is intense, is weighted heavily in the direction of release and hope rather than in the direction of doubt and skepticism. Only thus have black people been able to maintain sanity and trust in life.

Thus, the black theologian must be anxious to let the experiences that blacks have had with life under difficult social circumstances provide the myths and the symbols for theological discourse. The black experience is a melody of aspirations, liberation, protest, survival, and meaning. We blacks have known great suffering, but we have known the meaning of victory over suffering through faith as well. This means that God as Lord of history and the Christ of Good Friday and Easter can be understood right out of the black man's encounter with life. "I am so glad trouble don't last always; Glory hallelujah!"

Black theology is to be *political* theology.* All of life and the whole person must be in focus at all times as black theology develops. We blacks take our direction from African traditional religions. Religion is a seven-day-a-week living experience for Africans. The health and wholeness, family and social life, economics and politics are as sacred as tribal ritual. Life is religious and religion is life. It was out of economic necessity that the Christianity that permitted slavery made a distinction between freedom of the spirit and physical bondage. Unfortunately, Platonic dualism and theological scholasticism provided theologians with a frozen dogma. Paul's conservatism and legal doctrines aided in establishing the permanent split between spiritual and physical liberation from which American Christianity has not recovered. It is not to the advantage of black theologians to blindly follow this false trail. The recovery of the wholeness of man, both in the Bible and in the African roots of our religious experience, provides a good foundation for a new departure toward a theology of liberation for blacks and all oppressed people everywhere. A political theology will overcome quietism the privatization of religion, and will open up the possibility of a secular/sacred merger as well as a personal/public ethic.

Black theology is to be *church* theology. The black churches have preserved the African temperament of black

* An extended treatment of this theme is found in J. Deotis Roberts, *A Black Political Theology* (Philadelphia: Westminster Press, 1974).

religion. It is logical that black religious and cultural nationalism will find a strong ally in the black church. Furthermore, the black church is the one major "political" institution that is under black control. It is unrivaled as a political, economic, social, and cultural institution, and it has deep historic roots in the aspirations of black people for liberation from all types of bondage. Black theology can be authentic only as it sinks its roots deep in the history, life, and witness of the black church. The raw materials for a black Christian theology are embedded in the black church. Therefore, black theology must incorporate the experiences flowing from churches and their members. The folk religious tradition that has been chronicled in black sermons, spirituals, and the Gospels, as well as in the oral tradition, is the stuff of black religious experience. The contemporary experience of the black churches as they participate in the humanization of the black man's life must be dealt with. There must be endless conversations between black laymen and ministers and black theologians if black theology is not to die stillborn as a futile and abstract dialogue between a handful of so-called black theologians. If the task of black scholars who happen to be theologians is to be fruitful and authentic, they must stay in touch with their people.

Black theology is to be *community* theology. We blacks desire that our people be set free. This means all black people. Those who are followers of non-Christian movements or those who are secular cannot be written off. We must seek a fuller understanding of all the "isms" in the black community. We must constantly assess why some other movements are more successful in liberating black people than our churches. We must determine whether there are deficiences in our theology and in the manner it is being applied in practical situations. We must also look carefully at the programs of other liberation movements at work in the community, and we must seek an "operational unity" with these groups in the cause of black liberation, even if we cannot arrive at an ideological unity.

Black theology is to be *ecumenical* theology. Blacks separated from the white churches primarily for *social* reasons rather than for *theological* ones. The black churches have not been interested in serious theological construction until now. What black scholar/theologians do now must not open deep wounds of doctrinal differences. Black theology can do without dogmas and charges of heresy. There has been a remarkable unity in the black consciousness of Christians that has elevated our struggle for liberation above any form of sectarian pettiness. Even the critical and constructive stage of black theology upon which we are entering should center in substantive matters of thought rather than in dogmatic polemics. We must be open to black theologies, allowing for different spiritual and intellectual autobiographies of the several theologians that provide their programs. We must not, however, spare each other that rigorous constructive criticism without which there can be no maturity. There is a remarkable meeting of minds among black Roman Catholics, Baptists, Methodists, and other branches of Christianity regarding our common foe (racism) and our common heritage. The black religious experience is the contact out of which black theologians are developing a fresh interpretation of the Christian faith. Black ecumenism is a reality among black churchmen and theologians, as together they chart the course of black liberation.

Black theology is to be *universal*. In speaking of the indigenizing dimension of black theology, I implied its ethnic origin. Black theology should bring liberation in touch with reconciliation. Only thus may liberation be elevated to its highest theological and ethical level. When reconciliation is properly understood in theological terms, liberation takes on its distinctive Christian character as well. Blacks are able to consider the terms of reconciliation in reference to the this-worldly and social-consciousness aspects of reconciliation as well as the personal and otherworldly interpretation of the white oppressor. Blacks are also able to view the possibility that the oppressed may need to be set free from their self-imposed fears and chains.

The means that what we blacks choose for our own liberation will be seen in the context of reconciliation. If a total experience of reconciliation of the estranged groups is the final goal, then all matters must be placed in Christian theological perspective. Means, values, and results are to be explored theologically and ethically. The liberating experience of reconciliation will be one in which black theology will speak redemptively to all sorts and conditions of men, women, and children the world over.

This brief essay has provided an opportunity to do several important things. I have had to seek a provisional definition of some terms, that is, *liberation* and *theism*. I have tried to make my stance clear over against other faith-claims and points of departure of some of the most outspoken black theologians. No adequate treatment of these differences or similarities has been offered, but the dialogue has been initiated. Further, I have staked out the province of this interest in liberation theism and have outlined the constructive task in light of a description of the program. The details of the program await further investigation.

10
A Feminist Looks at Black Theology

LETTY M. RUSSELL

As black theology moves beyond the phases of "legitimization" and "critical expansion" toward "systematic construction," is it important to look at ways in which insights from a variety of liberation theologies might strengthen this undertaking.[1] Although each liberation theology emerges out of the experience of a particular oppressed group and reflects the experience of a particular oppressed group and reflects the meaning of the Gospel from its own perspective, there is a basic commonality that springs from the horizon of freedom found in the biblical basis of reflection. The struggle for human liberation that goes on in both complementary and conflicting ways is, nevertheless, a common struggle, for "all discrimination is eventually the same thing—antihumanism."[2]

In my view, feminist theology and black theology have much to gain through a sharing of insights with each other and with other Third World liberation theologies. In the initial phases of work, a great deal of energy has been devoted to legitimization of black theology against white (racist) theology, and of feminist theology against male (sexist) theology, and some of the common ground between liberation theologies has been overlooked. In fact, many of us feminists have fallen into the oppressors' old trap of "divide and conquer." So busy have we been in asserting the importance of our own perspectives that we have exercised horizontal violence among each other, and played games, vying for top place on the list of the "Hit Parade of Oppressions." Recognizing that racism is the most serious cancer in American society, we must, nevertheless, remember that sexism and classism are intertwined with racist oppression, and that all these appear in worldwide manifestations of cruelty that might make our own present positions seem enviable.

Black and feminist theologies, in all their variety, have emerged out of struggles against oppression that are interlocked. Racism and sexism, along with classism, are manifestations of "the same social process which both justifies and helps perpetuate the exploitation of one group of human beings by another." [3] From the days of the abolitionist movement, the struggles of blacks and women have been intertwined in both a mutual and a conflicting struggle against the "overarching system of domination by white males." [4] Both women and blacks have been searching for ways to "be somebody" in American society.

Although women have shared the social fate of their partners, and have been numbered with both the oppressors and the oppressed, it is clear that the future of black liberation includes the liberation of black women. They make up over half of the black population and are, along with their other nonwhite sisters, the most oppressed group in the society. For this reason, black theology needs to address itself to the problems and aspirations of black women as well as black men, and to listen to the voices of these women as they begin to speak their own mind in the churches and in society. Already black women are speaking up about their own perspectives, and soon additional voices from this camp will be heard from within black theology.[5] Feminist theology, on the other hand, can never hope to gain a hearing among the Third World women of this country and abroad unless it addresses itself to the particular oppressions experienced by those who make up over half of the oppressed majority of the world.

Feminist theology that ignores the experience of economically and racially oppressed women can never move beyond middle-class elitism to construct a sound theology that reflects the spectrum of experience of the entire group. Black theology that ignores the experience of black sisters can never move beyond chauvinistic elitism to construct a theology expressive of the many groups in its own constituency. For this reason, it seems important to make a small beginning in looking at black theology and feminist theology in such a way that each shares its insights with the other as they work on their agendas of liberation theology.

I FEMINIST THEOLOGY

There are, of course, many types of feminist theologies, but for the purpose of this discussion I will describe *feminist theology* as:

> an attempt to reflect on the meaning of God's will for full human liberation in order to advocate the partnership of women and men in church and society.

This theology is *feminist* because it is done by those actively engaged in advocating the equality of the sexes. It is *theology* because persons are using their *logos* (mind and whole being) in the perspective of God as they experience the liberating power of God's action in the world.

Such theology is not necessarily *female,* for this word refers to the biological characteristics of women in contrast to those of the male and, specifically, to woman as "breast feeder" (*femina*). Nor is it necessarily *feminine,* a word that connotes the cultural-psychological traits associated with women in contrast to masculine traits in a particular society. This theology is *feminist* in the political sense of the word, which means those who advocate changes that will establish political, economic, and social equality of the sexes. The opposite of a feminist is a *sexist*, a person whose actions or words declare others to be inferior because of their sex. Feminist theology is written out of the experience of oppression of women in an androcentric society that considers women to be "not quite human." [6] A society that sets up *white, male* as the standard of what *human* means, inevitably considers those with certain biological characteristics which do not conform to this standard as less than human, and reinforces certain cultural myths about inferior traits that are internalized by the oppressed groups. The result is the formation of racist and sexist castes in the society. Feminist theology is a search for liberation from oppression by those who advocate human personhood for all. As such, it can be done by both males and females, and it can emphasize a variety of feminine and masculine traits. Its distinctive message concerns not the *female* or the *feminine*, but the *feminist* advocacy of full personhood for women as well as for men.

Feminist theology as a developing discipline brings with it many *problems*, as well as *insights*, which can be shared. As I investigate some of these, it is important to remember that there are only a few books specifically in the area of feminist theology, although the number of articles is increasing and several books have recently been published. [7]

Problems. Like other liberation theologies, feminist theology has a tendency to be what is sometimes called *genitive theology:* a theology *of* women. Writers sometimes think that it is not only *by* women, but also *about* women. Yet feminist theology is not necessarily written by women, and it is *not* about women. It is about God. Otherwise it should be called *ego-logy* instead of *theo-logy*. When women do it, they speak of feminist theology in order to express the fact that the experience from which they speak and the world out of which they perceive God's words and actions and join in God's actions is that of women seeking human equality. Another way of expressing this is to say that the *ecology of their theology* is that of women living in a particular time and place.

The importance of women's reflecting theologically is the same as that of any group around the world. Women make a contribution to the unfinished dimension of Christian thought. They want to add to the understanding of the Christian faith, not replace the other insights that have been contributed by others. As they add to all the other pieces their small piece of experience about the way God is known to them, the totality of Christian thinking becomes more wholistic and comprehensive.

The *problem* with their contributions, however, is that they are sometimes so overwhelmed with their new consciousness of selfhood or with bitterness toward the injustices of the church that their focus is narrowed to only the self-story of women. This frequently happens when there is such a strong identification with the women's liberation ideology that the center of the Christian message in Jesus Christ is lost.[8] Here the problem of Christian tradition surfaces, as women struggle to distinguish between culturally oppressive patriarchal traditions in the Bible and church history, and the core of tradition itself as reflected in God's will to hand over Jesus Christ to all generations and groupings of people.

Two key problems in feminist theology that are related to this narrowing of focus that leads to genitive theology are those of *racism* and *classism*. Women who are writing most of this literature are mainly educated, white, Western women. In order for their writings to speak to black and other Third World women, they need to include the particular experiences of oppression of the latter groups. Only as the women's movement begins to include more and more of these women and to reflect their concerns will it truly be a "Fourth World Movement" of women in every race, class, and country.[9] In the same way, if it is to avoid a narrow parochialism of one class and culture of women, feminist theology must speak to the various situations of women's oppression and interpret these clearly in the light of the Gospel message.[10]

Feminist theology as written by white women should also

reflect a deep consciousness of the oppressive roots of their own history and should work through this experience of continually reflecting on their history *as women*. Otherwise, the danger is always present that it too will "cop out" from addressing itself to the interlocking system of racism, classism and sexism that is operative in society.[11] It needs to assist in the prophetic task of critcizing the women's movement when the movement is geared to obtaining equal privileges for white, middle-class women at the expense of the vast remainder of the economically and racially oppressed peoples of the world.

Insights. Over the past few years, feminist theology has developed insights out of the corporate history of women that can be shared with black and other liberation theologies. Many of these insights relate to the basic content of Christian tradition that is shared by all those engaged in such reflection. Here I would like only to suggest some of the insights that relate to this *style* of theology.

One such insight is the emphasis on sisterhood that has led to *collective efforts at doing theology* in groups.[12] Much of the theology written has come out of extensive group discussion and feedback, so that it is not "handed down from the top" as doctrine but emerges from group consciousness and struggle.[13] Women have gone this route partly out of necessity. It was necessary to overcome horizontal violence among women in order to learn to be pro-woman and to support one another. This called for intentional cooperative efforts. Also, the lack of interest by male theologians and the lack of female theologians as role models caused women to turn to each other in carrying out their research in an experimental manner.

Other insights are also derived from this emerging corporate style. For instance, women discovered that they need not be rigorously linear or systematic in style. As they began to speak out of their own life stories, women discovered that their enculturated traits relating to a *wholistic view of life*— inclusive of emotions and the totality of experience along with the mind—could be brought to play in the theological enterprise. For this reason, much reflection is done among women through drama, celebration, music, and story, and not just through argumentation.[14]

Consciousness raising as an intentional key to aiding persons to discover the political, social, economic, and theological contradictions in their own situation has led to the development of new stories of faith out of the biographies of women, past and present. This in turn has led to new research and interpretation of the biblical story and Christian history, and to efforts to evolve a new language that is clearly inclusive of women in the Christian tradition.[15] Women are seeking to find *human pronouns* that reflect the fact that *both* women and men are included in the words expressed. The English use of such words as *man, men, his, mankind, brotherhood,* and so on in the generic sense has been increasingly called into question. However much a particular person or organization may protest that the words *really mean* human, human beings, his and hers, humankind, personhood, and so on, the fact remains that women are frequently left out of both the mental and the social structures of our culture. This struggle with language extends to the reconsideration of the words and images for the Trinity as well as for other theological issues.[16]

Of course, many other insights could be described besides these that are related to the style of corporate and inclusive theology. Yet these must suffice to point to some of the developing ideas in feminist theology that could lead to more dialogue with black theology.

II Black Theology

The many types of black theology and their various approaches are reflected in other chapters of this volume on *Black Theology II.* It is not within the scope either of this discussion or of my experience as a white woman to try to give a definition of black theology.[17] For the purpose of this discussion I will describe *black theology* through the words of James Cone:

Black Theology is a theology of liberation because it is a theology which arises from an identification with oppressed blacks of America, seeking to interpret the gospel of Christ in the light of the black condition.[18]

This theology is *black* because it reflects on the experience of oppression among American blacks.[19] It is *theology* because it uses one's *logos* in the perspective of *theos* as the liberating power of God's action is experienced in and through the world.

In relation to the distinctions in terms made in feminist theology, one finds that he or she is dealing not only with a distinct experience, but also with a different set of terms. Black theology, like Asian, African, native American, or latin-american theology, is ethnocentric in character and comes out of both a specific situation of oppression and a common tradition. *Black* refers to biological characteristics. It also denotes cultural-psychological traits. Last, *black* is a political term referring to those who advocate changes that will establish political, economic, and social equality of the races. The opposite of *black* seems to be (white) *racist,* a person whose actions and words declare others to be inferior because of their race.

Against the white male "norm" of society, *black* is also considered "not quite human," but this dehumanization is experienced by black men and women in different and more physically and economically obvious forms of exploitation. The word *black* denotes the total biological, cultural, and political situation of those oppressed in an American caste system. It is difficult for whites to "think black," and they are not considered qualified to write black theology because *black* is usually associated directly with biological characteristics.[20] Nevertheless, it would be possible to say that whites can write black theology and are "thinking black" when they seek to advocate racial equality in addressing themselves to the problem of white racism in their own lives.

Feminist theology can be written by males because the term *feminist* itself does not necessarily include the biological characteristics of the person who advocates changes in society. But feminist theology written by men also has an ambiguous character in the sense that members of an oppresor group may be setting out to define the reality of the oppressed "for them." At the same time it takes on strength and meaning when men address themselves to the problems of their own sexist situation in the light of the experience of women.[21]

In comparison to those on feminist theology, books on black theology have been published in greater numbers, yet it (black theology) too is a developing discipline that raises many *problems* and shares many *insights,* only a few of which can be mentioned here.

Problems. Black theology also has a problem with *genitive theology* because its stress on the black experience leads to a theology of, by, and about blacks. As various writers have moved further into systematic construction, they have been at pains to try to separate black ideologies from a theology (about God) that springs from the rooted tradition of black and African oppression. This appears to be one of the purposes of J. Deotis Roberts in his emphasizing that a full theology must affirm both liberation and reconciliation, and not just "[turn] the tables of oppression." [22] James Cone has been concerned to defend himself against making blackness, rather than Jesus Christ, his "ultimate reality." In his inaugural address at Union Theological Seminary, his answer to this charge was to state

> emphatically that, like Scripture, the black experience is a *source* of the Truth but not the Truth itself. Jesus Christ is the Truth and this stands in judgment of all statements about truth. But . . . there is no truth in Jesus Christ independent of the oppressed of the land—their history and culture.[23]

The focus on black experience has sometimes tended toward preoccupation with one story at the expense of the universatility of the gospel message of liberation for all oppressed people, no matter what color or country. Gradually, blacks' talk of oppression has expanded to include other people of color, but the very self-definition of black theology as relating to American black experience has a tendency toward parochialism.[24] The vast majority of blacks and people of color live outside the United States. It is to their cultures and to Islamic and African religions that many black people are turning in search of nonwhite history and new roots. Perhaps if, in addition to its biblical roots, black theology placed more emphasis on its worldwide Christian heritage, going far back into history with such groups as the Donatists and up to the present with Independent African churches, it would not be so heavily dependent on the American experience of black as an oppressed minority.

Another problem of black theology is that it not only tends to be *about* blacks, but it also tends to be only about *black males*. Thus, consciously or unconsciously, some black theology tends to be *sexist* in much the same way as some feminist theology tends to be *racist*. The style seems to have developed out of emulation of the oppressor, in this case, the white male theologians. The tone is authoritarian, with little consideration of the cultural myths that have doubly oppressed black women.[25] Speaking of the Black Power movement, one black woman has commented that the black male

> sees the system for what it really is for the most part, but where he rejects its values and mores on many issues, when it comes to women, he seems to take his guidelines from the pages of the *Ladies' Home Journal*.[26]

This comment might well be considered by black theologians as a call to reexamine their ethical stance on issues that are related to the importance of the partnership of black women as equals in the struggle for liberation, and what that might mean in the encouragement of black women to tell their own story. It is "normal" for human beings to want to look down on someone, and that someone for those who are oppressed is usually their women. But this is no excuse for Christian liberation theologians to adopt that stance. It is the false reasoning of white males with a win-lose mentality to say that in order for black men to be strong, black women must become weak and emulate the pedestaled femininity of their white sisters.[27]

One way of combating tendencies to sexism in black theology is to encourage black women to begin to do theology on their own, so that a more complete black experience of the meaning of the Gospel in the context of black oppression might emerge. Another way might be a conscious effort to change the sexist language so that it more clearly represents the universal dimension of liberation theology as it relates to both women and men. If the language used oppresses others, it would seem that black men could well risk a little of their masculine identity to make the Gospel even more clearly good news for *all* of the oppressed. Language is important because it is the way people name and symbolize their social reality, and changing language and mental habits is part of changing that reality.[28]

A third problem that affects black theology is that of *classism*. Within the American, racial, caste structure, class is operative in stratifying the bourgeois above the black lower classes.[29] Black theology reflects this class stratification just as much as does feminist theology, for it is largely middle-class and academic in its focus, and not necessarily always in contact with either the mass of the black church people or those alienated from the church.[30] These economic and class distinctions may tend to inhibit the power of black theology to speak of liberation to its own constituency, however much impact it may have on white academic theology.

Insights. A key insight that black theology shares with other "indigenous theologies" is that of the *exposure of what has been called Christian theology* as actually a white male theology that has dominated Western Christian tradition through a form of "cultural imperialism." The emphasis on reflecting out of the black situation has been a pioneering effort on the American scene in interpreting the meaning of the biblical message as good news for all races and subcultures. This emphasis on the experience of oppression and suffering provides a much-needed model that can be shared with others, even as black theologians continue to explore and develop the motifs.[31]

The methodology of *"turning white, male theology on its head"* and asking what each element—salvation, justification, Christology, and so on—means for black Christians is important for all those engaged in liberation theology.[32] It helps provide the courage and energy for the continued struggle to reexamine the entire Christian tradition as it relates to contemporary social experience.

Another helpful insight is the *attention given to the ideology of black power* and the political struggles of black people as a basis for action-reflection on both the Gospel and social realities. This is extremely important, though sometimes risky, because it situates theology squarely in the midst of struggles for liberation, rather than allowing it to take place only in academic monologue about doctrine that tends to relegate "applications" to a later time or place. As Cone so well states, the *heresy* of the church today is not its doctrines, but its denial of the Lordship of Jesus Christ by refusing to join in the struggle for justice and freedom.[33]

The list of problems and insights could be extended, but those briefly mentioned here appear to be especially important in the dialogue between black and feminist theology that, hopefully, is beginning to take place in a common search for human liberation.

III LIBERATION THEOLOGY

Feminist theology, and black and other Third World theologies, share a common ground in what is coming to be called *liberation theology*. They are, by definition, concerned with the gospel message of liberation that is interpreted as good news for the oppressed. There are many types of liberation theology, and there is no one narrow school that dominates because it grows out of a struggle to interpret the meaning of the Gospel in the light of concrete actions for social change.

For the purpose of stressing the *common methodologies* and *common perspectives* that many of the theologians share, it is possible to describe *liberation theology* as:

an attempt to reflect upon the experience of oppression and divine-human actions for the new creation of a more humane society.

It interprets the search for salvation as a journey toward freedom, and process of self-liberation in community with others in the light of hope in God's promise.

This perspective is related to *political theology* or *theology of hope*, as seen in such writers as Jürgen Moltmann, Johannes Metz, and Dorothee Soëlle.[34] According to Moltmann, Christian political theology is an attempt to relate the eschatological message of freedom to sociopolitical reality. The focus of Christian hope is not simply on the open future, but on the future of the hopeless.

Common methodologies. In general, liberation theologians stress an *inductive* rather than a deductive approach. Instead of deducing conclusions from first principles established out of Christian tradition and philosophy, many people today do theology by reflecting on their life experience as it relates to the gospel message. Stress is placed on the *situation-variable* nature of the Gospel as good news to people only when it speaks concretely to their particular needs of liberation.

For this reason, liberation theologians try to address themselves to experiences that illuminate their own situation and can be shared with others. They try to express the Gospel in the light of the experiences of oppression out of which they are written, whether racial or sexual, social or economic, psychological or physical. Such a method draws on many disciplines that illuminate the human condition, and not just on a particular theological tradition.

This inducive approach is experimental in nature. It becomes a theology of constantly revised questions and tentative observations about a changing world, rather than the type of theology described by Thomas Aquinas as a "science of conclusions." For instance, in trying to develop new models for thinking about God in a Christian context, women discover a vast quantity of questions addressed to biblical and church tradition and to the concepts of creation, redemption, sin, salvation, and incarnation. No doctrine is left unchallenged in the search for a faith that can shape life amid rapid and sometimes chaotic change. "[T]hese doctrines are no longer taken so much as answers than as ways of formulating questions." [35]

Such an approach is heavily dependent on the *corporate support* of the community out of which it grows. Just as black theology grows out of the American black community and black churches, feminist theology grows out of small communities that experiment in action and reflection for new meaning for living.

This communal search is doubly important because liberation theology is intended to be put into practice. The purpose of this type of theology is *praxis*. It is a tool for doing something that can become a catalyst for change among those who believe in the biblical promises for the oppressed. The direction of thought flows not only "downward" from the "theological experts," but also upward and outward from the collective experience of action and ministry. It is practical theology that brings action and reflection together. Thus, liberation theology is usually not "systematic" theology. The purpose of doing it is not to place all the discoveries or conclusions into one overarching system (although the thinking is logical, consistent, and documented), but rather to apply the discoveries to a new way of acting to bring about change in society.

Common perspectives. Liberation theologies share at least three common perspectives. The first perspective is that the *biblical promises* of liberation are an important part of theological reflection.[36] Two major motifs of the Bible are liberation and universality. God is portrayed in both the Old and New Testaments as the Liberator. God is the Liberator not just of one small nation or group, but of all humankind. This theme is an important part of the biblical understanding of God's *oikonomia*, or action for the world in the history of salvation.

God's *oikonomia* provides an eschatological perspective. Because we see ourselves as part of "God's utopia," we participate as Christians in the work of liberation. As Paul says in I Corinthians 9:17, we are "entrusted with a commission (*oikonomian*)." Participation in God's work is the way in which people express their hope and confidence in God's intention of liberation and salvation. No longer are lines drawn between Christian and non-Christian, or between one confession or another. Instead, Christians join with *all* those involved in the revolution of freedom, justice, and peace.

Such theology stresses the Gospel's good news of liberation. Christ has set the captives free, and therefore, there is future and hope. This hope stems not just from one's own actions and strategies, which are often weak and misguided, but from God's promise for all humanity. In the women's movement many reject the Bible as the basis for theology because of the patriarchal, cultural attitudes that it reveals. Yet those who would do *Christian* theology cannot abandon the story of Jesus of Nazareth. They find instead that they must use the best tools of scholarship in wrestling with the texts to find out how liberation and universality apply to their own experience.

A second perspective shared by most liberation theologies is that both humanity and the world are to be understood as *historical,* as both changing and changeable.[37] The Bible views the world as a series of meaningful events that are moving toward the fulfillment of God's plan and purpose of salvation. Each human being is made up of his or her individual history, and society is formed out of collective events or histories.

To view the world as history is not just to think of it as records of past events, but also as a process of change from past to present to future. This process takes on meaning as we interpret the events that shape our future. The future that evolves out of the past (*futurum*) is placed at the disposal of those who are aware of their own historical possibility and seek out political, economic, and social ways of planning for tomorrow. For Christians there is also a vision of a future that comes toward them (*adventus*) and is placed by God at their disposal.[38] In hoping for the coming of God's future, they find new courage and strength to enter into the difficult process of planning and acting on behalf of human liberation.

Christians enter the struggle against oppression because they hope for God's promise of liberation and because they are driven by the knowledge that the "Gospel's business is the liberation of human beings. . . . Having faith, [they] put our wager on the liberation of all people." [39] They also enter the struggle because to be human is to take part in this historical process or historicity, and it is to have an opportunity of transforming the world and shaping the future.[40]

To view the world as history is to become involved in the development of ideologies, or sets of ideas, that can be used to change and shape this reality. Christians, along with others, make use of these interpretations in order to participate in the revolutions of freedom. Christian women make use of the ideology of women's liberation. Some Christian blacks relate to the ideology of Black Power, just as some Latin Americans tend to ally themselves with Marxian ideology.

The difficulty of this dangerous but important mixture of faith and ideology is that all ideologies are only partial interpretations of social reality. Yet ideologies gain their power to change the situation in line with that one set of ideas. For Christians this means that all ideologies must be subject to constant critque in the light of the Gospel. Neither God nor ideologies provide a blueprint of the future. God's promise leads Christians to a confidence that the future is open, but not to an exact knowledge of how liberation will be accomplished, or what it will look like. We Christians must live by the poverty of that knowledge.

A third common perspective of most liberation theologies is that of *salvation as a social event*. In Christian theology today human beings have a new awareness in their body, mind, and spirit, and in their social relationships. This has led to a broadening of the understanding of individual salvation in the afterlife to include the beginnings of salvation in the lives of men and women who identify with

Jesus, the Liberator.[41] Often the Old Testament concept of salvation as *shalom*, or wholeness and total social well-being in community with others, is stressed.

Emphasis is placed on the longed-for eternal life as a quality of existence in the here and now. It is expressed through Christian actions in sharing God's gift of liberation to all people. Thus, salvation is not an escape from fated nature, but is concrete social liberation in oppressive situations: the power and possibility of transforming the world, bringing a new creation, and seeking to overcome suffering.

In this perspective, sin is also seen differently. As the opposite of liberation, sin is *oppression,* a situation in which there is no community, no room to live as a whole human being.[42] Sin "is eminently a political, a social term." [43] It includes the sins of one's own people, race, and class. Therefore, Christians are faced with responsibility not only for admitting their collaboration, but also for working to change the social structures that bring it about.

Obviously, not all people doing liberation theology would choose to underline these particular common methodologies or perspectives. Certainly there are many other themes and emphases that could be lifted up along with these. Yet, insofar as various liberation theologians are engaged in a common enterprise, this provides ground for fruitful exploration by black and feminist theologians as they seek out the meaning of Jesus Christ in the midst of a world groaning for freedom (Rom. 8:18–25).

In spite of different and even contradictory agendas, each liberation movement strengthens the others, for each is an added thrust for breaking the chains of oppression, and each works in the knowledge that *no one is free until all are free.* As the work of action-reflection in feminist, black, and other Third World theologies progresses, the dialogue will be greatly strengthened by the reflections of women from all different cultures and subcultures. But the dialogue can still begin, regardless of whether men or women are doing the reflection. Each has a part to play in contributing to the ongoing development of a more complete Christian theology. The universal horizon of God's freedom beckons to all, and within this horizon all can journey together.

NOTES TO CHAPTER 10

1. William Jones, "Toward An Interim Assessment of Black Theology," *The Christian Century*, May 3, 1972.

2. Shirley Chisholm, "Women Must Rebel," *Voices of the New Feminism*, ed. Mary Lou Thompson (Boston: Beacon, 1970), p. 216.

3. Marlene Dixon, "Why Women's Liberation?," *Up Against the Wall, Mother.* . . , ed. Elsie Adams and Mary Louise Briscoe (Beverly Hills, Calif: Glencoe, 1971), p. 422; Cellestine Ware, *Woman Power* (New York: Union Theological Seminary, Tower, 1970), p. 16.

4. Rosemary Ruether, "Crisis in Sex and Race: Black Theology vs. Feminist Theology," *Christianity and Crisis* 34, no. 6 (April 15, 1974): 67; Helen Mayer Hacker, "Women as a Minority Group," *Masculine/Feminine*, ed. Betty and Theodore Roszak (New York: Harper, 1969), pp. 140–44.

5. Pauli Murray, "The Liberation of Black Women," in Thompson, ed., *Voices*, pp. 87–102. Pauli Murray is now studying for the Episcopal Priesthood. Note also the emergence of such groups as the National Black Feminist Organization, founded in May 1973.

6. Dorothy L. Sayers, *Are Women Human?* (Grand Rapids, Mich.: Eerdmans, 1971), pp. 37–47.

7. Some of these publications are: Rosemary Radford Ruether, *Liberation Theology: Human Hope Confronts Christian History and Power* (New York: Paulist, 1972); idem, ed., *Religion and Sexism: Images of Women in Jewish and Christian Tradition* (New York: Simon and Schuster, 1974); Mary Daly, *Beyond God the Father: Toward a Philosophy of Women's Liberation* (Boston: Beacon, 1973); Alice Hageman, ed., *Sexist Religion and Women in the Church: No More Silence* (New York: Association, 1974); Eric Mount, *The Feminine Factor* (Richmond, Va.: John Knox, 1973); Letty M. Russell, *Human Liberation in a Feminist Perspective—A Theology* (Philadelphia: Westminster, 1974).

8. This sort of tendency can be seen in Daly, *Beyond God the Father*.

9. Barbara Burris, "The Fourth World Manifesto," *Notes from the Third Year: Women's Liberation*, ed. Anne Koedt and Shulamith Firestone (P.O. Box AA, Old Chelsea Station, N.Y., 10011, 1972), p. 118; Ware, *Woman Power*, p. 98. Burleigh B. Gardiner, "The Awakening of the Blue Collar Woman," *Intellectual Digest* (March 1974), p. 17.

10. An attempt is being made to include the world dimension of women's experience through the World Council of Churches. Cf. "Sexism in the 1970's," Consultation of women from the six continents, *RISK* (WCC, Geneva, December 1974).

11. Ruether, *Liberation Theology*, pp. 1–7.

12. *Women Exploring Theology at Grailville, 1972* (Church Women United, N.Y., N.Y., 10027).

13. One example of this was Letty M. Russell, *Women's Liberation in a Biblical Perspective* (Concern/National Board, YWCA, 1971), which was written as a result of the work of 40 pilot study groups across the country.

14. *Women Exploring Theology at Grailville, 1972.*

15. Nelle Morton, "The Rising Woman Consciousness in a Male Language Structure," *Andover Newton Quarterly* 12, no. 4 (March 1972): 177–90.

16. Russell, *Human Liberation,* chap. 3, "Search for a Usable Past."

17. For a description of this process, see Jones, "Toward an Interim Assessment," and William R. Jones, *Is God a White Racist?: A Preamble to Black Theology* (New York: Doubleday, 1973), pt. 2.

18. James Cone, *A Black Theology of Liberation* (Philadelphia: Lippincott, 1970), p. 23.

19. J. Deotis Roberts, "Introduction," *Quest for a Black Theology,* ed. James J. Gardiner and J. Deotis Roberts (Philadelphia: Pilgrim, 1971), p. lx.

20. John David Maguire, "The Necessity of Thinking Black," mimeographed (Paper delivered at the Student YWCA, University of Illinois, May 1970).

21. Mount, *The Feminine Factor.*

22. Jones, "Toward an Interim Assessment"; J. Deotis Roberts, *Liberation and Reconciliation: A Black Theology* (Philadelphia: Westminster Press, 1971).

23. James Cone, "The Dialectic of Theology and Life or Speaking the Truth," *Union Seminary Quarterly Review* 29, no. 2 (Winter 1974): 86.

24. For a discussion of the World Council of Churches, see "Symposium on Black Theology and Latin American Theology of Liberation," *RISK* 9, no. 2 (WCC, Geneva, 1973).

25. For a discussion of these stereotypes of black women as "nonfeminist matriarch," "depreciated sex object," "loser," and "invisible," see Mae C. King, "The Politics of Sexual Stereotypes," *The Black Scholar* 4, nos. 6–7 (March–April 1973): 12–13.

26. Frances Beale, "Double Jeopardy: To be Black and Female," *The Black Woman,* ed. Toni Cade (New York: Signet, 1970), p. 92.

27. Murray, "The Liberation of Black Women," pp. 88–92.

28. For instance, the omission of any women's names from the signatures to the "Black Declaration of Independence" in the *New York Times,* July 3, 1970, ignores the personhood and contributions of black women to the cause of human rights and seems to accurately represent the power structure in black churches represented by the National Committee of Black Churchmen; cf. Murray, "The Liberation of Black Women," p. 94.

29. Ruether, "Crisis in Sex and Race," p. 70; Trellie Jeffers, "The Black Woman and the Black Middle Class," *The Black Scholar* 4 nos. 6–7 (March–April 1973): 37–41.

30. Allen H. Smith, "Black Liberation and Black Churches," *Reflection* 69, no. 2 (January 1972).

31. Jones, *Is God a White Racist?*.

32. Cone, *A Black Theology of Liberation;* Albert Cleage, *The Black Messiah* (New York: Sheed and Ward, 1969).

33. Cone, "The Dialectic of Theology and Life. . . ," pp. 88–89.

34. Jürgen Moltmann, "Political Theology," *Theology Today* (April 1971), pp. 8–23; cf. Johannes Metz, "Political Theology," *Sacramentum Mundi* (New York: Herder, 1970), chap. 5, pp. 34–38; Dorothee Soëlle, *Political Theology* (Philadelphia: Fortress, 1974); C. Clark Chapman, Jr., "Black Theology and Theology of Hope: What Have They to Say to Each Other?," *Union Seminary Quarterly Review* 29, no. 2 (Winter 1974): 107–30; M. Douglas Meeks, *Origins of Theology of Hope* (Philadelphia Fortress, 1974); Joseph Petulla, *Christian Political Theology: A Marxian Guide* (Maryknoll, N.Y.: Orbis, 1972).

35. Ruether, *Liberation Theology*, p. 3.

36. Jones, "Toward an Interim Assessment."

37. Rubem Alves, *A Theology of Human Hope* (Washington, D.C.: Corpus, 1969), pp. 85–100; James Cone, "The Social Context of Theology: Freedom, History and Hope," *RISK* 9, no. 2 (1973): 11–33.

38. Jürgen Moltmann, *Hope and Planning* (New York: Harper and Row, 1965), pp. 178–84.

39. Dorothee Soëlle, "The Gospel and Liberation," *Commonweal*, December 22, 1972, p. 270.

40. Paulo Freire, *Pedagogy of the Oppressed* (New York: Herder, 1970), p. 72.

41. Joseph A. Johnson, Jr., "Jesus, the Liberator," *Quest For a Black Theology*, pp. 108–11.

42. Cone, *A Black Theology of Liberation*, pp. 186–96.

43. Soëlle, "The Gospel and Liberation," p. 273.

11
Process Thought and Black Theology

RANDOLPH C. MILLER

My thesis is that process thought can serve as a neutral philosophical base for black theology. If theology is the truth about God in relation to persons, it needs to be grounded in experience. Experience is understood in both its broad and its narrow sense. It can be the experience of human beings dealing with the objective aspects of reality as in mathematical physics and the awareness of God as universal; or it can be narrowed down in terms of racial, ethnic, and cultural factors and ultimately to the individual in his or her solitude. Thus, one can take a world view that has universal significance and relate it to the biblical sources, African roots, and the black experience. The results at the level of particularism will differ from those of people with a chicano background, or with women's concerns, or with cultures other than Afro-American.

Except for the most primitive tribes that are isolated from the current scene, no one can escape the impact of a world view based upon the findings of science and technology. Some may deny this on Sunday when they worship according to a theology that reflects ancient world views, but as soon as they face the world they live in during the week, they have to come to terms with a culture that is heavily dependent on and formed by technical results of modern science. There is no escape from this world during the week, and a religion that provides the illusion of such an escape is not to be trusted.

Black theologians, in addressing the world of their own experience, deal with specific questions. These questions may be seen to have a universal significance, but they are sharpened by the specific forms of evil and oppression that are emerging from the experiences of slavery. Many people are oppressed, many people seek liberation, many pople want political and religious freedom, many people try to demonstrate their sense of worth; but each culture, sub-culture, ethnic group, social class, or male/female identity takes on a specific form.

It is against this background that I seek to look carefully at process thought and indicate ways in which such a world view can contribute to the questions asked by black theologians.

i Process Thought

The key analogy for process thinking is the human body. Paul's analysis in 1 Corinthians is helpful: "For just as the body is one and has many members, and all the members of the body, though many, are one body, so it is with Christ. . . . For the body does not exist of one member but of many." We know how the eye or ear or foot contributes to the total health and functioning of the body, so "as it is, there are many parts, yet one body" (1 Cor. 12:12, 20, 20, RSV).

This human body is a constant process of becoming and perishing. It keeps changing from one moment to the next. Yet throughout all this becoming and perishing there is a self-identity. A baby that becomes an adult is in some sense the same person throughout life, although even one's identity changes somewhat. Finally the perishing overcomes the becoming, and one is not sure what happens next.

The body is an experiencing one, and animals survive

due to the keenness of their senses. Human beings learn through their senses, and what cannot be seen or heard or touched remains in the area of doubt. But the human body, at least, also has a strong sense of the whole. Human beings have experiences that draw in the whole body rather than just the senses in particular. This is a way of interpreting an act of commitment of the whole self—in aesthetic experience, sex relations, and worship. Human beings experience the totality of the event and do not sense it piecemeal.

This is particulary true of certain kinds of human relations. Human beings have a kind of empathy for others, a feeling of their feelings, a mutual interpenetration. The biblical verb *to know* refers both to Abraham's sexual relations with Sara and to the way in which he "knows" God. In the Gospel of John the same language is used: "If you had known me, you would have known my Father also; henceforth you know him and have seen him. . . . Believe me, that I am in the Father and the Father in me. . . . You will know that I am in my Father, and you in me, and I in you" (John 14: 7, 11, 20). Such an experience has been called a *prehension,* which is a vague affective tone, a feeling or concern or grasping by which the whole body becomes related to another whole body. Men and women can prehend God and He can prehend them.

This points to the social nature of reality. "For by one Spirit we were all baptized into one body—Jews or Greeks, slaves or free—and were made to drink of one Spirit" (1 Cor. 12:13). Human beings become persons throughout interpersonal relations, and they are deeply influenced by the way they are treated. Often these relationships break down, and this leads to people's failures to realize their potentialities. They experience alienation, loneliness, and opposition. Thus the body is broken. But the ideal remains. "If one member suffers, all suffer together; if one member is honored, all rejoice together" (1 Cor. 12:26).

The analogy of the human body is a model for understanding the whole of reality. And it is backed up by some of the theories emerging from modern science. Men discover that this earth is not the center of the solar system, and that the solar system is only one among many. Furthermore, an Einstein perfects a theory of relativity, so that space and time are understood as parallel to mass and energy. Most people do not understand modern physics, but they can see the results in the development of nuclear energy, and see them as demonic in the bombing of Hiroshima. When astronauts read the story of creation from behind the moon on Christmas, men and women realized that their relation to God is more than what happens in some earthly Garden of Eden.

Quantum theory states that all elements of experience are ultimately too small to be known through the senses, and that the behavior of electrons can only be known mathematically. Furthermore, there is an element of chance or indeterminacy at the center of things. One can predict accurately the outcome of an experiment, but one cannot tell what a particular electron will do. Knowledge at this level is statistical, similar to that of a life insurance company that can predict how many people will die next year but cannot point out which ones.

When people turn to the theory of evolution, they discover that changes have taken place in the developments of history, but only at great cost. When they look at the amount of waste, the chance variations that lead to new forms of life, the mutation of genes, and the suitability for survival, they are likely to be appalled at the great cost of evolution. Creativity, chance, and limitation are at work, and survival of the fittest is something other than animal strength. Men and women discover that survival depends on being a part of a community of organisms. Ants, bees, and chimpanzees survive because they form communities. Organisms, whether animal or man, create their own environments and have the power to destroy them.

The element of novelty in this stream of evolution accounts for the fact that man has trouble locating the missing links. But somewhere along the line mind emerged, at least in human beings, and possibly to a lesser extent in some higher animals. Everything that exists is composed of the same particles, and yet chance mutations occur. With human beings, the mind at work has the capacity to think, to invent, to control the environment, and to do new things. Thus they develop a sense of worth. They move beyond the level of morality to that of religion.

One of the great process philosophers, Alfred North Whitehead, had this to say: "In mankind, the dominant dependence on bodily functioning seems still there. And yet the life of a human being receives its worth, its importance, from the way in which unrealized ideals shape its purposes and tinge its actions. The distinction between men and animals is in one sense only a difference of degree. But the extent of the degree makes all the difference. The Rubicon has been crossed." [1]

In this kind of world, the emphasis is on the dynamic qualities of life, the elements of chance and change, the limitations that keep process from becoming chaos, and the becoming and perishing of all organisms except God. God is the potentiality of man's becoming, and He is participating in the process and sharing with His creatures in the creative adventure that is life.

II RELIGION

The view of religion that emerges from this approach is complex, and an oversimplified interpretation ought to be mistrusted. "Religion," wrote Whitehead, "is the vision of something which stands beyond, behind, and within the passing flux of immediate things; something which is real, and yet waiting to be realized; something which is a remote possibility, and yet the greatest of present facts; something that gives meaning to all that passes, and yet eludes comprehension; something whose possession is the final good, and yet is beyond all reach; something which is the ultimate ideal, and the hopeless quest." [2]

The focus is right. Men can know something, and yet it dissolves in mystery. A God of persuasive love is working for all men and with all men for the coming of the kingdom, but He does not use coercive power. "The power of God is the worship He inspires." [3] Men follow Him in their own freedom as a response of their worship of Him. They know Him because of their experience of Him, which is a part of their normal experience.

The Christian tradition made a mistake when it moved from a God of love to a God of power. Instead of taking its leave from "the brief Galilean vision of humility," it borrowed its models from Egypt, Persia, and Rome, and it put a monarch on the throne of God. "The essence of Christianity," said Whitehead, "is the appeal of the life of Christ as a revelation of the nature of God and of his agency in the world. . . . There can be no doubt as to what elements in the record have evoked a response from all that is best in human nature. The Mother, the Child, and the bare manger: the lowly man, homeless and self-forgetful, with the message of peace, love, and sympathy : the suffering, the agony, the tender words as life ebbed, the final despair : and the whole with the authority of victory." [4]

The God of process thought may be seen from two perspectives. He is both beyond the world and in it. He has an abstract and primordial nature, that which does not change and which is the principle of limitation so that creative processes do not degenerate into chaos. Men do not literally know God in His abstract nature, but He becomes the necessary principle and the chief exemplification of all the principles of life. [5] This is one pole of God's bipolar nature.

The other pole is known through man's experiences of God in action as persuasive love. This is God in action, fully actual, taking into Himself the meanings of the past so that the future can emerge. What happens does not fade from God's memory. He is conscious and personal, patient and loving, and the source of all values. "The purpose of God is the attainment of value in the temporal world." [6] "He saves the world as it passes into the immediacy of his own life. It is the judgment of tenderness which loses nothing that can be saved. It is also the judgment of a wisdom which uses what in the temporal world is mere wreckage." [7]

In such a world, evil is real. But it is not due to God, for God's power is not coercive. Traditional theology has always struggled with an all-powerful and all-good God who permits or even wills evil. So evil has to be good in disguise, or God's goodness is different from that of man and the analogy of goodness is strained to the breaking point, or there is a devil that God allows to exist. But process thought will allow none of this. Evil is real and is opposed to God's love; it comes about due to the reality of freedom, the occurrence of chance or accident, the emergence of novelty, and the sheer malvolence of human beings. There is destruction when God's ultimate purpose is completely ignored. "The fact of instability of evil is the moral order of the world," says Whitehead.[8]

But if evil is real and God does not will it, what does this say about God's perfection? Men can still claim that God is unsurpassable, but He is a changing God who takes into Himself the suffering and evil as well as the joy and good that occur. Thus He is surpassable, but only by Himself. His perfection is that of love, and love must always be open to suffering and joy or it ceases to be love. There is an element in God, however, that does pronounce judgment with a certain remorselessness and that stands against any ultimate opposition.

Human beings, in their freedom, may or may not align themselves with God's will. God does not coerce them, but He loves them. Thus man must accept his own moral responsibility, and he cannot blame God for the mess he is in. He can only look at himself and his fellow human beings and ask to what extent their wills are aligned with God's. At the same time, he sees that it is God's intention that human beings should dwell together in meaningful relationships, recognizing their differences as legitimate ones, and seeing that all men function together as members of the same body. This means that all need to work for the overcoming of evil, for the liberation of those who are frustrated in their efforts to be fully members of the body, and for the redemption of those who have wandered away from their human functions in meaningful living. Because there is chance, because novelty is constantly emerging, because there is freedom, there is always the opportunity to be transformed by renewal into a higher order of human personality, to be reconciled with brothers and sisters, and to recognize that all human beings have a sense of their ultimate worth.

iii BLACK THEOLOGY

If I understand correctly some of the major themes of black theology, I have a hunch that process thought, which is neutral as far as race or subcultures or ethnic groups are concerned, might serve as a proper background for the further development of black theology. Let us look briefly at seven areas: (1) theodicy, (2) suffering, (3) liberation, (4) freedom, (5) reconciliation, (6) worth, and (7) Jesus Christ.

Christian theology around the world is now subject to a process of indigenization, making it intelligible within a particular culture or subculture and basing it upon the experiences of the people. In the United States there have always been particular theologies of various denominations as drawn from their earlier foreign cultures. Episcopalians still look to England and Lutherans to Germany to discover their roots. But in the case of blacks, a dominant white theology has been imposed on them, though it must be noted that much theology as expressed in the spirituals and blues reflected the black religious experience.

Black theology today, as I understand it, has arisen out of the past and current black experiences of oppression and suffering due to racism. The task of black theology is "to analyze the black man's condition in the light of God's revelation in Jesus Christ with the purpose of creating a new understanding of black dignity among black people, and providing the necessary soul in that people, to destroy white racism." [9] This is not just a problem for a separated black culture, however; for blacks exist in a pluralistic society that includes many subcultures and ethnic groups, and theology has to make sense of the total human environment in relation to God. The dominant note, however, is oppression; and the way out is in terms of liberation and reconciliation—in that order.

(1) *Theodicy.* Not only process thought but most black theologies begin with the assumption that creation is good. In some sense, man "is a co-creator with God in the act of creation." [10] Yet it is evident that oppression, evil, and suffering are dominant notes of the black experience. This can be accounted for if God is a white racist or an indifferent deity or not a good God. But the assumption is that God is a good God, and that He loves all human beings regardless of color. Then why should blacks suffer more than their share, and primarily at the hands of white racists who claim to worship the same God? The situation is much the same for the Jews throughout their history, made especially vivid by the genocide under Hitler. It leads many blacks and Jews to deny the existence of a good deity.

These facts make theodicy central to black theology. William R. Jones says that blacks cannot blame God, that they must refute the charge of divine racism, that they must avoid the claim of divine punishment, and that they must not leave the question in some realm of mystery where "God knows best." [11] Jones suggests that the power of God rests in His persuasion, which among persons is the highest form of power. The sovereignty of divine love allows for freedom and therefore for disobedience.

Process thought can contribute some insights at this point. If God acts through persuasion, and if His power is found in men's worship of Him, there is a basis for understanding the sin of oppression, which is the coercive use of power over those who cannot resist. The misuse of freedom is sufficient to account for the entire history of oppression, once one looks at the motives of those who seek power over others. Because God acts through persuasive love, He does not take away His gift of freedom, and only as His persuasion takes hold is there any hope of the transformation of human beings or society. However, because love is persuasive and transforming, the conversion of human beings and of society always remains a possibility and therefore the basis for hope.

This view fits into the wider scene in which any suffering must be placed. Process thought sees the universe not as a tightly knit system with God running the show as a dictator, but as an area in which chance, novelty, and accident are possible, thereby making possible both growth or evolution and disastrous setbacks. Animals that develop through chance mutations may survive if the conditions are right, and especially if they learn how to live together as a community or herd or clan; but if they develop in another way or turn on each other, the result is extinction. There are enough archaeological studies of extinct creatures to serve as a warning, as well as enough developments to provide for hope for the future. But the future remains open, even for God, and what men do makes a great difference.

(2) *Suffering.* If the key to black theology is to refuse "to embrace any concept of God which makes black suffering the will of God," [12] perhaps blacks are on the right track. Suffering takes many forms, of which oppression is paramount, but blacks have known all the other aspects as well, such as slavery, lynching, poor health, starvation, poverty, broken families, and all kinds of racial slurs, for none of which they are responsible. And what does God do about it? He does not by divine fiat eliminate suffering. There is no record in the Bibile that God intervenes when men inflict suffering on other men, and even Jesus died as a young man on the Cross.

But reference to Jesus' suffering indicates that one must make a distinction between negative and positive suffering. In his case the suffering was overcome and the results were positive, even though on the Cross he felt that God had forsaken him. There are much suffering and sacrifice that are seen to be redemptive, and other suffering that is the cost of something greater that is achieved, as in the martyrdoms of many Christians from Polycarp to Martin Luther

King. Suffering *may* become the basis for communication, healing, and redemption. Christians must never lose sight of this fact. Process thought goes beyond traditional theology by saying that God takes our suffering unto Himself as He participates in the ongoing life of creation.

Most suffering that fails to be redemptive is what human beings inflict on each other, and racism is a supreme example. Suffering in such a case is due to the sin of the one who inflicts and not the one who receives. Thus, suffering *per se* is not a punishment from God through the agency of men, but is the result of anti-God forces at work, which God does not stop except as men respond to *His* power of pesuasion.

(3) *Liberation*. Whitehead talked about God's subjective aim, which is very close to what is meant by *purpose*. When men have a right relationship with God as He is at work in their midst, their subjective aim or purpose may be in alignment with His. If so, they are free to be themselves, which is what liberation is all about. Yet, because men are bound together, they recognize that no one is free until all are free, so that God's intention is frustrated by the oppressors, and liberation is not achieved for the oppressed or the oppressors.

Black theologians have made this their basic theme in many cases, but they see clearly that "white American theologians have been virtually silent on black liberation, preferring instead to do theology in the light of a modern liberalism that assumes that black people want to integrate into the white way of life." [12] It is not always clear what the goal is, for black nationalism points to complete segregation by black choice, and others are opposed to both separatism and integration and seek a middle ground in which blacks and whites meet as equals in a pluralistic society that grants the integrity of both groups.[13] The problem still remains, however, that blacks are a minority as far as political power is concerned, and this leads to great difficulties even in a fragmented, pluralistic society. However, a just society still provides for the human rights of every person regardless of race, sex, or status, and this America has failed to provide, except for some white males.

Process thought has something to say at this point. Reality is primarily social, so that everything is related throughout the whole of nature. Each entity has to some extent a purpose of its own in relation to other entities, and its survival depends on its own health-in-relation. If liberation is interpreted as being one's basic self in relation to others, then there is a social interpretation that holds water even in troubled times. This, then, one can believe to be God's subjective aim or intention for all human beings.

The problem is that many people do not understand themselves or others in such a relationship. Christian faith looks upon Jesus as the liberator who gives human beings both freedom and self-understanding, who identifies with the poor and downtrodden, who says that those who serve the least of these are serving the Father, who comes to free the captives and prisoners, and to announce the year of the Lord. But is anybody listening?

(4) *Freedom*. Process thought, because it takes seriously the principles of relativity and of indeterminacy, has room for novelty and chance in a universe that is a process of becoming and perishing. It also assumes a limited freedom for its lesser creatures and genuine freedom for human beings. Freedom is a process of becoming. "A man is free when he sees clearly the fulfillment of his being and is thus capable of making the envisioned self a reality." [14] Freedom is a gift that must be exercised or it will be lost; and its existence depends on others. Freedom is both internal and external. Bonhoeffer had a degree of freedom even in a concentration camp. Paul's letters from jail give indications that he was locked up but not oppressed. Yet freedom is more than freedom to think or speak; it includes freedom to act out what one really is in a society that is sufficiently permissive to allow of many variations. A law-and-order society, whether fascist or communist or pseudodemocratic, denies this kind of freedom.

However, genuine freedom requires some kind of structure. The universe would become chaos without a principle of limitation. A child would become wild without parental restraints. Yet the universe is not completely determined, and a child is not rigidly controlled, else men would become automatons. So it is freedom under just law that provides for full development. Blacks learned the limitations on their freedom at an early date, but they found ways to express their freedom through music, not only in the spirituals and blues, but through the development of jazz. If one examines a jazz band, especially as the tradition developed in New Orleans, the relation of freedom and structure may be clearly discerned. There is a structure provided by the tune, the key, and the beat, but each musician is free to improvise in turn, and in the final chorus they improvise together. This improvisation depends on the capabilities of each musician, so that some of them sound more creative than others, but each one expresses his own being and aptitudes within the structure. There is no dictation from inside or outside the band. This is an expression of genuine freedom and an analogy for understanding it in other situations.

(5) *Reconciliation.* Process thought makes use of the concept of prehension, in which one feels the feelings of another, achieves a kind of empathy, and grasps the meaning of the other. This is the way in which a person comes to know others. There is a possibility of a mutual prehension that leads to a relationship of love. Because God is persuasive love, God prehends humans and they prehend God— if they will. Thus, God influences them and is influenced by them. All can share in God's suffering and joy. "We enjoy God's enjoyment of ourselves," says Charles Hartshorne.[15]

Such a deity works for reconciliation between human beings and Himself and among all who are estranged in any way. "In Christ God was reconciling the world to himself" (2 Cor. 5:19); "If a man says, 'I love God,' while hating his brother, he is a liar. If he does not love the brother whom he has seen, it cannot be that he loves God whom he has not seen. And indeed this command comes to us from

Christ himself: that he who loves God must also love his brother" (1 John 4: 20–21, NEB).

The problem here is the definition of *brother*, which includes the right to be a person in relation to others. It is in this sense that love can occur only between equals.[16] Cone suggests, following Paul Tillich, that love, power, and justice must go together. Yet the one thing a human being lacks is the power to make another love him or her. One can offer love, but only at the risk of being rebuffed. God offers his love, at the cost of crucifixion.

What is clear, however, is that love has a certain unconditional element about it. Reconciliation between blacks and whites on white racist terms is obviously impossible. Cone sees as a precondition to reconciliation a full emancipation or liberation of black people. But, as Roberts says, "liberation must never overshadow reconciliation."[17] The redemption promised in Jesus Christ includes both liberation and reconciliation. The dignity or worth of a person is found in the Christian promise that the value God sets on a person is paramount. One is to treat other persons as ends in themselves and never as means.

(6) *Sense of worth*. It is clear that the black experience in relation to white racism has threatened and sometimes destroyed the black's sense of worth. Yet, if men are to understand the worth of humanity as a whole, which is a deliberately color-blind statement, they need to see in what this worth consists. Whitehead has written that "for animal life the concept of importance, in some of its many differentiations, has a real relevance. The human grade of animal life immensely extends this concept, and thereby introduces novelty of functioning as essential for varieties of importance. Thus morals and religion arise as aspects of this human impetus towards the best in each occasion. Morals can be discerned in the higher animals; but not religion. Morality emphasizes the detailed occasion; while religion emphasizes the unity of ideal inherent in the universe."[18]

Human beings are shaped by unrealized ideals. For the Christian, these ideals are relatively clear—especially the unrealized ones! The brotherhood of human beings, the right to be different from others, the liberation from oppression through the experience of freedom within a moral framework so that justice becomes an expression of love in action, the recognition that racial and sexual differences do not affect one's sense of worth—these are some of the goals that are far from realization, even though some halting steps may be evident.

Reconciliation is a process involving a sense of separation or alienation, a willingness to forgive, and an openness to the transforming powers of God. "Do not be conformed to this world, but be transformed by the renewal of your mind, that you may prove what is the will of God, which is good and acceptable and perfect" (Rom. 12:2, RSV). This sense of worth as a basis for action is what Cone is suggesting when he writes that "black people cannot talk about the possibilities of reconciliation until full emancipation has become a reality for *all* black people." [19] Of course, it would help if there were full emancipation for any of us, for white people caught up in racism are not emancipated either, nor do those of any race have full political, social, or economic rights. It is hard for anyone to have a sense of worth if he is only a number; the black experience is only a more profound expression of such a human predicament.

(7) *Jesus Christ.* Men's sense of worth as Christians turns on what they think of Jesus as the Christ. Process thought has not yet worked out a full Christology,[20] but there are some important suggestions. If men can see the fullness of God dwelling in Jesus Christ, they can say that Jesus prehended God more fully than other men; or they can say that God had a particular subjective aim or purpose for Jesus of Nazareth that was different from His purpose for others; or they can say that the action of God in Jesus lives on in the life of the church; or they can say that the living Christ is prehended by them because he lives on in the memory of God. Jesus is the "chief exemplification" of what it means to accept fully the leading of God's persuasive love in their own lives.

By following Christ, men find liberation and reconciliation in spite of the society in which they live. I can know my own integrity before God, even when others do not recognize it. Thus "black is beautiful," even in a white racist society, although full reconciliation does not come until both black and white can be seen as beautiful (and red and yellow as well).

Thus the concept of a black messiah is legitimate, for it identifies Jesus with a particular group for whom he died and rose again. It is important to note that white churches have always created the Christ in their own image. If one were to seek historical accuracy, he would portray Jesus as a Jewish peasant much like those who live today in Nazareth —short, wiry, and dark-skinned. But Europeans created images that were Italian, British, and German, just as Japanese, Indonesians, and Africans have created their own images reflecting their own cultures. If one takes any of these images as literal portrayals of the historic Jesus, he is mistaken, but, as representing the universal Christ in a particular culture, they are valid.

Process theology at this point frees man from many traditional images and models. God as the supreme monarch, borrowed from the Greek, Egyptian, and Roman views, is inconsistent with the "brief Galilean vision" of a God who is persuasive love, and thus man has the right to re-create the fundamental vision in terms of his own culture and of a world view that fits the twentieth century. Even some biblical imagery may be questioned on these grounds. Furthermore, if the God of process thought is the God that is discovered or revealed to some extent in all religions, Christians have a responsibility to interpret Him so as to exclude no one, even though they need to particularize their image of Him in order to worship Him in their own way.

IV Conclusion

What I have suggested in this treatment of process thought as a basis for black theology is that those who share deeply in the black experience and are aware of the various black theological traditions can make use of a process view to clarify many of the deepest concerns of the black community. This is not the job of a white theologian, but, if process thought is racially neutral, he can offer it for consideration.

Some implications of process thought are similar to the conclusions of William R. Jones. He describes "humanocentric theism" as a live option for black theologians. It is a position that stresses human responsibility for the evil men suffer and for the ways of overcoming it, but at the same time sees God as an active factor. If the God that men believe in is open to the future and has not predetermined their future activities, then He can be as surprised as they are at future developments. "Divine responsibility for the crimes of human history is thus eliminated." [21] Thus there is no moral escape for the oppressor, for he cannot blame others and he cannot accept quietism as long as racial injustice continues. God acts through human beings when they are open to His divine persuasion, but men can block God's purposes. Jones sees the possibility of fitting these conclusions into the writings of other black theologians.[22] It avoids the claim that God is only the God of blacks and therefore a failure at obtaining liberation; it avoids the claim that God is on the side of whites, for God is opposed to injustice and takes on Himself the suffering of all. God, then, is identified with the sense of justice and the suffering of love. God works in and through men, and when they suffer He takes on Himself their suffering. But He also rejoices in their victories over injustice, and He becomes for them the source of their vision of a kingdom of God on earth.

This vision, noted Whitehead, "claims nothing but worship. . . . The power of God is the worship He inspires. That religion is strong which in its ritual and its mode of thought evokes an apprehension of the commanding vision. The worship of God is not a rule of safety—it is an adventure of the spirit, a flight after the unattainable. The death of religion comes with the repression of the high hope of adventure." [23] Man's adventure today must be the elimination of white racism and the emancipation of the oppressed, for men can respond to the will of God if they so choose; else there will be judgment.

Process thought comes very close to an early Christian passage from *The Epistle to Diognetus:* Did God send Christ "like a tyrant with fear and terror? Not at all. But with gentleness and meekness, like a king sending his son, he sent him as man to men; he sent as seeking to save, as persuading, not compelling, for compulsion is not the way of God. He sent him as one calling, not pursuing; he sent him as loving, not judging. For he will send him as judge, and who will endure his coming?" [24]

NOTES TO CHAPTER 11

1. Alfred North Whitehead, *Modes of Thought* (New York: Macmillan Co., 1938), p. 39. Significant process thinkers include Charles Hartshorne, Schubert Ogden, Daniel Day Williams, John B. Cobb, Jr., Bernard Eugene Meland, Norman Pittenger, David Griffin, Eugene Peters, Gene Reeves, and Delwyn Brown.

2. Alfred North Whitehead, *Science and the Modern World* (New York: Macmillan Co., 1925), pp. 267–68.

3. Ibid., p. 269.

4. Alfred North Whitehead, *Adventures of Ideas* (New York: Macmillan Co., 1933), pp. 213–14.

5. Alfred North Whitehead, *Process and Reality* (New York: Macmillan Co., 1929), p. 521.

6. Alfred North Whitehead, *Religion in the Making* (New York: Macmillan Co., 1926), p. 100.

7. Whitehead, *Process and Reality*, p. 525.

8. Whitehead, *Religion in the Making*, p. 95.

9. James H. Cone, *Black Theology and Black Power* (New York: Seabury Press, 1969), p. 117.

10. J. Deotis Roberts, *Liberation and Reconciliation: A Black Theology* (Philadelphia: Westminster Press, 1971), p. 84.

11. William R. Jones, *Is God a White Racist? A Preamble to Black Theology* (Garden City, N.Y.: Doubleday/Anchor, 1973), pp. 174–75.

12. James H. Cone, *The Spirituals and the Blues* (New York: Seabury Press, 1972), p. 107.

13. Roberts, *Liberation and Reconciliation*, pp. 176–77.

14. Cone, *Black Theology and Black Power*, p. 39.

15. Charles Hartshorne, *The Divine Relativity* (New Haven, Conn.: Yale University Press, 1948), p. 141.

16. Cone, *Black Theology and Black Power*, p. 53.

17. Roberts, *Liberation and Reconciliation*, p. 69.

18. Whitehead, *Modes of Thought*, pp. 36–37.

19. Cone, *Black Theology and Black Power*, p. 146.

20. See David R. Griffin, *A Process Christology* (Philadelphia: Westminster Press, 1973); W. Norman Pittenger, *The Word Incarnate* (New York: Harper & Row, 1959).

21. Jones, *Is God a White Racist?*, p. 195.

22. Ibid., pp. 200–201.

23. Whitehead, *Science and the Modern World*, pp. 268–69.

24. "The Epistle to Diognetus," 7.4–6, in Edgar J. Goodspeed, *The Apostolic Fathers: An American Translation* (New York: Harper & Row, 1950), p. 280.

Notes on Contributors

WILLIAM H. BECKER is Department Chairman and Associate Professor of Religion at Bucknell University, Lewisburg, Pennsylvania.

CALVIN E. BRUCE is a Ford Foundation Doctoral Fellow studying ethics and theology at Yale University, and has served as Teaching Fellow in Christian Ethics at Yale Divinity School.

CLYDE A. HOLBROOK is Danforth Professor of Religion and Department Chairman at Oberlin College, Oberlin, Ohio.

WILLIAM R. JONES is Professor of Religion and Director of Black Studies at Florida State University.

EDWARD LEROY LONG, Jr., is Professor of Christian Ethics at Drew University.

RANDOLPH C. MILLER is Horace Bushnell Professor of Christian Nurture at Yale Divinity School.

HENRY H. MITCHELL is Director of the Ecumenical Center for Black Church Studies of the Los Angeles Area and Adjunct Professor of Black Church Studies at Southern California School of Theology at Claremont and Fuller Theological Seminary.

J. DEOTIS ROBERTS, SR. is Professor of Systematic Theology at Howard University School of Religion, Washington, D.C., and editor of *The Journal of Religious Thought*.

LETTY M. RUSSELL is Associate Professor of Theology and Women's Studies at Yale Divinity School.

DAVID T. SHANNON is Dean of Faculty at Pittsburgh Theological Seminary.

GEORGE B. THOMAS is Director, I.T.C. Research Action-Advocacy Project: Religious Heritage of the Black World, Atlanta, Georgia.